THE RIGHTS OF SHAREHOLDERS

Other books of interest from BSP Professional

The Law of the Investment Markets
R.R. Pennington
0–632–02372–4

Directors' Personal Liability
R.R. Pennington
0–00–383294–5

Management Buyouts – The Legal Implications
M. Sterling, M. Wright and P. Yerbury
0–632–02202–7

Making Commercial Contracts
John Parris
0–632–01862–3

The Law of International Trade
David Tiplady
0–632–02376–7

The Right to Dismiss
Second Edition
Michael Whincup
0–632–01893–3

Contracts of Employment
Vivien Shrubsall
0–632–02145–4

THE RIGHTS OF SHAREHOLDERS

Peter G. Xuereb

Dip. N.P., LL.D. (Malta), LL.M. (Lond.),
Ph.D. (Cantab.), Advocate (Malta)

BSP PROFESSIONAL BOOKS

OXFORD LONDON EDINBURGH

BOSTON MELBOURNE

First published 1989

British Library
Cataloguing in Publication Data
Xuereb, Peter G.
  The rights of shareholders
  1. Great Britain. Companies. Shareholding.
  Law
  I. Title
  344.106′666

ISBN 0-632-02148-9

BSP Professional Books
A division of Blackwell Scientific
  Publications Ltd
Editorial Offices:
Osney Mead, Oxford OX2 0EL
  (Orders: Tel. 0865 240201)
8 John Street, London WC1N 2ES
23 Ainslie Place, Edinburgh EH3 6AJ
3 Cambridge Center, Suite 208, Cambridge,
  MA 02142, USA
107 Barry Street, Carlton, Victoria 3053,
  Australia

Set by DP Photosetting, Aylesbury, Bucks
Printed and bound in Great Britain by
Mackays of Chatham PLC, Kent

Contents

regulation; The regulatory structure; Obligations flowing from authorisation; Consequences of breach: investor remedies

Preface

The author's first aim in writing this book was to cut through the mass of legislation, case law and academic writing on the law on the rights of shareholders in the registered company limited by shares with a view to exposing the underlying principles which support the edifice. These principles are not static – they are constantly being developed, refined, revised and even challenged. The second aim was therefore to try to expose current trends and to indicate their likely implications.

I have concentrated on the law of England and Wales. However, in general, the companies legislation (but not the case law) applies also to Scotland. Reference has therefore, where thought appropriate, been made to the position in Scotland. The Financial Services Act 1986, which largely came into force on 29th April 1988, extends also to Northern Ireland and company law in the Republic of Ireland, Northern Ireland and Great Britain is virtually identical in substance and practice with the general exception at the moment of insolvency law. Cross-reference works have been produced by the Department of Economic Development for Northern Ireland enabling the reader in Northern Ireland to make good use of books on English company law. Northern Ireland insolvency law will be brought into line with the Insolvency Act 1986 by 1989. It is hoped that the book, whose purpose is to expose the underlying principles and trends informing the development of company law, will be of use also to readers in these and other jurisdictions. Reference has been made to proposals for the harmonisation of the company law of the EEC Member States. Occasionally, some detailed comment on these proposals has been made. There are many such proposals of importance in the pipeline, but as they are still being debated in Brussels it was decided in most cases to restrict comment to a reference to the gist of the proposals. As and when they are adopted, it is hoped that a subsequent edition of this book (or a supplement) will evaluate their impact on the rights of shareholders in this country.

It is anticipated that this book will be published at a time when the Financial Services Act of 1986 is fully in force. At the time of writing, Part V of the Act is scheduled to come into force in the latter half of 1988. The previous law on prospectuses is not covered and the reader who is interested in that law should consult earlier works on Company Law. The law and self-regulatory rules are those in force at the time of writing and every effort has been made to take account of all developments up to July 1988.

My thanks go to the publishers – Mr Richard Miles in particular – and to Mrs Anne Waters aided and abetted by Ms Tricia Day, both of whose typing skills and stamina made meeting my deadline a possibility.

The book is dedicated to my family, namely Angela, Simon *et al.*

Peter G. Xuereb
Exeter
July 1988

Table of Cases

References are to section numbers.

Table of Statutes

Table of Statutory Instruments

Table of Rules of the Supreme Court

Part One
The Internal Dimension

Chapter 1

Introduction

1.1 *Background*

1.1.1 Shareholder rights

There can be many different types of shareholder. The sum total of any individual shareholder's rights are determinable only by a perusal of the particular company's registered documents (namely the memorandum and articles of association), the terms of issue of his shares, the general law, the relevant legislation, and what can for the moment be called 'secondary sources' (extrinsic contracts, shareholder agreements). A company can issue shares to which different rights have been attached if its memorandum or articles so declare; for example, it is common for articles to provide that preference shares carry no voting rights except in the event of a failure on the company's part to pay the contractual rate of dividend on those shares (see Chapter 7). Yet one might have been forgiven for thinking that the right to vote was so fundamental a right as to be inherent in any shareholder's 'status', whatever the type of share held by him. This is a very good example of the basic principle that the primary source of shareholder rights is his contract with the company as embodied in the memorandum and articles (see Chapter 2) and generally the terms on which his shares were issued (see Chapter 7) and that the matter is largely left by law to the sphere of private contract. There is no such thing as a settled fixed set of rights which by law inheres in some abstract notion of 'shareholder status', although statute law (particularly the Companies Act 1985) sets out certain inderogable shareholder rights (see Chapter 2).

1.1.2 Shareholder interests

Moreover, it must not be forgotten that shareholders do not all have identical *interests* or, if they do, they do not necessarily prioritise those interests in the same way, even when they are given identical rights by the company contract. A shareholder's interests are wider than his rights. He hopes, of course, that his rights will secure the satisfaction of his interests. The 'short-termism' debate – about whether there ought not to be greater control over the single-minded pursuit of the greatest possible short-term profit with the subordination, to a greater or lesser degree, of the need to invest in the future by investing in research and development – is an ongoing one. It is all to do with conflicting shareholder interests. The big institutional investors (pension funds, unit trusts, investment trusts, insurance companies) have not traditionally taken an active role in the shareholders' forum, the general meeting (see Chapter 3). However, they have been accused of putting pressure on company managements to improve dividend performance. Yet company management's view of their role under the law, and their role in practice, is that of ensuring continued profitability and future growth above all else. This is not, then, simply a clash between management and shareholder interests. It is argued that the committed shareholder (we can also refer to this type of investor as the typical shareholder) takes precisely the same view as management does or should. 'By 'committed shareholder' is meant the typical or 'hypothetical shareholder' – another cryptic description first employed by Lord Evershed MR in *Greenhalgh* v. *Arderne Cinemas Ltd* [1946] 1 All ER 512 to indicate the typical shareholder who is committed to the company on a long-term basis, who anticipates and expects a share of the profits (i.e. dividends) but not at the cost of compromising future performance. Despite the probable preponderance of 'short-term' shareholders – in large companies at least – it is arguable that some rules of company law are inspired by the need to pursue the hypothetical shareholder's interests, and that in the interests of the general good those interests should be preserved as the ultimate yardstick of management decision-making. As counsel said in the *Savoy Hotel Investigation* in 1954 (HMSO, 1954):

> 'The "Company" does not mean "the sectional interest of some (it may be the majority) of the present members or even ... of all the present members, but of present and future members of the company ... on the footing that it would be continued as a going concern, [balancing] a long-term view against short-term interests of present members.'

Not only this, but the directors' task is to balance the differing and conflicting interests in the company (e.g. shareholders' and employees' interests) in order to reach decisions which they genuinely believe to be in the company's overall best interests (*Report of the Committee of Inquiry on Industrial Democracy*, January 1977, HMSO, Cmnd 6706, Chapter 8 para 39).

1.1.3 The interests of the company: other interests

However, the law is not entirely consistent in this regard. While the directors are obliged to perform a delicate balancing act, a shareholder voting in general meeting has traditionally been free to vote as he pleases even where his interests (and this includes 'outside', non-shareholder interests) conflict with those of the company as a going concern, i.e. the enterprise. However, the majority of shareholders in general meeting are under a duty to act *bona fide* in the interests of the company as a whole when altering the articles of association and there is strong evidence in the more recent court judgments that the duty will soon be regarded as a general duty restricting the free exercise of all general meeting power (see Chapter 4). The main obstacle to this development has so far been the idea – firmly rooted in company law – that the shareholders 'own the company' through the ownership of their shares and that the company exists for the benefit of the current shareholders. Since a company is governed in part by the shareholders, and since these exercise their power democratically by majority vote in general meeting, the majority has been viewed as entitled to govern free of all outside interference. The courts have been only too happy to stay out of corporate decision-making. In 1812 (*Carlen* v. *Drury* (1812) 1V & B 154), Lord Eldon said: 'This court is not to be required on every Occasion to take the Management of every Playhouse and Brewhouse in the Kingdom'. On one view, this has meant power without responsibility, and puts in stark contrast the role of the general meeting and that of the board of directors. It is for the policy-makers to decide, in the public interest, whether it is not time that the general meeting was recognised for what it is – an organ of the company – and it was also recognised that shareholders are not the only parties who are interested in the company's welfare. As the law stands other interested parties (employees, creditors, consumers) must stand impotently by while the general meeting decides issues of concern to all without any legal obligation to consider any interests but their own, even where these conflict with those of the company. Reform in the area of general meeting responsibilities is a direct attack on 'short-termism'.

1.1.4 Institutional investors: short-termism

Institutional investors, accounting for well over 50 per cent of the market value of listed equity securities in the United Kingdom, have in the past been inactive shareholders as a rule. Where they have been active they have rarely fared better than any 'individual' minority shareholder in bringing management or the general meeting to book (see Chapter 8). The more active they become in monitoring day to day management (and this is a perceived trend) the greater the opportunity of checking the worst forms of abuse and breach of duty on the part of those in control of a company's affairs, for institutional investors tend to have the resources necessary for the waging of protracted legal battles. However, at the same time the pressures on management to pursue short-term goals may increase in a manner which is detrimental to long-term success. This makes the development of realistic and fair duties to be owed by the board of directors and by the general meeting of shareholders all the more important. Provided that these duties were fulfilled the decisions taken by these organs would be unassailable. It would never fall to the courts to substitute their business judgment for that of the company organs; they would simply continue to develop and apply principles to regulate the proper exercise of power.

1.1.5   The 'group of companies'

The 'group of companies' is a fact of life of which little account has been taken by United Kingdom company law. The evolution of group enterprise has created many problems for the law, which was devised with the single independent company in mind. Even today we have a 'unitary' or 'single company' system of company law in the United Kingdom. The central problem raised by the group enterprise is: How can the group be allowed to operate as a group while at the same time ensuring full protection to minority shareholders in (and creditors of) the subsidiary company or companies? The law has failed to answer this very difficult question, and the economic reality is ignored in favour of the legal reality, namely that each and every company within the group is a separate legal entity, and that therefore the directors of each company owe an overriding duty to that company to act honestly in the interests of that company irrespective of the interests of other companies in the group or of the 'group enterprise' (of which there is no legal definition). An EEC initiative to harmonise the law on groups of companies (*Draft Ninth Directive on the Conduct of Groups of Companies Containing a Public Limited Company as a Subsidiary* – see DTI Consultative Document, February 1985) is still being discussed. It has profound implications for UK company law.

Moreover, growth and the pooling of resources has led to the emergence of so-called 'pure' conglomerates with subsidiaries in a number of different and totally unrelated industries. In such cases, there is no discernible 'group enterprise' in the sense of a principal group activity and it becomes unreal to speak of a 'group interest' in anything other than purely financial terms and from the viewpoint of the holding company, although in corporate strategy terms conglomerates aim to balance long-term growth and short-term performance in the same way as the single company. The law's failure to grapple with the 'group' issue is most evident in connection with the law on directors' duties, in which context the failure is most felt. This general question is outside the scope of the present work but some manifestations of the problem will be referred to later (see, for example, [8.4.4]).

1.1.6   The shift of control and short-termism

A major phenomenon which has shaped the present corporate scene is the well documented shift of control from the 'owners' (the shareholders) to management and the increase in minority control brought about by the wide dispersion of share ownership in the large public companies. This has coincided with the increasing preponderance in such companies of the 'short-term investor', resulting in the tensions which lie at the root of the short-termism debate. The *de jure* controllers (the shareholders) may tend to be short-term-oriented while the *de facto* controllers (the directors) tend to take a long-term view for a number of reasons ranging, it is said, from exemplary professionalism to the most naked self-interest in the pursuit of power. While the shift of control to management is incontrovertible, it does not follow that management will be at odds with the typical shareholder. The means to the satisfaction of both their ends is the long-term prosperity of the enterprise. However, this presumes that the typical shareholder's interests extend beyond short-term maximised profit – an unrealistic assumption in many cases. This assumption being unrealistic, there is a tension between 'typical shareholder in fact' on the one hand and management and 'typical shareholder in law' on the other. This tension occasionally manifests itself in terms of internal rebellion within the company and more rarely in minority actions and petitions in the courts, but as a rule operates as a potent market force.

In the small private company, on the other hand, the roles of shareholder, director, manager, and employee often coincide in the same persons. The *modus operandi* within such companies is easily guessed at, but it must be borne in mind that the possibility of such companies being taken over is remote and that short-term pressures are correspondingly weaker on such companies than on others. It would come as no surprise to learn from an empirical study of managerial decision-making in such companies (if it could be undertaken) that Professor Wedderburn and Dr Paul Davies were correct in their assertion that no one particular interest is entitled to, or will, predominate always ((1977) 6 ILJ 197).

Which particular interest prevails in any set of circumstances is determined *ad hoc* on the basis of the company's overall continuing best interests. For example, there is no point in declaring huge dividends to oneself as shareholder if the result is to prejudice oneself as an employee. The challenge which the policy-makers face is that of allowing public companies to operate in the same way, balancing the short-term and the long-term. In the large company the shareholding employee is probably the best point of reference, assuming that he possesses a substantial shareholding. He would want the company to take a balanced strategic stance. Of course, in his capacity as an employee he is not well placed to argue or to enforce such a policy even if the law required every company organ to follow it. As an employee he can do little more than rely on the system of industrial relations. As a minority shareholder he can risk prohibitively expensive and difficult litigation to oblige directors to act according to law but he can do comparatively little to control or influence the general meeting (see Chapter 8).

1.1.7   Sources of shareholder rights

The foregoing will indicate that there is no such thing as a fixed and definite 'shareholder status', whether in legal or in practical terms. In legal terms, the shareholder has such rights as his contract with the company or the law (statute or common law) accord him. There are different classes of shareholder. Furthermore, identity of rights does not necessarily entail identity of interests. Crucial to the understanding of the individual position of each shareholder is an understanding of the 'sources' of his rights and obligations. It is to this that we first turn in Chapter 2. The principles which we consider there apply equally to all classes of shareholder and irrespective of identity or otherwise of interests. The specific position of different classes of shareholder is dealt with in Chapter 7.

1.2 The book's approach

1.2.1 Emphasis

This book is intended to guide the reader through the essential law on the rights of shareholders in the registered company (i.e. registered under the Companies Acts) limited by shares. The author has concentrated on the company law of England and Wales. The companies legislation also applies to Scotland. The law of Northern Ireland is virtually identical, except for the law of insolvency which will be brought into line with English law by 1989; the law of the Republic of Ireland is also very similar.

The approach is to examine the principal areas of company law (using company law in the widest sense to embrace the law as it applies to investment in, and the conduct of business through, companies) which are of prime relevance to the shareholder or potential shareholder. 'Indirect participation', such as through investment in unit trust schemes, is not discussed directly. The applicable law is discussed from the point of view of shareholder rights (and obligations) while taking due account of shareholder interests. The rights and interests of other groups – for example, creditors, employees, consumers, the public at large – are adverted to in order to place those of the shareholders in context (see, for example, [8.6]) but the emphasis throughout is on the latter. For a 'rounder' picture the reader will need to refer to mainstream works on company law. (These include L.C.B. Gower, *Principles of Modern Company Law*, 4th ed.; R.R. Pennington, *Company law*, 5th ed.; J.H. Farrar, *Company Law*; Northey and Leigh, *Introduction to Company Law*, 4th ed. Some excellent practitioners' works exist, e.g. *Gore-Browne on Companies*, 43rd ed.; *British Company Law and Practice*, Commerce Clearing House Editions UK Ltd; *Palmer's Company Law*.) The main purpose of the book is to cut through the detailed rules as contained in the vast number of cases and statutory provisions with a view to (a) clarifying the principles which underlie the detailed rules and (b) making manifest the trends which currently inform the direction being taken by company law. For this reason, too, the book is not a comprehensive compendium or exposition of all the relevant cases on particular topics. The discussion of the cases is intended to be selective, but representative, of the law and the reader who wishes to pursue a particular point to its ultimate conclusion will wish to continue his researches through one of the excellent general works on company law (see above). However, it is hoped that the reader will find enough here to set him on the right track armed with a knowledge of of the applicable principles and legal rules and an insight into the current state of development, and likely direction, of the law.

1.2.2   Pressures for change in the law

Company law is subject to constant pressures for change. Of these, one of the most significant is the harmonisation programme of the European Economic Community and reference is made to EEC proposals in this respect, some of which are commented upon. However, many of these proposals are far from being agreed and it has not been felt advisable in a book of this size to deal with them in any detail for this reason.

Other pressures are 'internal', of which a good example is the demand for the lessening of administrative and bureaucratic burdens on small business. The Government is always considering the removal of such burdens, for example in relation to accounting requirements (see Chapter 5). Other 'pressures' underlie certain perceivable trends in the law.

1.2.3   Perceivable trends in the law

Perceivable trends will be highlighted in the course of the book. These include the increased awareness of the need to protect the legitimate interests, as well as rights, of shareholders (see Chapters 2 and 8). Another is concern with ensuring the credibility of the 'securities industry' and the desire thereby to encourage share ownership on a hitherto unprecedented scale (see Chapter 10). This is mirrored by a trend to ensure that the individual shareholder is adequately protected from the abuse of power by the board of directors and, increasingly, by the majority of shareholders in general meeting (Chapters 4 and 8). Again, there is a trend in the case law to differentiate between the larger 'anonymous' type of company and the more closely held type of company in which the 'personal element' actually plays some part in the relations between the shareholders, and between the shareholders on the one hand and the company and management on the other (see Chapters 2 and 8). Also, the law is increasingly concerned, as it has been put, with returning some real control over the company's affairs to the shareholders. The ill-fated Companies (Audit Committees) Bill, which would have given shareholders more rights to appoint independent outside directors onto the boards of large companies (had it survived its passage through the House of Lords in May 1988), would have been a step in this direction (see, on this theme, Chapter 3). The disclosure of information about company affairs remains a pillar in the protective structure for the benefit of creditors, shareholders and potential investors alike (Chapters 4, 5, 9, 10; the ECC *Draft Fifth Directive on Company Law* (OJ 1983 Vol 26, C 240 pp 2-38)) and the 'Vredeling' proposal for a Directive on procedures for informing and consulting employees (OJ 1983 Vol 26 C 217 pp 3-16) will eventually extend the disclosure obligation for large companies in the interests of industrial harmony. This latter proposal has encountered fierce opposition and agreement on its content appears to be some way off into the future.

One particular trend in the law is worth emphasising and will be highlighted time and again. It is the first trend noted above, namely the courts' increased willingness to take account of 'legitimate expectations' and 'interests' in addition to 'rights'. It will be noticed that the courts increasingly accept a model of 'the company' according to which, while the company is still regarded as existing primarily for the benefit of its members, it is not to be confused with the sum of its current members. For example, while the board has a discretion in setting profits aside for future company needs, this longer-term requirement must be balanced against the short-term interest of members in an annual dividend (See *Re a Company* No. 00370 of 1987, *The Times* July 5 1988, and [8.5]). The balance is to be struck apparently by reference to the concept of 'reasonable necessity'. Individual shareholder rights and interests must be respected, but may be ignored where this can be said to be *reasonably required* in the interests of 'the company'. The writer has adverted to this trend elsewhere ((1985) 6 Co Law 199; (1986) 7 Co Law 53; (1988) 51 MLR 156) and would simply point out here that the courts are really asking the board (and sometimes the general meeting) to operate on the assumption that members have a continuing interest in their company. The long-term interest and success of the company is therefore also their own interest and success. It is management's task to perform a balancing act between long-term (or 'continuing') interests and short-term interests, and the courts are increasingly prepared to inquire into whether this balancing act has been performed with the proper considerations in view (see especially Chapters 2, 4 and 8).

Chapter 2

The Sources, and the Enforcement, of Shareholder Rights and Obligations

2.1 Introduction: Sources of rights and obligations

Shareholder rights stem from two main sources: (a) The company's constitution and (b) the law, including the common law – or 'case law' – and statute law (mainly the Companies Act 1985). The company's constitution is referred to as the 'statutory contract' because it embodies reciprocal undertakings between the company and the shareholder and also between the shareholders themselves, and is binding in virtue of a statutory provision, namely section 14, Companies Act 1985. It consists of a *memorandum of association*, the company's 'basic document' which must list particulars specified by law such as the company's objects (section 2, Companies Act 1985), and the *articles of association*, which set out the rules on corporate governance. Model forms of memoranda and model sets of articles have been set out in statute over the years and will apply to relevant companies in the absence of lawful contrary provision. Current statutory provision is made by The Companies (Tables A to F) Regulations 1985 (SI 1985 No 805). For example, 'Table A' of the Schedule to these Regulations sets out the model 'Regulations for the Management of a Company Limited by Shares'. It is to this model that reference will primarily be made throughout this book, the reference being to 'Table A'. It must be noted that a company is governed (saving contrary lawful provision) by the model regulations in force at the date of its registration (see further, sections 2,3,7,8 Companies Act 1985).

2.2 The statutory contract: contractual force

Section 14 of the 1985 Act provides that:

'Subject to the provisions of this Act, the memorandum and articles shall when registered, bind the company and the members thereof to the same extent as if they respectively had been signed and sealed by each member, and contained covenants on the part of each member to observe all the provisions of the memorandum and of the articles.'

The wording of the section can be traced back to the original Act of 1844 which adopted the existing method of forming a joint stock company by deed of settlement and merely superimposed incorporation on registration. The 1856 Act substituted the memorandum and articles for the deed of settlement and introduced a provision on the lines of the present section 14. What is odd is that the vital new factor, namely that the incorporated company was a separate legal entity, was not taken into consideration and the words 'as if they respectively had been signed and sealed by each member' did not continue 'and by the company', though the phrase 'the memorandum and articles shall, when registered, *bind the company* and the members thereof...' is indicative of what was intended. There have indeed been numerous decisions to the effect that the company is bound (*Johnson* v. *Lyttle's Iron Agency* (1877) 5 ChD 687; *Wood* v. *Odessa Waterworks Co.*, (1889) 42 ChD 636, for example) and the omission referred to is not today generally regarded as a ground for justifying the way in which the courts have proceeded to interpret section 14 (but see Prentice in (1980) 1 Co Law 179). Other explanations have to be sought for the way in which the courts have 'cut down' the contractual effect of the company contract.

2.3 Limitations on contractual force

Therefore, while in the nineteenth century a major obstacle to shareholder relief was the courts' uncertainty on the question whether the company was a party to the statutory contract at all, this issue was settled in the affirmative by the House of Lords early in the twentieth century in *Quin and Axtens Ltd* v. *Salmon* [1909] AC 442. Today, instead of asking whether the company is a party to the contract the question is which terms of the memorandum and articles have contractual force as between the parties, assuming that Parliament cannot have intended *all* their provisions to have such force. This question is posed despite what appears to be the unequivocally comprehensive language of section 14. The sources of the current problem are two streams of judicial authority, the first restricting the ambit of the statutory contract to 'insider rights' and the second preventing a minority shareholder from suing where the infringement of the articles which is complained of can be classified as a mere 'internal irregularity' which the company can lawfully remedy by ordinary resolution in general meeting. In the latter case, the so-called rule in *Foss* v. *Harbottle* (1843) 2 Hare 461, operates to prevent vexatious litigation (see Chapter 8).

2.4   *Hickman's case*

Hickman v. *Kent or Romney Marsh Sheep-breeders Association* [1915] 1 Ch 881 at 897, is the classic case on the first stream of authority. Mr Justice Astbury said, in a passage which is even today taken to reflect the legal position:

> 'I think this much is clear, first, that no article can constitute a contract between the company and a third person; secondly, that no right merely purporting to be given by an article to a person, whether a member or not, in a capacity other than that of a member, as for instance, as solicitor, promoter, director, can be enforced against the company; and thirdly, that articles regulating the rights and obligations of the members generally as such do create rights and obligations between them and the company respectively ...'

The first proposition merely states the doctrine of privity of contract. The second proposition declares 'outsider rights' to be outside the ambit of the statutory contract. The third proposition emphasises that the company is bound towards its members and *vice versa* but restricts this effect to 'articles regulating the rights and obligations of the members generally as such'. It may be added here that it is now settled that it is possible for one member to sue another on the satutory contract without joining the company as a party (*Rayfield* v. *Hands* [1960] Ch 1).

Hickman's case was endorsed by the Court of Appeal in *Beattie* v. *E. and F. Beattie Ltd* [1938] Ch 708. Here the defendant, a director, sought to rely on an arbitration clause in the articles requiring all disputes between the company and its members to be submitted to arbitration, having been sued by his company for the return of sums allegedly improperly received by him. The court ruled that since he was being sued in his capacity of director and not that of member he could not invoke the article referred to.

2.5   *Quin's case*

A considerable body of legal literature exists which points out that

Hickman's case did not accurately reflect the state of the law at the time. In particular, it is difficult to reconcile the House of Lords judgment in *Quin and Axtens Ltd* v. *Salmon* [1909] AC 442. The facts of this case were that the company's articles provided that the company's business should be managed by the directors, who might exercise all the powers of the company. The articles also provided that no resolution of the directors on the sale or lease of company land should be valid if either of the two managing directors dissented from the resolution. One of the managing directors dissented from one such resolution, but the company in general meeting purported to 'ratify' the resolution by ordinary majority. The aggrieved managing director, who was a shareholder, sued the company and the other directors for an injunction restraining them from acting on the resolution. He won. In the Court of Appeal, Mr Justice Farwell said:

'These resolutions are absolutely inconsistent with the articles; in truth this is a simple attempt to alter the terms of the contract between the parties by a simple resolution instead of by a special resolution.'

The judgment was affirmed by the House of Lords.

2.6   Reconciling the cases

Professor Lord Wedderburn cites *Quin's case* as a central plank in his argument that a member has a personal right to have all the provisions of the company's constitution observed, even where this would have the consequence of indirectly enforcing 'outsider rights', as long as he sues in his capacity as member (see (1957) CLJ 194 and (1958) CLJ 93). There seems therefore to be direct conflict between *Quin's case* and the *Hickman* line of cases which Wedderburn explains by reference to the capacity in which plaintiff sued in each of the cases. Wedderburn's point of substance is that a member has a general right to enforce every provision of the company constitution. However, this is directly contradicted by the two streams of authority referred to above (see [2.3]).

The cases are notoriously difficult to reconcile. Goldberg has suggested that the member's right is confined to that of insisting that the company's affairs are conducted by the particular organ of the company which is specified as the appropriate body in the Act or in the company constitution ((1972) 35 MLR 362; (1985) 48 MLR 158). Prentice modifies this to a right to enforce those provisions which relate to the company's power to function ((1980) 1 Co Law 179). Drury ((1986) CLJ 219) has followed Baxter ((1983) CLJ 96) in explaining the limits on the contractual force of the company contract by saying that all shareholder rights are relative and not absolute, i.e. that any right conferred by one article is in any event subject to the rights of other members including the right of the majority to ratify breaches of the articles, and by pointing out that the court will in any case not allow pointless litigation to proceed ((1986) CLJ 219). Smith ((1978) 41 MLR 147) and Gregory ((1981) 44 MLR 526) have argued that the only sensible way forward is for the courts to allow section 14 to mean what it says, i.e. all the provisions of the company contract are binding and enforceable. As Dr L.S. Sealy has said, none of the attempts to reconcile the cases is entirely convincing (L.S. Sealy, *Cases and Materials in Company Law*, 3rd ed., p132). They all involve *ex post facto* rationalising which must do some violence to the cases in an attempt to reconcile the essentially irreconcilable. The result of this conflict is of course that it is practically impossible to advise a member in advance in every case as to the chances of enforcing a particular provision in the company contract. It is possible to make a statement of the generally accepted current position in broad terms but with two important qualifications *viz.* (1) firstly, it is always a difficult question to decide which principle governs a particular case, and (2) secondly the very principles are under some attack.

Principle No. 1

Articles which confer rights of a 'personal' or 'proprietary' nature on shareholders in their capacity as such (i.e. *qua* shareholders) are enforceable; e.g. the right to vote (*Pender* v. *Lushington* (1877) 6 ChD 70); the right to a declared dividend (*Wood* v. *Odessa Waterworks Co.* (1889) 42 ChD 636); the right to have one's name entered on the register of members (*Re British Sugar Refining Co.* (1857) 26 LJ Ch 369 and *Re Hackney Pavilion Ltd.* [1924] 1 Ch 276 followed in *Moodie* v. *W. & J. Shepherd (Bookbinders) Ltd.* [1949] 2 All ER 1044); to enforce delivery of a share certificate in accordance with the articles (*Burdett* v. *Standard Exploration Co.* (1899) 16 TLR 112; see art. 6 Table A); to transfer shares (*Cannon* v. *Trask* (1875) 2 Eq 669); to enforce preferential rights and class interests, such as the right of first refusal (*Staples* v. *Eastman Photographic Co.* (1896) 2 Ch 303); to prevent dividends from being distributed otherwise than in cash in accordance with the articles (*Wood* v. *Odessa Waterworks* (1889) 42 ChD 636); to prevent an irregular forfeiture (*Johnson* v. *Lyttle's Iron Agency* (1877) 5 ChD, 687); the right to the return of his capital on a winding up (*Griffith* v. *Paget* (1877) 6 ChD 511). The same applies to articles which impose *obligations* on the members in their capacity as members (e.g. to pay the unpaid balance of the issue price of their shares). The company can enforce these obligations.

In 'Hickman' terms these are articles which 'regulate the rights and obligations of the members generally as such'. However, it is not possible to give an exhaustive list of such rights and obligations because the courts have not done so. One could be tempted to say that any right or obligation connected with (a) the attendance and voting at general meeting, (b) the payment for or the transfer of shares, (c) the participation in the profits or surplus assets of the company on a winding up, must all fall within this category. However, in *MacDougall* v. *Gardiner* (1875) 1 ChD 13, the right under the articles to demand a poll on the question of adjourning a meeting was breached. The Court of Appeal, *per* Mr Justice Farwell, held that no 'personal' right had been infringed because:

> 'Everything in this bill ... if it is a wrong is a wrong to the company, because every meeting that is called must be...for the purpose of doing or undoing something which is supposed to accrue for the benefit of the company.'

The distinction between the right to demand a poll and the right to vote (see *Pender* v. *Lushington*, above) is not an obvious one. In both cases the member is prevented from exercising his voting power. Nor can *Pender's case* and *Macdougall's case* be distinguished on the basis that by the time of the Court of Appeal's decision in *Macdougall* no purpose would have been served by court intervention because MacDougall had by then obtained control, and it was expressly stated in *Pender's case* that the right to vote was personally enforceable irrespective of such 'futility' arguments. In the words of Sir George Jessel MR:

> 'Mr Pender ... is a member of the company, *and whether he votes with the majority or the minority he is entitled to have his vote recorded.*'

In other words, once it is established that a proprietary right has been infringed it seems that it is not open to the company to argue that it would be futile to force the company to do properly what had been done improperly. In technical language, the *Foss* v. *Harbottle* point cannot be taken. However, all depends on whether a proprietary right can be identified. Apparently there is no right, for example, to have a poll taken (*MacDougall* v. *Gardiner* (1875) 1 ChD 13); to have directors retire in accordance with the articles of association (*Mozley* v. *Alston* (1847) 1 Ph 790); to relief when the value of their shares is eroded by the wrongdoing of directors which directly prejudices the company, and only indirectly prejudices the members through the consequential diminution in the value of their shares (*Prudential* v. *Newman Industries Ltd* (No. 2) [1982] Ch 204 at 223); to enforce a provision in the articles which requires the annual accounts to be prepared in accordance with the Companies legislation (*Devlin* v. *Slough Estates Ltd.* [1983] BCLC 497, see [2.13.1]).

Principle No. 2

By necessary implication from Principle No. 1, articles which confer rights or impose obligations on members in a non-member capacity are not enforceable under section 14. For example, in the classic case of *Eley* v. *Positive Government Security Life Association Co. Ltd* (1876) 1 ExD 88, the articles of defendant company provided that Eley should be the company's solicitor. When the company ceased to employ him he sued for breach of contract. Lord Cairns LC, seemingly ignoring the fact that Eley became a member after the articles were signed, treated him as an 'outsider' and said that the relevant article was 'either a stipulation which would bind the members or else a mandate to the directors. In either case it is a matter between the directors and the shareholders, and not between them and the plaintiff'. The principle which is thought to underlie this rather 'difficult' case was clearly stated in *Hickman's case*, as we saw above. Defining 'proprietary right' is not easily done. Bastin proposed that a proprietary right is one which is connected to the value and marketability of the share, and would include any right conferred by the articles which can be exercised and enjoyed by a shareholder without the concurrence of others ((1977) JBL 17). However, 'outsider rights' may be incorporated in a special contract which is independently enforceable. (See [2.10] and [2.11] below).

In the light of recent developments in other areas of company law, the application of this proposition to particular cases may be in need of qualification, quite apart from Wedderburn's arguments (see [2.6] above). The courts have been prepared in the context of so-called 'quasi-partnership' companies (companies in which the personal relationship of the parties is an important consideration) to hold that a shareholder is treated unfairly or inequitably if his legitimate expectations, as opposed to rights, are wrongfully ignored. The courts have done this in the context of petitions for winding up under what is now section 122 of the Insolvency Act 1986, and of petitions for relief from unfairly prejudicial conduct under what is now section 459 of the Companies Act 1985 (see Chapter 8). While relief may not be available at common law, therefore, statute may provide alternative relief (see further [2.10] below).

Principle No. 3

Articles which do not fall within the scope of Principle No.1 above are likely to be regarded as unenforceable by an individual shareholder because of the so-called 'rule in *Foss and Harbottle'*. The classic example of this is *MacDougall* v. *Gardiner* itself (above). As it was put by Jordan CJ in the Australian case of *Australian Coal & Shale Employees' Federation* v. *Smith* (1938) SRNSW 48:

'Now, the rule that the company is itself the proper plaintiff to sue for wrongs done to the company applies not only to wrongs done to the company by matters arising *dehors* the articles of association, but to wrongs done to the company in the nature of failure on the part of shareholders to observe the articles. As to this, the rule is that if as the result of non-compliance by members with the articles of association something has been done which constitutes a wrong to the company, or brings about the doing of a wrong to the company, the company alone can sue to remedy the wrong; and the court will not, subject to the exceptions already indicated, entertain a suit by shareholders purporting to act on the behalf of all the members to enforce the strict rights of the company ...

Further, the constructive deed constituted by the memorandum and articles is one of a very special character, and it does not follow that every breach by the company of one of its terms gives rise to a right of action which a court of equity will enforce. Where there has been a breach of the articles to which the company has been a party, to the extent that it has acted on it without having done anything to regularise it, the breach may in one aspect constitute a wrong to the company, and in another a wrong done by the company to a shareholder in the company in the nature of a breach of the shareholder's right to have the articles observed by the company. In this case, if the breach is one which the company in general meeting or acting by its directors can, if it chooses, lawfully condone by adopting the correct procedure, the court will not at the instance of a shareholder prevent the company from acting, merely because the correct procedure has not been adopted ...This is regarded as a matter of internal management, and the court will not interfere merely to check irregularities in the doing by a company of that which it has power to do regularly ...

An individual member can, however, sue alone to restrain the company from doing an act which is *ultra vires* the memorandum of association ... And if the company commits a breach of the articles of a kind which it cannot lawfully regularise by means of a general meeting or by the action of its directors, it would appear that an individual shareholder may sue to restrain the breach ... Thus, if a company by its agents in breach of the articles denies to a shareholder his right to vote, the shareholder may maintain his suit against the company to enforce his right: *Pender* v. *Lushington.*'

This, of course, begs the whole difficult question of which breaches are ones which the company 'cannot lawfully regularise by means of a general meeting or the action of its directors'.

The difficulty of compartmentalising is seen in *Australian Coal & Shale* itself where Jordan CJ went on to hold:

'If a person who is entitled to act as director of the company is unlawfully prevented from acting, this in one aspect constitutes a wrong done to the company by the person responsible and in another a wrong done to the director by those persons and also by the company if the company is responsible for their action. If a person not entitled to act as director assumes to act as such he is thereby committing a wrong against the company; and it has been said that it is for the company to determine whether it will restrain him from so doing, and that a suit cannot be maintained by an individual shareholder for the purpose, nor can he sue on behalf of himself and all other members, bringing the company before the court as defendant, at any rate unless the case can be brought within the exceptions to the rule in *Foss* v. *Harbottle*: *Mozley* v. *Alston*. But if the company by its agents permits an unqualified person to act as director, its conduct may constitute a breach by the company of its obligation to its shareholders to abide by the articles of association.

It is stated in *Hickman* v. *Kent Sheep-Breeders' Association*, in reliance upon the *Eley* v. *Positive Life Assurance Co.* type of case, that the rule that no right purported to be given by the articles to a person in any other capacity than that of member can be enforced against the company extends to a right to act as director. But provision for the appointment of directors to manage the business of the company was one of the essential features of the old deed of settlement, as was recognised by section 7 of the English Companies Act 1844 (7 & 8 Vict. c. 110), and has always been treated by statute as a matter to be provided by the articles of association. Both upon principle and upon authority, I see no reason why a member who by virtue of the articles of association and of things done thereunder is also a director, cannot as against the company, at any rate whilst it is a going concern, insist upon his right to act as director ... or why, indeed, any shareholder cannot as against the company and its agents insist that a person who under the articles is entitled to act as director and whom the company in general meeting cannot under the articles lawfully dismiss as director shall not be prevented from acting as director, and insist also that the company and its agents shall not permit to act as director a person whom under the articles of association the company is not entitled to employ as director: *Cousins* v. *International Brick Co. Ltd* [1931] 2 Ch. 90. In practice, in suits by individuals, injunctions have been granted against unqualified persons restraining them from acting as directors ...'

The issue is nothing if not difficult and the reader is referred back to the various academic arguments already mentioned.

2.7 Ratifiability a criterion?

As *Australian Coal & Shale* demonstrates, there are cases where the articles involved have not appeared to fall within the category covered by Principle No.1 above yet where the court has allowed an individual shareholder to sue to enforce the article against the company. In *Catesby* v. *Burnett* (1916) 2 Ch 325 a shareholder sued successfully to prevent directors from holding office in breach of the articles. On no possible interpretation did the relevant article confer a right on the objecting shareholder. Therefore one is left to ask what right was being enforced and what made it enforceable? The same dilemma is raised by other cases, notably *Quin & Axtens Ltd* v *Salmon* (see [2.5] above). What was Salmon's 'proprietary' interest?

To say that the matter can be approached from a different direction by asking whether the breach is such as can be cured (i.e. ratified) by ordinary resolution of the company in general meeting (so that the rule in *Foss* v. *Harbottle* prevents suit) is really to beg the question, for we then have to decide which breaches are ratifiable and why (see further on this point, Smith (1978) MLR 147). Furthermore, in some cases where the breach was clearly of a 'procedural' article (and therefore ratifiable in *MacDougall* terms) the individual shareholder has been allowed to sue (*Hodgson* v. *NALGO* [1972] 1 All ER 15), but special circumstances obtained in *Hodgson* in that insistence on corporate action would have meant a denial of justice as there was no time in which the majority could act effectively. An additional point is that, assuming one has classified the breach as a mere 'procedural irregularity', it is not clear whether the *probability* of ratification is a relevant criterion so that the personal action will fail only where there is a likelihood (as opposed to the mere theoretical possibility) of the majority ratifying a 'procedural irregularity' (see Smith, (1978) MLR 147 at p.152).

2.8   The courts' dilemma

The courts' dilemma was stated in this way by Lord Justice Lawrence in *Cotter* v. *NUS* ([1929] 2 Ch 58, 107):

> 'I think it would be lamentable if a technical breach of the rules were held to entitle a dissentient member or minority to obtain an injunction to restrain the carrying out of a resolution.'

This, of course, begs the question: when is a breach of the rules merely 'technical'? Also, Smith (in the article cited above) makes the point that where a breach of the articles (e.g. by the directors holding office in breach of the articles) is a wrong both to the company and to the shareholder, even if it be permissible for the company to ratify a breach of the articles, it seems illogical to extend the effect of this ratification to the prejudice suffered by the shareholder. In any case, many breaches are not 'ratifiable', as we have seen.

2.9   Summary of the legal position

This rather unsatisfactory state of the law can be summarised in this way. The law may be moving in a direction which extends the scope of the personal action (*Quin & Axtens* v. *Salmon*; but see against this the line taken by the Court of Appeal in *Prudential* v. *Newman Industries (No.2)* [1982] 1 All ER 354). The current position can broadly be stated as follows: until the articles are lawfully altered a shareholder has a right 'to maintain himself in full membership with all the rights and privileges appertaining to that status' (Lord Justice Jenkins in *Edwards* v. *Halliwell* [1950] 2 All ER 1064). However, there are problems with the definition of these 'rights' and 'privileges' (the 'personal right' limit). In particular, does his 'status' entitle him to expect compliance by the company and its organs with each and every provision in the articles? Some further support for an affirmative answer to this question may have come in *Re A Company No. 005136 of 1986* ([1987] BCLC 82) where a member complained that the directors had used their power under the articles to allot shares for an improper purpose (see [3.4]). Mr Justice Hoffmann said that:

'Although the alleged breach of duty by the board is in theory a breach of its duty to *the company* (see Chapter 8), the wrong to the company is not the substance of the complaint ... The true basis of the action is an alleged infringement of the petitioner's individual rights as a shareholder. The allotment is alleged to be an improper and unlawful exercise of the powers granted to the board by the articles of association, which constitute a contract between the company and its members ... *An abuse of these powers is an infringement of a member's contractual rights under the articles.*'

When it comes to enforcing compliance with 'procedures' (the internal irregularity limits) laid down in the articles, as Jordan CJ put it in *Australian Coal and Shale Employers' Federation* v. *Smith* (1938) 38 SRNSW 48, the courts feel that

'the need is for some principle which disregards mere trifles (for example the order of business) yet hits out at breaches of rules designed for the shareholders' protection',

while bearing in mind that

'(rules of procedure) are in many ways just as much the essence of the agreement as the right to share in profits, and the man who is deprived of his rights at meetings may see his profits dwindle in direct proportion' (Chumir, (1955) 4 Alb LR 96 at 100).

According to the 'ratifiability' analysis;

'... In each case a line has to be drawn through the articles. On one side stand clauses the breach of which cannot be ratified; on the other side stand those in the grip of the ordinary majority' (Wedderburn, (1957) CLJ 194).

The difficulty of drawing this line is illustrated by the fact that some articles which appear to deal more with 'management' rights than shareholder rights have been held to be enforceable (*Pulbrook* v. *Richmond Consolidated Mining Co.* (1878) 9 ChD 610 – the right to act as director) while articles which could be regarded as conferring a shareholder 'proprietary' right have not (*MacDougall* v. *Gardiner*, above – the right to demand a poll). The traditional way of explaining the majority of cases and reflecting the two limitations placed on the contractual force of the statutory contract, can be illustrated diagrammatically as follows.

The traditional explanation for the cases

The 'Wedderburn line'

Enforceable	Dividing Line	Unenforceable
(Because a breach is not ratifiable)	A R T	
Articles conferring personal rights (or imposing obligations) on shareholder as a shareholder	I C L E	Articles which *do not* confer personal shareholder rights *either*
	S	(a) because they confer 'outsider' rights *or* (b) because they merely lay down rules of procedure (the breach of which is ratifiable by the company)

This traditional way of viewing 'the cases' is constantly being rethought in the light of a number of cases which do not quite fit the pattern. Hence, alternative explanations have been suggested as we have seen. The main ones can be summarised as follows:

Unsettled Questions (which double as alternative Suggested Explanations for the cases)

(1) Whether there is a general personal right, *provided* one sues as a member, to force the company to observe all the provisions of its constitution until this is changed according to law subject only to those matters of internal management on which the courts have seen fit to defer to majority rule in the past? (Wedderburn, [2.6] above).

(2) Whether the only right a shareholder has is a right to insist that the 'proper' organ, as designated by the memorandum or articles be allowed to function in the particular case? (Goldberg, [2.6] above).

(3) Whether the only right a shareholder has is a limited right to intervene to enforce those provisions which affect the power of the company to function? (Prentice, [2.6] above).

These last two views narrow 'the general right' to that of enforcing provisions of a 'constitutional character' (proffering two possible definitions of this concept).

2.10   A new development?

One way around the 'outsider rights' restriction on the contractual force of the articles has been highlighted by recent cases. (Another way would be to point to an 'extrinsic contract'; see [2.11] below.) For example, in *Diligenti* v. *R.W.M.D. Operations Kelona Ltd.* [1976] 1 BCLR 36 the Supreme Court of British Columbia held the petitioner to be entitled to relief under a provision equivalent to section 459, 1985 Act (see Chapter 8). Here, the articles provided that members would be directors. One such member was ousted from his position as director. The court held that the right to act as director had been given to and enjoyed by petitioner *qua* member; therefore, a breach of the right affected petitioner *qua* member and the remedy was available.

A similar line has been taken by the English courts when applying section 459, 1985 Act to 'quasi-partnership' type companies, i.e. companies which are in essence akin to partnerships (see Chapter 8). This may cut the legs from under the *Eley* line of cases because it becomes possible in appropriate circumstances to argue that *prima facie* all rights embodied in the articles are granted to a member in view of his membership and ought to be regarded as terms of his membership. Therefore, they would be enforceable under section 14(1) directly. They would be enforceable (subject to lawful alteration of the articles for the future, but not with retrospective effect) as terms of his 'global' 'contract of membership'. This involves the recognition of a link between Mr Justice Astbury's second and third propositions in *Hickman's case* (above, [2.4]), narrowing the second and expanding the third in appropriate circumstances, those 'appropriate circumstances' being limited possibly to the 'quasi-partnership company' context. This goes further than saying that the court may find that an extrinsic contract has been concluded with an outsider on the basis of the articles. This latter route of argument has operated in the context of directorial appointments, whether the appointees were also members or not (*Swabey* v. *Port Darwin Gold Mining Co.* (1889) 1 Meg 385 CA; *International Cable Co.* (1892) 66 CT 253 and *Re New British Iron Co., ex parte Beckwith* [1898] 1 Ch 324).

There is equal reason for applying this to contracts entered into with prospective 'insiders', i.e. prospective shareholders. The artificial dichotomy between a member's capacity as member and his capacity as 'director' or other 'outsider' would thus disappear. Of course, this is to ask the courts to accept that the 'personal rights of members' can embrace rights pertaining to some non-member capacity, i.e. that a member's membership rights may *include* his right to be the company's director, solicitor etc. (the *Hickman* line of cases states the opposite as far as section 14(1) is concerned). In Chapter 7 [7.2.3.5]) we shall refer to further judicial support for such an approach. Be this as it may, the articles are only one possible source of a particular individual's basket of rights against the company, the others being the law and 'extrinsic contracts'.

2.11   *Extrinsic contracts*

Shareholders, and non-members, are free to enter into any lawful contract with the company and thereby acquire rights against the company. The courts are able to infer the existence of an extrinsic contract, outside and possibly additional to the section 14 contract, from the conduct of the parties, and to use the articles as evidence of the terms of that contract (see *Re New British Iron Co.* (1898) 1 Ch 324; *Shuttleworth* v. *Cox* [1927] 2 KB 9; *Southern Foundries Ltd* v. *Shirlaw* [1940] AC 801).

It would not matter in practice that such rights as were enjoyed in virtue of such a contract could not properly be termed 'shareholder' rights if an enforceable extrinsic agreement could in any case be pointed to. Indeed, while rights granted and enjoyed purely in virtue of the articles would be variable prospectively by an alteration of the articles, if it appeared that the rights were enjoyed under some 'extrinsic' contract (albeit evidenced by the articles) then while the company could not be prevented from altering the articles it would be liable in damages for breach of contract if it acted on the alteration (*Southern Foundries Ltd* v. *Shirlaw* [1940] AC 701). This is because extrinsic agreements are governed by the ordinary law of contract and may in principle only be varied by the agreement of the parties to them. Therefore, even if nothing is said in the articles about the '*prima facie* oursider' right, the member may be able to invoke what we have so far called an 'extrinsic contract' which is in reality and in legal terms a separate (albeit possibly a collateral) contract which together with the memorandum and articles constitutes the bundle of rights and obligations a member has *vis à vis* the company. The contract is 'collateral' where it is entered into as a pre-amble to the contract of membership, but of course there can be a contract whereby a person who is already a member agrees to something quite independently of his membership, for example to serve as director under a service contract.

An interesting question is whether an outsider right enjoyed under the articles by only one or more members, but not by all members, constitutes them the holders of a separate class of shares from those held by the other members. If so, that right could only be taken away – or varied – if at all, by the company following the variation of class rights procedure (see Chapter 7). Subject to this point, it would seem that the grant of an 'outsider right' in the memorandum or articles affords less protection (because of the power of alteration enjoyed by the company) rather than more (subject to section 27, 1985 Act – entrenchment in the memorandum; see [2.12] below).

The courts' apparently blanket insistence that outsider rights granted by the statutory contract are not enforceable under section 14 is to be contrasted with their liberality in allowing the most drastic remedy, *viz.* winding-up, when such 'rights' are denied and with their willingness to provide relief under section 459 (see Chapter 8). Surely, the courts must soon acknowledge the principle that 'outsider rights' granted in return for membership are membership rights. This will amount to a redrawing, if not a reversal, of the *Hickman* line of cases. Also, it will require reconsideration of the interesting question whether, on a transfer of shares, such 'outsider rights' 'run with the shares' held by the member to whom they were initially granted by the 'extrinsic' contract. In *Shalfoon* v. *Cheddar Valley Co-op Dairy Co. Ltd* (1924) NZLR 561), a New Zealand case, Mr Justice Salmond said in a case dealing with *obligations*, not rights:

'There are two distinct ways in which an obligation may come into existence as between a company and one of its shareholders. In the first place it may have its source in a regulation validly made by the company and inserted in the articles of association in pursuance of the authority conferred by section 22 and 122 of the Companies Act 1908. In the second place it may have its source in a contract made between the company and the individual shareholder. This distinction is of practical importance for several reasons. In the first place an obligation imposed by a regulation is not merely personal, but is appurtenant to the share of the company so as to run with those shares in the hands of successive owners and to bind all shareholders for the time being; but a contractual obligation is purely personal and binds only the individual shareholder who has become a party to the contract, and cannot be made to run with the shares as appurtenant thereto in the hands of successive owners. In the second place a regulation can always be altered or repealed by the company and the rights and obligations created thereby may be thus modified or destroyed; whereas a contract between the company and a shareholder can only be altered or cancelled by the mutual consent of both parties. In the third place a regulation to be valid must be within the scope of the legislative authority given to a company by the Companies Act over its shareholders; whereas a contract made between the company and its shareholder is subject merely to the general provisions of the law of contract, a company being entitled to make any contract with a shareholder which it might lawfully make with an outsider. A shareholder may therefore take upon himself by contract with the company many obligations which could not be imposed upon him by the company by the making of regulations ...'

Assuming these principles to apply in general to rights as well as obligations, a court taking the *Diligenti* approach (see [2.10] above) would need to decide whether to maintain these principles intact. Could a member who by virtue of a provision in the articles had the right to be a director assign this right by transferring his shares? That he could in principle would seem to follow from Mr Justice Salmond's first 'consequence', unless the transferor and the company had agreed that it would not be assignable. But rights are not assignable if of a personal nature and the right to be a director, for example, would appear to be such a right. Therefore if the *Diligenti* approach were applied to section 14 this exception to assignability would require Mr Justice Salmond's first consequence to be tempered. As between the initial shareholder and the company, however, section 14 would be interpreted as binding the company to allow the shareholder to act as director, solicitor etc. or pay damages, while also risking a petition under section 459, Companies Act 1985 or even under section 122(1)(g), Insolvency Act 1986 (see Chapter 8). The only way out for the company would be to alter the articles to remove the right, something it could only do if the right emanated solely from the articles (and not from an extrinsic contract) and even then perhaps only by following the available procedures for varying class rights. This argument will be reverted to in the context of class rights (Chapter 7).

2.12   *Entrenchment of contractual rights in the memorandum*

2.12.1   The company's constitution

The Companies Act 1985 envisages that a company's constitution will comprise two documents, the Articles of Association which regulate a company's workings (or the 'internal relations' within a company), and the Memorandum of Association, which has been called the company's 'basic statute'. It is in the memorandum that persons dealing with the company will find such vital information as the company's name, its objects, the place of its registered office, whether the liability of its members is limited, the amount of its proposed share capital and its division into shares of a certain amount (section 2, Companies Act 1985). The Memorandum takes priority over the articles in the event of a conflict between their respective provisions (*Andrews* v. *Gas Meter Co.* [1897] 1 Ch 361).

2.12.2   Alteration of the memorandum

For our present purposes the important point concerns the alteration of the memorandum. While the articles may be altered by special resolution (section 9, 1985 Act), the 'conditions' contained in the memorandum may only be altered in the cases and in the mode (sometimes by ordinary resolution) and to the extent, for which express provision is made in the 1985 Act [section 2(7), 1985 Act]. In other words, one would need to look at the detailed provisions of the Act in each case, and in particular for present purposes at section 17. This section provides two rules which are of relevance here.

First, any 'condition' contained in the memorandum which could lawfully have been contained in the articles instead of in the memorandum, is alterable by the company by special resolution with the rider that if an application is made to the court for the alteration to be cancelled, the alteration does not have effect except in so far as it is confirmed by the court. Section 17 provides that the power of alteration by special resolution [besides being subject to the conditions of section 17(1) itself] is subject to section 16 and to Part XVII of the Act. This means that a member's liability to subscribe for shares or to otherwise pay money to the company may not be increased without his express consent in writing (section 16), and that the power is lost if the court has so directed in a minority-protection order under Part XVII (see Chapter 8). As far as the grounds on which an application to set aside the alteration, and on which the court will deny confirmation to an alteration, are concerned, these are the same as apply in the case of an objection to an alteration of the objects clause, with certain modifications [section 17(3), 1985 Act].

Secondly, section 17 provides that the power to alter conditions which could have been inserted in the articles does not apply where the memorandum itself either provides for or prohibits the alteration of those conditions. Therefore, it is possible to 'entrench' certain rights by the expedient of inserting them in the memorandum and declaring them to be unalterable. Of itself, of course, this does not guarantee success in enforcing any such condition, for the court could still conceivably classify the right as an 'outsider right' and the member seeking a remedy might need to point to an extrinsic contract or try to argue for the application of the above 'new' analysis, i.e. that it is a term of *his* membership. However, if 'ratifiability' is the criterion for the application of the rule in *Foss* v. *Harbottle* (the accepted view is that it is), it is arguable that this rule cannot pose an obstacle to enforcement, because if the members acting unanimously are unable to alter the memorandum it seems impossible to argue that a simple majority can ratify the breach of a provision in the memorandum. This would allow a simple majority to do that which all the shareholders could not do (arguing from *Edwards* v. *Halliwell* [1950] 2 All ER 1064). However, it would seem that rights contained in the memorandum and declared to be unalterable may be altered by utilising section 425, 1985 Act (see [9.2.2] below).

2.12.3   Class rights

The power given by section 17(1) does not authorise the variation (or abrogation) of class rights, which is governed by special rules laid down in the Act (see Chapter 7). Suffice it to say here that if class rights are set out in the memorandum and there is no provision for their variation either in the memorandum or in the articles, those rights are alterable only with the agreement of all the members of the company.

2.13   *Statutory rights – individual and qualified minority rights*

2.13.1   Introduction

A major source of shareholder rights is statute and in particular the Companies Act 1985. This statutory entrenchment of rights operates as a restriction on the power of the majority in general meeting, for section 9 of the Act empowers the company to alter the articles by special resolution 'subject, *inter alia*, to the provisions of the Act'. Therefore, a right vested in members by the Act cannot be inserted in the articles and then altered. This would be for the company to usurp the role of Parliament. A clear statutory right can only be taken away by new legislation. It should follow that a breach of a statutory right by the company cannot be ratified by it, so that the rule in *Foss* v. *Harbottle* cannot prevent individual suit for redress. The classic expression of this principle is that for the company to act in such a way is to act illegally and *ultra vires* (beyond its capacity) so that even unanimous shareholder agreement cannot cure the infringement (*Ashbury Railway Carriage and Iron Co. Ltd* v. *Riche* (1875) LR 7 HL 653).

The common law therefore allows a single shareholder to sue to restrain the breach (*Simpson* v. *Westminster Palace Hotel* (1860) 8 HL Cas 712; *Poole* v. *G.W.R.Co.* (1867) 3 Ch App 262 at 277). However, a distinct line of authority (exemplified by *Re Oxted Motor Co. Ltd* [1921] 3 KB 32) imports the same distinction, between rules of substance and rules of mere procedure, which bedevils the 'statutory contract rights' cases (above, paras [2.2] *et seq.*), into this area.

The Court of Appeal has recently appeared implicitly to affirm the validity of the approach taken in this line of cases, according to which a violation of a mere 'procedural rule' of statute is, at least prior to liquidation, ratifiable by general meeting resolution (*Precision Dippings Ltd* v. *Precision Dippings Marketing Ltd & Ors* (1985) 1 BCC 99, 539). In *Precision Dippings Ltd* v. *Precision Dippings Marketing Ltd & Ors* the facts were that a dividend was declared following a breach by the company of section 43(3)(c) of the 1980 Companies Act (now section 271(4), 1985 Act) which required an auditors' statement to be annexed to their report where the report is qualified. The test applied by the Court of Appeal was whether the statutory provisions concerned were intended as a major protection for the interests of creditors and members, and the court held that sections 39-43 of the 1980 Companies Act were of this nature, so that a breach of them was not ratifiable by the members.

Nevertheless, in another recent, but prior, case (*Devlin* v. *Slough Estates* [1983] BCLC 497) the court held that an individual shareholder could not sue for a declaration that the company's accounts had been drawn up in breach of the companies legislation. It was held that while the annual accounts (which by article 150 of the company's articles had to be prepared in accordance with the companies legislation) were obviously very important, providing the only information to which a shareholder was entitled, and the only information for the public at large, yet it would be strange if the court could be approached by any shareholder, asking the court to settle the company's accounts in accordance with the statute. It was held that article 150 did not give a shareholder the right to insist that the accounts were prepared in accordance with the statute. The court did say that there were many matters relating to accounts which had to be a matter of business judgment, for which there was no single correct answer. However, this does not seem adequate reason for interpreting an 'article 150' provision in the articles as conferring no personal right on a shareholder and denying him *'locus standi'* (the right to sue) though it might ground a finding that the accounts had in fact been properly drawn up.

The court's reasoning in *Devlin* does not square very comfortably with the general approach taken in *Precision Dippings* by the Court of Appeal and cannot be explained simply by reference to some distinction between 'statutory' and 'contractual' shareholder rights. Pennington (R.R. Pennington, *Pennington's Company Law*, 5th ed., p.727) has sought to explain the cases on the memorandum and articles (the 'statutory contract rights' cases) by saying that a distinction needs to be drawn between 'personal' and 'corporate' rights, and that only if a shareholder has a special interest in its observance (distinct from the general interest which every member has in the company adhering to the terms of its constitution) can a provision in the memorandum or articles be said to confer a personal right on him. Can *Devlin* v. *Slough Estates* be regarded as an application of this rationalisation to the sphere of statutory rights? It would seem that the area of statutory rights is as uncertain as that of contractual rights in the memorandum and articles, and Pennington's rationalisation would support a very narrow view of the ambit of 'personal rights'.

2.13.2   Examples of statutory individual rights

(All references are to the Companies Act 1985, unless otherwise stated.)

(1) S.16.	Without his consent in writing, a member may not be compelled by a resolution of the company to take or subscribe for more shares or in any way have his liability to contribute to the company's share capital or otherwise to pay money to the company increased.
(2) S.459	A member has the right to petition for relief from actual or proposed unfair prejudice.
(3) S.124(1) Insolvency Act 1986	A contributory, among others, may apply to the court for a winding-up order. (For the statutory definition of 'contributory' see section 74 Insolvency Act 1986.)
(4) S.371(1)	A voting member may apply to the court in certain circumstances for an order calling a

general meeting of the company.

S.367(1)	A similar application may be made to the Secretary of State for Trade and Industry in relation to the annual general meeting.
(5) Ss.430A-C	In certain circumstances, a member has a right to require a take-over offeror to acquire his shares, to object to the acquisition of his shares or to apply to the court for a revision of the terms of acquisition.
(6) S.240	A member is as a rule entitled to receive advance notice (21 days prior to the general meeting at which they are to be laid) of the company's accounts (i.e. profit and loss account, balance sheet, directors' report, auditors' report and, if applicable, the company's group accounts).
(7) S.356, S.19	Each member has the right to inspect various registers and documents to be held at the company's registered office or to be sent certain documents (e.g. a copy of the memorandum, section 19).
(8) S.359	Any member may apply to the court for rectification of the register of members.
(9) S.582(5)	In connection with the power of the liquidator of a transferor company to accept shares, etc. in a transferee company, a dissentient member may require the liquidator either to abstain from carrying the special resolution effecting such a scheme into effect or to purchase his interest at a price to be determined by agreement or arbitration.
(10) S.369	The effect of this provision is to give a member who has the right to receive notice of general meetings the right to be given certain specified minimum periods of notice (see Chapter 5).
(11) S.89	Subject to important exceptions, a company proposing to allot equity securities must offer them first to existing holders (pre-emption rights; see Chapter 6).
(12) S.372	Subject to some exceptions and limitations, any member entitled to attend and vote at a

	meeting is entitled to appoint an agent (a proxy) to attend and vote on his behalf.
(13) S.176	A member of a private company may object to a payment being made out of capital for the purchase or redemption of its shares, provided he did not consent to or vote in favour of the relevant special resolution.
(14) S.174(3)	Notwithstanding anything contained in the company's articles, any member of the company may demand a poll on the question whether a resolution shall be passed by a private company for the payment out of capital for the purchase or redemption of its own shares under section 173.
(15) S.164(5)(b)	Notwithstanding anything contained in the company's articles, any member has the right to demand a poll on the question whether authority be conferred on the company to make an off-market purchase of its own shares (or on the variation, revocation or removal of such authority) pursuant to section 164(2).
(16) S.16 Company Directors' (Disqualification) Act 1986	Any past or present member, among others, may apply to the court for the making of a disqualification order against any person who has committed or is alleged to have committed an offence or other default.
(17) S.212(3) and (5) Insolvency Act 1986	A 'contributory' (see section 74, Insolvency Act 1986) may, with the leave of the court, apply to the court for an examination into the conduct of officers of the company and others [see section 212(1), Insolvency Act 1986] with a view to compelling such person (a) to repay, restore or account for any money or other property of the company, with interest, or (b) to contribute such sum to the company's assets by way of compensation in respect of misfeasance or breach of duty as the court thinks just.

2.13.3   Examples of statutory qualified minority rights

While individual membership rights can be exercised by an individual shareholder, the exercise of 'qualified minority' rights requires the co-operation of a minority group of specified size. There is a link between the two concepts which is also of relevance to contractual rights and which will be referred to after some examples of qualified minority rights are given.

A qualified minority enjoys the following rights, among others:

(1)	S.370(1)(3)	In so far as the articles do not make other provision in the matter, two or more members holding not less than one-tenth of the issued share capital (or, if the company does not have a share capital not less than 5 per cent in number of the members) may call a meeting.
(2)	S.368	Members holding not less than one-tenth of the paid-up share capital which carries the right to vote at general meetings (or, in the case of a company not having a share capital members representing not less than one-tenth of the total voting rights) may requisition the holding of an extraordinary general meeting. The directors have twenty-one days from the date of the deposit of the requisition at the company's registered office within which to convene the meeting.
(3)	S.376	Members holding not less than one-twentieth of the total voting rights, or not less than 100 members holding shares in the company on which there has been paid up an average sum, per member, of not less than £100, may by complying with section 377, require the company to circulate certain resolutions and statements to members.
(4)	S.373	The effect of section 373 is:

(a) For the following minorities, the right to demand a poll at a general meeting on any question other than the election of the chairman of the meeting or the adjournment of the meeting is absolute and a poll must be taken.
    The 'minorities' are:

(i)   not less than 5 members having the right to vote, or

(ii) a member or members not having less than 10 per cent of all the votes, or

(iii) members holding shares (conferring a right to vote) which on the aggregate of the sums paid up equal not less than 10 per cent of the total sum paid up on all shares conferring the right to vote.

(b) The articles may not prohibit the right (individually or collectively) to demand a poll on any such question as is referred to in (a). At common law, every member having the right to vote may demand a poll and this right may only be excluded by express provision to that effect (*R. v. Wimbledon Local Board* (1882) 8 QBD 459) or special custom (*Campbell v. Maund* (1836) 5 A&E 865).

(5) S.5   The holders of not less in the aggregate than 15 per cent in nominal value of the issued share capital or any class of it (or, if the company is not limited by shares, not less than 15 per cent of the company's members) may apply to the court for a resolution altering the objects of the company to be cancelled.

(6) S.17   A similar right of objection exists to the alteration of conditions in the memorandum which could lawfully have been contained in the articles.

(7) S.127   Where class rights have been varied, the holders of not less in the aggregate than 15 per cent of the issued shares of the class in question (being persons who did not consent to or vote in favour of the resolution for the variation), may apply to the court to have the variation cancelled.

(8) S.431   The Secretary of State may appoint one or more inspectors to investigate, and report on, the affairs of a company on the application, *inter alia* (i.e. among others),

(i)   in the case of a company having a share capital, either of not less than 200 members or of members holding not less than one-tenth of the shares issued, or

(ii) in the case of a company not having a share capital, on the application of not less than one-fifth in number of the persons on the company's register of members.

(9) S.442   A similar right to the one just cited exists to request the Secretary of State to institute an investigation into the membership of the company, and otherwise with respect to the company, for the purpose of determining the true persons who are or have been financially interested in the success or failure (real or apparent) of the company or able to control or materially influence its policy.

(10) S.214   The holders of shares representing one-tenth or more of the amount paid up on shares carrying a right to vote at general meetings of a public company may requisition it to use its powers under section 212 (investigation into interests in its shares). The company must exercise these powers on deposit of a requisition complying with section 214.

(11) S.54   Where a special resolution by a public company to be re-registered under section 53 as a private company has been passed, an application for its cancellation may be made to the court, within 28 days, by (a) the holders of not less in the aggregate than 5 per cent in nominal value of the company's share capital or any class thereof; (b) if the company is not limited by shares, by not less than 5 per cent of its members; or (c) by not less than 50 of the company's members. Persons who have consented to or voted in favour of the resolution may not apply.

(12) S.157(3)   A similar right exists to apply for the cancellation of a special resolution approving the giving of financial assistance by a private company for the acquisition of its own shares under section 155. The application may be made by (a) the holders of not less in the

aggregate than 10 per cent in nominal value of the company's issued share capital or any class thereof, or (b) if the company is not limited by shares, by not less than 10 per cent of the company's members. The application may not be made by a person who has consented to or voted in favour of the resolution.

2.13.4 Purpose of qualified minority rights

Having cited some main qualified minority rights, it should be clear that these are rights whose purpose is normally to provide access to a competent forum in which an impartial decision on the disputed measure can be obtained. For example, if the dispute is with management, a minority can requisition an extraordinary general meeting; if it is between warring groups of shareholders, minority rights give access to the court (sections 5, 17, 127) or to the Department of Trade and Industry (sections 431, 442). They represent a compromise between, on the one hand the necessity of protecting certain interests and, on the other hand that of ensuring that the safeguards are not resorted to vexatiously.

2.13.5 The link between individual rights and qualified minority rights

The question here is: what are qualified minority rights in 'individual membership right' terms? The following considerations apply equally to statutory as to contractual qualified minority rights (i.e. those contained in the company constitution). To take an example, suppose the articles entitle any two members having the right to vote to demand (and, by implication, to be granted) a poll on the question of the election of the chairman of the meeting (article 46, Table A). Suppose that two such members make the demand but the right of one of the members to join in this demand is denied in breach of the articles. The question is: what is the proper analysis of the thwarted shareholders' rights? It is submitted that the answer is that either of those two members has the right to say:

'I have the right, as a voting member of the company,

(i) to join in demanding a poll [since this is a common law right which is not excluded by the articles], and

(ii) to have the poll granted if my demand is joined by one other member having the right to join in demanding a poll, for the contract assures me that such a demand will be effective.'

In other words, this qualified minority right breaks down into two 'personal' and 'individual membership' rights. In the above example, article 46 would be read as actually conferring the right to join in demanding a poll. This analysis is confirmed by section 373(2) of the Act which provides that 'the instrument appointing a proxy to vote at a meeting of the company shall be deemed also to confer authority to demand *or join in* demanding a poll ...'

2.14 *The general law as a source of rights*

As it happens, the common law vests the right to demand a poll in a shareholder, subject to the articles (*R.* v. *Wimbledon Local Board* (1882) 8 QBD 459). This illustrates the fourth source of shareholder rights, *viz.* the general law. Other examples of a right emanating from this source are the right to restrain the company from acting *ultra vires* and, *a fortiori*, illegally; the right to have 'fraudulent' general meeting resolutions altering the articles declared invalid (see [4.5.3]); the right to receive sufficiently informative notice of the content of proposed general meeting resolutions (*Kaye* v. *Croydon Tramways Co.* [1898] 1 Ch 358); the right to have a reasonable opportunity to speak at meetings (*Wall* v. *London and Northern Assets Corpn* (1898) 2 Ch 469); the right to move amendments to resolutions (*Henderson* v. *Bank of Australasia* (1890) 45 ChD 330); the *prima facie* right to transfer shares (*Re Smith, Knight & Co., Weston's case* (1868) 4 Ch App 20. These common law rights are all subject to being cut down by contrary agreement, e.g. in the memorandum and articles. We turn now to the question of remedies.

2.15 *Remedies for the breach of shareholder rights*

2.15.1 Statutory rights

Statutory rights, whether individual or qualified minority rights, cannot be taken away by the company whether through a provision in the memorandum and articles or by general meeting or board resolution. Any such provision or resolution is unlawful and void.

However, there appears to be no general right to compel the

company to observe each and every provision of the Companies Act.
While it is sometimes said that a member can restrain the company
from acting *ultra vires* or unlawfully, there are exceptions and the
dividing line is none too clear (see [2.13.1] above). The exceptions
purport to be examples of the infringement of legal provisions which
do not in terms confer personal rights on members, so that the
infringement falls within the sphere of operation of the rule in *Foss* v.
Harbottle. However, a member may sue to restrain the company from
holding a general meeting of which insufficient notice has been given.
Again, any equity shareholder may seek an injunction to prevent a
proposed issue of equity shares or securities in the absence of
compliance with the existing holders' statutory preferential subscription rights (see Chapter 6) or to restrain the company from passing a
resolution of which insufficiently informative notice has been given.
On the present state of the authorities, it is impossible to predict with
certainty when a breach of the Companies Act will be remediable by
declaration or injunction at the instance of an individual shareholder,
and the sort of arguments touched on above will have to be employed.

2.15.2   Rights under extrinsic contracts

As far as the breach of personal rights enjoyed in virtue of extrinsic
contracts are concerned, the normal contractual remedies, primarily
damages, are available.

2.15.3   Rights under the statutory contract

As far as breaches of the memorandum and articles are concerned, it
would seem that the special nature of this 'statutory contract'
precludes the usual remedies. The remedies available appear to be
limited to actions for an injunction or a declaration (and these only
where 'personal rights' have been infringed), or for a liquidated sum
due to the member as a member (for example, where a dividend has
been declared but not paid). Damages for breach of the section 14
'contract' appear not to be recoverable from the company (apparently
in the interests of upholding the 'maintenance of capital principle' in
favour of non-member creditors) but there is some (albeit old and
weak) authority to the contrary (*Moffat* v. *Farquhar* (1878) 7 ChD 591).
Nor is rectification available where articles are registered in the wrong
form by mistake (*Scott* v. *Frank Scott (London) Ltd.* [1940] Ch 794, CA).
  It has been said that an injunction is always available to restrain a
proposed breach of the memorandum or articles, whatever the nature
of the provision which it is proposed to breach (Smith, (1978) MLR

147). This is because the shareholders in general meeting cannot authorise a future breach (this would be to alter the articles without a special resolution (*Boschock Proprietary Co. Ltd* v. *Fuke* [1906] 1 Ch 148) or 'ratify' a future breach of the articles. The power of ratification only arises after the breach has occurred (*Irvine* v. *Union Bank of Australia* (1877) 2 App Cas 366, *Grant* v. *U.K. Switchback Rys* (1888) 40 ChD 135). Some would extend this to those provisions of the memorandum which are alterable by ordinary resolution (Pennington, *op. cit.* p.731) on the ground that alterations can only operate prospectively. However, after the breach has occurred it becomes necessary to draw the 'Wedderburn line' through the articles in order to decide whether an individual shareholder has a remedy (unless the courts pin their sails to one or other of the Wedderburn, Goldberg, Prentice or Gregory views – see above, [2.6]). The position is, of course, illogical. Why should it be possible to prevent the proposed breach of a 'mere procedural rule', but not to sue to have the ensuing resolution declared invalid? We come back to this point in Chapter 3 (at [3.8.4]).

2.16 Shareholder obligations

2.16.1 Sources of obligations

All that has been said above in relation to rights applies also to shareholder obligations. Therefore, obligations arise from contract (in the shape of the memorandum and articles) and from the general law (in particular the 1985 Act). Further obligations may arise in the usual way from 'extrinsic' contracts.

2.16.2 Remedies

One important difference applies as regards remedies. Where a shareholder acts in breach of the articles, the reasons which prevent the recovery of damages do not apply since here it is the company which is plaintiff. Damages are recoverable by the company.

2.16.3 Liability to contribute to capital

In a company limited by shares (the type of company with which this book is concerned), the shareholder's principal obligation relates to his capacity as a provider of capital to the company, i.e. to his liability towards the company to contribute the amount in cash or in kind agreed as the consideration for the share or shares allotted to him. Once this agreed consideration is paid over to the company the share is 'fully paid' and all further liability ceases. A shareholder in a company limited by guarantee pays nothing or only a nominal amount on becoming a member but undertakes to make payment to an amount specified in the articles or the terms of issue of his shares in the event of the company being in the red on liquidation (section 1(2)(b), 1985 Act). A shareholder in an 'unlimited company' (section 1(2)(c), 1985 Act) is liable to contribute without limit to the debts of the company on a winding-up in proportion to the nominal value of his shares. For this reason it is common for this type of company to make no arrangements for capital contribution. Unlimited companies are rare.

Guarantee companies may not (since 22 December 1980) have a share capital (i.e. issue shares), and only receive capital contributions on winding-up. They are therefore an inappropriate vehicle for the carrying on of a business and are usually adopted for the carrying on of a charitable undertaking. We shall therefore concentrate on the registered company which is limited by shares, this being the vehicle adopted for the purpose of raising capital with a view to pursuing commercial objects. This is the type of company which this book is about. References are to the Companies Act 1985 unless otherwise stated.

2.16.4

The memorandum of a company limited by shares (the word 'company' will be used from now on) will expressly limit the liability of the members to the amount, if any, unpaid on the shares respectively held by them (section 1(2)(a)). On formation, each subscriber to the memorandum will undertake to take at least one share. The number of shares taken by each subscriber must be stated in the memorandum (section 2(5)(b)(c)).

If a company is initially registered as a public company, it may not commence business until a 'trading certificate' has been obtained from the Registrar of Companies (section 117). This is granted only after the Registrar is satisfied that the company has allotted shares which together amount in terms of nominal value to the 'authorised minimum capital' (currently £50,000; section 118) of which one quarter of the nominal value must be paid up immediately. (There are no minimum capital requirements or minimum payment requirements for a private company and its shares.) These requirements apply also on the re-registration of a private company as a public company. The point is that the holder of shares in a public company will be obliged to pay one quarter of the nominal value of each share immediately. The memorandum or articles or terms of allotment can, and usually do, require the payment of the whole of the nominal value (plus any premium), as can the memorandum of a private company set down payment requirements. Indeed, section 101 provides that a public company may not allot a share except as paid up *at least* as to one quarter of its nominal value and the *whole* of any premium on it. However, once the nominal value of the shares has been fixed by the memorandum, then (notwithstanding any provision in the memorandum or articles) no shareholder is bound by any alteration to the memorandum made after the date on which he became a member which purports to oblige him to take or subscribe for more shares than the number held by him at the time of the alteration, or to increase his liability to contribute to the company's share capital or to pay money to the company. The only exception is where he agrees in writing to be bound, whether in advance of the alteration or subsequently to it (section 16). It is possible for a private company to apply for re-registration as an unlimited company (in which case all members would become liable without limit for the company's debts), but this requires the unanimous assent of all members, consistently with section 16 (section 49).

2.16.5 Calls – forfeiture and surrender in lieu of forfeiture: the company's lien

Apart from any contractual requirement (in the terms of allotment) to pay the whole of the nominal value of shares (plus any premium) on subscription or allotment (nowadays the rule is that shares will be issued as fully paid), the shareholder may be called upon to pay the balance due (if any) at any time at the behest of the board, or if necessary in the course of winding-up. As far as calls are concerned the articles usually provide that the board give members a minimum of fourteen days' notice (article 12, Table A). (Table A is the model form of articles for a company limited by shares and is set out in the Schedule to the Companies (Tables A to F) Regulations 1985, SI 1985 No. 805 as amended from time to time.)

Joint holders of a share are jointly and severally bound to pay all calls in respect of the shares held jointly. Interest is usually payable on calls which remain unpaid after the due date of payment, the rate of interest being fixed by the terms of allotment of the share or in the notice of the call; if no rate is fixed in this way, the rate payable is that fixed in the Act unless interest is waived by the directors (article 15). Subject again to the terms of allotment, on an issue of shares the directors may impose different amounts and times of payment on different holders (section 119(a); article 17, Table A).

When a call is unpaid, the directors must give fourteen days' notice demanding payment of the call plus interest from the due date, stating the place where payment should be made and warning that in default of payment the shares in respect of which the call is made will be liable to be forfeited (article 18, Table A). If this notice is not complied with, the relevant shares may be forfeited by board resolution, this to include all dividends or other moneys payable in respect of the forfeited shares and still not paid before the forfeiture (article 19, Table A). The forfeiture may be cancelled on such terms as the directors think fit at any time before sale, re-allotment or other disposition (article 20, Table A).

The normal effect of forfeiture is that the company gets its shares back (and, if a public company, must cancel them or dispose of them within three years, section 146) and the former owner is discharged from all liability on the shares (*Re Bolton* [1930] 2 Ch 48 at 59 *per* Luxmore J). But by article 21 of Table A the effect of forfeiture is modified so that the person whose shares have been forfeited ceases to be a member 'in respect of them' and is obliged to surrender the relevant share certificate but remains liable to the company for all moneys which at the date of forfeiture are presently payable by him to the company in respect of those shares plus interest. Moreover, the directors may enforce payment (they may also waive it) without making any allowance for the value of the shares at the time of forfeiture or for any consideration received on their disposal. The former member is an ordinary debtor of the company, and not a 'contributory' (*Ladies' Dress Assocn Ltd* v. *Pulbrook* [1900] 2 QB 376; see [2.16.6] below regarding 'contributories'). This liability ceases when the company receives full payment for the shares, and the company cannot receive more than the difference between the calls due and the amount received on any re-issue of the shares (*Re Bolton* [1930] 2 Ch 48).

Article 22, Table A provides that a statutory declaration by a director or the secretary that a share has been forfeited on a specified date shall be conclusive evidence of the facts stated in it as against all persons claiming to be entitled to the share. The same considerations apply where the articles permit a shareholder to surrender his shares in lieu of forfeiture (section 143(3)(d) permits the articles to so provide but Table A makes no provision for this). Section 143(3)(d) of the Act expressly excepts forfeiture or surrender in lieu for non-payment of any sum payable in respect of the shares from the general prohibition (in section 143(1)) against a company acquiring its own shares. The legislator's approach is to allow a company to return capital to the defaulter while imposing restrictions on the duration for which forfeited or surrendered shares may be held by a public company (section 146(2) and (3)), and setting out rules for capital reduction (section 146), possible reregistration as a private company (sections 140, 147) and disclosure (e.g. Companies Act 1985, Schedule 7, Part II and Schedule 9, para 13(3)). Creditors of public companies are offered a diminished but adequate level of protection by the Act.

Since it is unusual today for shares to be issued other than as fully paid, this brief review can suffice.

The company's lien

As a means of securing the payment of calls the articles may provide that the company shall have a charge (called a 'lien') on partly paid shares. Since the 1980 Act, a public company may not take a lien on its own shares other than to secure an amount payable in respect of partly-paid shares (see now section 150, 1985 Act). The only exceptions relate to 'old public companies', money-lending or credit-providing companies to secure moneys owing under transactions entered into in the ordinary course of business, and re-registering companies (section 150). Listed companies may not provide for a lien in their articles if they are to comply with the Yellow Book (Admission of Securities to Listing) of the Stock Exchange, by which all listed companies are contractually bound to the Stock Exchange.

Article 8 of Table A confers on the company a first and paramount lien on every partly paid share for all moneys (whether presently payable or not) payable at a fixed time or called in respect of that share. The directors may at any time declare any share to be wholly or partly exempt from this article; on the other hand, if the company is a private company and it is desired that the company possess a lien of wider ambit (to cover *any* moneys due by a shareholder to the company) article 8 would need to be expanded to provide for this. This is not necessary for a private company which has already adopted an article modelled on article 11 of the former Table A, Schedule 1, Companies Act 1948.

The lien over 'shares' extends beyond the shares themselves and covers any dividend payable on them but not yet paid (*Hague* v. *Dandeson* (1848) LR 2 Ex 741). Article 8, Table A, provides that the company's lien on a share shall extend to any amount payable in respect of it.

If the articles so provide, the lien entitles the company to sell the shares in such a manner as the directors shall determine (article 9). The sale can proceed when presently owing sums remain unpaid after the expiry of fourteen days from the giving to the shareholder (or person entitled to the shares in consequence of death or bankruptcy of the shareholder) a notice demanding payment and a statement that if the notice is not complied with the shares may be sold.

Under Scots law the right to a lien exists at common law, unlike the case in England where there is no lien unless the articles so provide (*Pinkett* v. *Wright* (1842) 2 Hare 120). The lien in Scotland covers any debts due to the company (*Bell's Trustee* v. *Coatbridge Tinplate Co. Ltd* (1886) 14 R 246). The company's articles may expressly confer this lien, or restrict it. However, public companies remain subject to section 150, 1985 Act (above). No automatic power of sale exists; so that a lien can be enforced by sale only if the power of sale is conferred by the articles, or a court warrant is obtained to that effect.

2.16.6　Liability as a 'contributory'

On the making of a winding-up order the liquidator (in England) and the court (in Scotland) will proceed to draw up a 'list of contributories' and collect the company's assets for application in discharge of the company's liabilities. A past or present member may find himself liable to contribute to the assets as a contributory (section 79, Insolvency Act 1986). (All references hereinafter are to this Act unless otherwise stated).

Section 74(1) provides that in principle on a winding-up every past and present member is liable to contribute to its assets to any amount sufficient for payment of its debts and liabilities, the expenses of winding-up, and the adjustment of the rights of the contributories among themselves. However, section 74(2) proceeds to qualify this principle. Thus:

(a) a *past member* is not liable to contribute

 (i) if he has ceased to be a member for one year or more before the commencement of the winding-up; nor

 (ii) in respect of any debt or liability of the company contracted after he ceased to be a member; nor

 (iii) unless it appears to the court that the existing members are unable to satisfy the contributions required to be made by them in pursuance of the Companies Act and the Insolvency Act;

(b) in the case of a company limited by shares, no contribution is required from any member exceeding the amount (if any) unpaid on the shares in respect of which he is liable as a present or past member;

(c) nothing in the Companies Act or the Insolvency Act invalidates any provision contained in a policy of insurance or other contract whereby the liability of individual members on the policy or contract is restricted, or whereby the funds of the company are alone made liable in respect of the policy or contract;

(d) a sum due to any member of the company (in his character of a member) by way of dividends, profits or otherwise is not deemed to be a debt of the company, payable to that member in a case of competition between himself and any other creditor not a member of the company, but any such sum may be taken into account for the purpose of the final adjustment of the rights of contributories among themselves.

Section 74(3) provides that in the case of a company limited by guarantee, no contribution is required from any member exceeding the amount undertaken to be contributed by him to the company's assets in the event of its being wound up, but that if it is a company with a share capital, every member of it is liable (in addition to the amount so undertaken to be contributed) to contribute to the extent of any sums unpaid on shares held by him. Further important provisions deal (sometimes in derogation of what has been said above) with the liability of directors or managers of limited companies whose liability is unlimited (section 75); the liability of past directors and shareholders where the company being wound up had made a payment out of capital for the purchase or redemption of its own shares (section 76); the liability of present and past members in the case where the company being wound up was at some former time registered as unlimited but had re-registered as a public company or as a limited company (section 77); the liability of members in the case of a company which was at some former time registered as limited but was re-registered as unlimited (section 78); the situation in the case of the death of a member (section 81); the effect of a contributory's bankruptcy (section 82); the situation in the case of companies not formed under companies legislation but authorised to register under section 680, Companies Act 1985 or its predecessors (section 83).

In England, calls on contributories are made by the liquidator with the leave of the court or the sanction of the 'committee of inspection' required to be set up by law (section 160). In Scotland, calls are made by the court (section 150). A debt owing to the contributory from the company may not be set off against calls except as allowed by the court (a) where all the creditors have been paid in full or (b) in the case of an unlimited company, where the debt is due to him on any independent dealing or contract with the company and does not consist of money due to him as a member of the company in respect of any dividend or profit. In the case of a limited company, the court may make a similar allowance as in (b) above to any director or manager whose liability is unlimited [section 149 (2) and (3)]. Set-off is also possible where the contributory is bankrupt (*Re Duckworth* (1867) LR 2 Ch App 578). At any time after the making of a winding-up order, the court may order any contributory on the list to pay any money, subject to set-off, to the company [section 149(1)].

The liability of a contributory creates a debt (in England and Wales in the nature of a specialty) accruing due from him at the time when his liability commenced, but payable at the times when calls are made for enforcing the liability (section 79).

2.17   *The right to dividends (or 'to share in the profits')*

The typical member's main expectation is that he shall share in the company's profits. However, a shareholder can so partake in a number of ways. Different investors have different interests or prioritise their interests in different ways. Certain types of investor prefer capital gains to dividend income. A company's dividend policy is a complex thing and will vary according to the type of company (i.e. whether listed, unlisted, closely held, etc.) and its future prospects, as well as according to taxation implications.

For these reasons there is no such thing as a member's absolute right to a dividend at common law, although since profit for the shareholders is the presumed product and at least one (traditionally the central) aim of commercial companies, no express power to pay dividends need be given in the memorandum or articles of such companies. Dividends need to be properly 'declared' in accordance with the articles and the Companies Act 1985 before they become a debt due from the company to the shareholder.

The maintenance of capital principle, whereby the company's *capital* is reserved in the first place for the company's creditors in preference to the shareholders, means that dividends are payable only out of profits. To pay a dividend out of capital would be to return capital to shareholders in breach of the above principle. This is why capital can be reduced only in accordance with stringent requirements set out in the Companies Act. This is also the reason why the Act sets out detailed provisions for ensuring that only profits available for distribution as dividend are so utilised (sections 263-281, 1985 Act – these provisions cannot be dealt with here and the reader is referred to broader works on company law). Suffice it to say here that dividends are only payable at all out of a company's accumulated realised profits less its accumulated realised losses (section 263(3), 1985 Act). In addition, a public company may only pay dividends if (a) the amount of its net assets is, at the relevant time, not less than the aggregate of its called-up share capital and its undistributable reserves, and (b) the amount of the proposed distribution will not lower the amount of those assets below that aggregate (section 264, 1985 Act). Alternative rules are provided for insurance and investment companies (sections 265-268, 1985 Act). If the above rules are breached, any shareholder who receives a distribution which he knows, or has reasonable grounds to believe, has been paid in breach of those rules, is obliged to repay the amount received to the company [section 277(1), 1985 Act]. Directors who are knowingly parties to such distributions are liable, jointly and severally, to repay to the company such sums as were distributed (*Flitcroft's Case* (1882) 21 ChD 519). If they make such repayments, they can be indemnified by those shareholders who received those dividends with knowledge of the breach (*Moxham* v. *Grant* (1900) 1 QB 88).

The articles will commonly set out the procedure to be followed by the company in making a distribution. As we have said there is no right to a dividend, unless (which is rare) the articles or the terms of issue of particular shares so provide (see, for example, *Paterson* v. *R. Paterson & Sons Ltd* (1917) SC (HC) 13). The directors are generally accorded the power to create reserves in the company's long-term interests and this power to balance long-term and short-term interests within the company is reflected in Table A and in the vast majority of articles of association. Article 102, Table A consequently provides that:

'Subject to the provisions of the Acts, the company may by ordinary resolution declare dividends in accordance with the respective rights of the members, but no dividend shall exceed the amount recommended by the directors.'

Article 102 refers to the 'final' dividend. The power to pay 'interim dividends', which can be paid at any time between two annual general meetings, is conferred on the directors by article 103. The directors are usually empowered to pay such dividends if it appears to them that this is justified by the profits available for distribution, but are usually prohibited from paying interim dividends on shares carrying deferred or non-preferred rights (see Chapter 7) if, at the time of payment, any preferential dividend is in arrear (Article 103, Table A). Article 103 also says that provided the directors act in good faith, they do not incur any liability to the holders of shares conferring preferred rights for any loss which these shareholders may suffer by the lawful payment of an interim dividend on any shares having deferred or non-preferred rights. The directors may also pay at intervals settled by them any dividend payable at a fixed rate, if it appears to them that the profits available for distribution justify the payment (Article 103).

As with the exercise of all their powers, directors must recommend dividends, or pay interim dividends, *bona fide* in what they consider to be the best interests of the company. Also, they must exercise due care *Re City Equitable Fire Assurance Co. Ltd* (1925) Ch 407; and see (*Re a Company No. 00370 of 1987, The Times* July 5 1988, below and Chapter 8, [8.5.]).

The 'profits available for distribution' are the profits of the company minus the amounts properly set aside by the directors for transfer to reserve. This means that even though the articles or terms of issue entitle preference shares to a fixed dividend in preference to ordinary shares, the payment of the dividend will depend on there being profits which are not transferred to reserve (*Re Buenos Aires Great Southern Ry Co. Ltd, The Company* v. *Preston* [1947] Ch 384). This is because there is, in principle, no debt until a dividend is recommended and declared. However, a shareholder may be entitled to object that he has been 'unfairly prejudiced' by a groundless decision by the directors to recommend no dividend or by an unjustified refusal by the general meeting to declare a dividend, and to petition for relief under section 459, 1985 Act (see Chapter 8). On the other hand, if the articles or terms of issue dispense with the need for a declaration and confer a right to a fixed dividend then provided that there are profits the preference shareholder can sue for his dividend on the basis of this contract with the company (*Evling* v. *Israel and Oppenheimer* [1918] 1 Ch 101).

Unless the articles make contrary provision, the position in English law is that dividends are payable in proportion to the nominal amount of the issued shares (*Birch* v. *Cropper* (1889) 14 App Cas 525). Article 104, Table A alters this common law rule to provide that, except as otherwise provided by the rights attached to shares, dividends are payable according to the amounts paid up, ensuring a fairer system of profit distribution. This is the common law principle in Scotland. (*Hoggan* v. *Tharsis Sulphur* (1882) 9 R 1191).

Where the articles speak of dividends being 'paid', payment must be in cash and not, for example, in the form of interest-bearing debenture bonds (*Wood* v. *Odessa Waterworks Co.* (1889) 42 ChD 636). Article 105, Table A overcomes this by expressly providing that the directors may recommend that a declared dividend be satisfied wholly or partly by the distribution of assets.

Although there is no *right* to a dividend unless the articles or terms of issue expressly so provide, every shareholder in a commercial company can be presumed to have a legitimate expectation that a dividend will be recommended by the board and declared by the general meeting if sufficient profits are made in any particular year and the company does not reasonably require that those profits be retained by the company (e.g. for research and development purposes). This has been categorically recognised by the courts which will intervene if this expectation is being unjustifiably ignored by the board. However, the appropriate remedy would appear to be the rather drastic remedy of petitioning for the compulsory winding-up of the company, for in most cases a less drastic form of relief will not be available under section 459, 1985 Act, due to the courts' interpretation of this provision (see Chapter 8, [8.5] on *Re a Company No. 00370 of 1987*, *The Times* 5 July, 1988).

Chapter 3

Shareholders and Management

3.1 Introduction

The title of this chapter reflects one of the main themes of this book, namely the relationship between the two primary organs of the company, i.e. the general meeting of shareholders and the board of directors. The chapter will explore their respective spheres of operation and highlight areas of overlap or even conflict. One of these areas of conflict (the issue of shares) will be explored in some detail. Indeed, on one view the law actually entrenches conflict by requiring of directors that they exercise their powers *'bona fide* (honestly) in what they consider to be the best interests of the company' while traditionally making no such demand on the shareholders who, both outside the general meeting and even when voting in general meeting, have had no-one other than themselves, and no interest other than their own, to answer to (but see Chapter 4).

For this main reason, a most important question in each case is: who has the power to perform this particular act or to decide on this particular course of action? Furthermore, the court will never interfere to overturn an exercise of business discretion but it will interfere to test the legality of the process by which that discretion is exercised. However, it can only do so when the law requires those exercising the discretion to take account of one or more particular interests. While the law does require this of directors (their main fiduciary duty to the company is that of acting *bona fide*, etc.) it is generally agreed that as a rule the law makes no such demands of the general meeting, although there are exceptions which have prompted some academics to question the traditional view. This will be explored further in Chapter 4. Suffice it to say here that increased pressure on shareholders to act responsibly (as opposed to selfishly on a short-term basis) may see restrictions being imposed generally on the freedom with which shareholders have hitherto been allowed to vote and to dispose of their shares (hitherto sacrosanct 'property' rights).

3.2 Some of the board's powers: law and practice

3.2.1 The organs of the company

'The company' as a creature of commerce and the law is an 'artificial' or a 'legal' person. This means that it is an 'independent' entity with its own property, capacity, objects, rights and obligations (contractual or otherwise) and is not to be confused with its members. Thus, a way needed to be found whereby this entity would 'act'. It can only act through living persons. These are the members of the board and the members of the general meeting (note that not all members are necessarily entitled to attend and/or vote at general meetings – this will depend on whether these rights are included in their personal 'basket of rights'). Clearly, the board and the general meeting cannot both manage the company's affairs. Indeed, the general meeting in any but the smallest company is too large a body to be able to conduct business effectively on a day to day basis. Hence, the obvious technique emerged whereby the shareholders, who may be regarded as the main 'organ' of the company with the prior claim to manage (a claim based on their 'ownership of the company') would delegate much of their 'sovereign' power to a 'board' which would be answerable to the general meeting. Therefore, while the duties (i.e. standards of conduct) of directors emanate from the general law and while specific legal obligations are imposed on directors by the 1985 Act and other legislation, the 'power' or 'authority' of the board derives from the shareholders themselves. In practice, the articles of the vast majority of companies will vest the function of managing the business of the company in a board of directors. Oddly, the law does not require this, although it does require that a public company have a minimum of two directors and that a private company have at least one (section 282, 1985 Act). The legislator assumes that the above practice of delegation will continue.

3.2.2 Article 70

Thus, article 70 (Table A) provides that:

> 'Subject to the provisions of the Act, the memorandum and the articles and to any directions given by special resolution, the business of the company shall be managed by the directors who may exercise all the powers of the company ...'

Before the positive aspect of this provision is discussed (*viz.* what is the extent of the delegation?) it is as well to consider the limitation enshrined in the opening words 'Subject to the Act, the memorandum and the articles'.

Some powers are vested by the Act in the general meeting to the exclusion of any other company organ or any other person, though the general meeting can act through an agent for the purpose of exercising the power. Where statute says 'by the company in general meeting', the power must be exercised by a properly convened general meeting, i.e. this means the general meeting and not 'all the shareholders outside general meeting', so that a meeting has to be held (e.g. section 121(4), *Re Duomatic Ltd* [1969] 2 Ch 365, and *dicta* in *M. Dalley & Co. Pty Ltd* v. *Sims* (1968) 120 CLR 603 at 614). Otherwise, the unanimous assent of *all* the shareholders entitled to attend and vote outside a general meeting is equivalent in effect to a general meeting resolution (*Cane* v. *Jones* [1980] 1 WLR 1451, a case on the alteration of the articles; Re *Express Engineering Works Ltd* [1920] 1 Ch. 466, a case on assent by all members expressed in board meeting). This applies also to the case where all the shareholders assent (including failing to object, *Re Bailey Hay & Co. Ltd* [1971] 3 All ER 693) to what is otherwise an irregular (but not fraudulent) exercise of power by the directors, and it does not matter whether assent is given by them at different times rather than simultaneously (*Parker & Cooper. Ltd* v. *Reading* [1926] Ch. 975). Assent must be unanimous (*EBM Co. Ltd. v. Dominion Bank* [1937] 3 All ER 555). The reason why extra-meeting agreement needs to be unanimous even though the law otherwise only calls for a simple majority or a qualified majority is that outside the general meeting a shareholder is deprived of the opportunity to influence a decision which the procedure of a meeting would normally afford him – through the giving of notice of the intended resolution and the exercise of the right to attend, speak and vote at meetings (see Chapter 4). Therefore, the typical form of articles will contain a clause akin to article 53, Table A, which declares that 'a resolution in writing executed by or on behalf of each member ... shall be as effectual as if it had been passed at a general meeting duly convened'. This requires extra-company assent to be unanimous and in writing. Otherwise, the common law as described above applies.

3.2.3   Board of directors not agent of shareholders

Powers allocated to the general meeting by statute cannot be allocated in a different way by the memorandum or articles. However, powers which are not so allocated can be, and often are, allocated by the articles. The general words of article 70 cannot as a matter of interpretation cover powers which could have been vested in the board by the memorandum or articles but which have been vested thereby in the general meeting. Indeed, article 70 reads: 'subject to the provisions of the ... memorandum and articles'. Moreover, powers covered by the general words of article 70, and thereby vested in the board, are subject to 'any directions given by special resolution'.

It will be apparent that the articles are framed in terms of a delegation by the general meeting *qua* (i.e. in its capacity as) primary company organ to the board *qua* agent of the general meeting. However the phrase *qua* company organ is an important one. Because the general meeting acts *qua* company organ (i.e. it is the company which is acting) the board, through the delegation, 'receives' the powers *qua* company organ. It is not the agent of the general meeting but rather that of the company. In strict law, the board owes its duties to the company and acts for the company. Except in exceptional and special circumstances no fiduciary duties are owed by the board to shareholders, whether individually or collectively. This partly explains the curious nature of the relationship between general meeting and board. The board is 'provisionally autonomous'.

3.3   *The autonomy question*

3.3.1   The *Automatic Self-Cleansing* line of cases

From the very moment when article 70 'bites', it is said, the board exercises its powers free from any influence by the general meeting. Indeed, it is a breach of duty on the board's part to fetter its discretion in advance. This was the explanation advanced for the *Automatic Self-Cleansing* line of cases. In *Automatic Self-Cleansing Filter Syndicate Co. Ltd* v. *Cunninghame* [1906] 2 Ch 34, the company's articles contained a clause similar to the current article 70, Table A, but requiring any intervention by the general meeting to be by extraordinary rather than by special resolution. At a general meeting, an ordinary resolution was passed directing the board to sell the company's undertaking to a new company. The directors disapproved of the terms of the sale and refused to carry out the sale. The Court of Appeal held that the general meeting had no power to interfere with the board's power of decision. Of course, the case was decided on the ground that the shareholders had sought to interfere by ordinary resolution, rather than by extraordinary resolution as the articles required. However, the 'agency theory' of board authority (i.e. the hitherto prevalent view, based on an interpretation of the current delegation article, that the board acted as agent for the majority in general meeting) was expressly thrown out.

In other words, the board came to be seen as an autonomous organ of the company (within the limits of its power) and entitled as such to disregard the views of the general meeting when acting within the scope of its power. Any power vested in it was regarded as exclusively so vested, i.e. to the exclusion of the general meeting. However, it really remained for the articles to determine the extent of this autonomy and if the articles provided that this autonomy should cease if a particular majority in general meeting so decided, then the article would be enforced. In this respect, the articles may provide that the general meeting (usually acting by special resolution, e.g. article 70, Table A) may override the board, but the articles impose the limit on the general meeting's power to do so.

The *Automatic* case is, therefore, an example of the then new practice of drafting articles so as to confer a measure of autonomy on the board. However, some have argued (Goldberg (1970) 33 MLR 177) that later cases emphasised the autonomy point in disregard of the actual wording of the articles. A clear statement of the autonomy principle is to be found in the case of *John Shaw & Sons (Salford) Ltd* v. *Shaw* [1935] 2 KB 113. In this case, the articles expressly vested all management powers in 'permanent directors' who, on behalf of the company, sought to sue other directors who were also shareholders in the company. The defendants passed an ordinary resolution in general meeting directing the board to discontinue the action. In the Court of Appeal, Lord Justice Greer said:

'A company is an entity distinct alike from its shareholders and its directors. Some of its powers may, according to its articles, be exercised by directors, certain other powers may be reserved for the shareholders in general meeting. If powers of management are vested in the directors, they and they alone can exercise these powers. The only way in which the general body of the shareholders can control the exercise of the powers vested by the articles in the directors is by altering their articles, or, if opportunity arises under the articles, by refusing to re-elect the directors of whose actions they disapprove. They cannot themselves usurp the powers which by the articles are vested in the directors any more than the directors can usurp the powers vested by the articles in the general body of shareholders.'

It is noted that a third possibility of 'control' would be for the general meeting to remove directors by ordinary resolution under section 303 of the 1985 Act. This was not available at the time of the case cited above. The above passage is sometimes taken as a reference to the effect of an article in terms of article 80 of the old Table A (Companies Act 1948, First Schedule; see [3.3.3] below) but it has been argued that Lord Justice Greer was presumably referring to articles, other than article 80, which vested powers especially in the board (Goldberg (1970) 33 MLR 176).

3.3.2 A matter of interpretation

The essence of the court's approach in *Automatic* is that the matter is one of interpreting the articles as a whole (as emphasised in *Automatic* and in other cases). However, the 'autonomy' argument has seemed to colour the interpretation issue, with a sort of assumption sometimes developing against 'overriding or even merely concurrent' general meeting power even where the only relevant article was article 80 (the current article 70's predecessor). Thus the word 'regulations' which featured, for example, in *Scott* v. *Scott* [1943] 1 All ER 582 and *Thomas Logan Ltd* v. *Davis* (1911) 104 LT 914 was interpreted to mean 'new articles' requiring the passage of a special resolution by special majority, i.e. three-quarters of the votes cast. Only in *Marshall's Valve Gear Co. Ltd* v. *Manning Wardle & Co. Ltd* [1909] 1 Ch 67 was the court prepared to interpret 'regulations' to include 'ordinary resolutions'. We shall now expand on these themes.

3.3.3 Article 80 of the 'old' Table A

This review is important because the form of words which arose in the last three cases cited was reproduced in Article 80 of the old Table A (1948 Act) which still appears in the articles of thousands of companies formed before the 1985 Regulations came into force (and can be adopted even now through an exclusion of article 70 and adoption of an article in article 80 form). 'Article 80' of the old Table A read, in essence, as follows (author's italics):

> 'The business of the company shall be managed by the directors, who ... may exercise all such powers of the company as are not, by the Companies Acts ... or by these regulations, required to be exercised by the company in general meeting, subject, nevertheless, to any of these regulations, to the provisions of the Companies Acts... and *to such regulations, being not inconsistent with the aforesaid regulations or provisions, as may be prescribed by the company in general meeting ...*'

Academics have usually taken one of two 'interpretive' positions. The first (see generally B.V. Slutsky (1968) 3 UBCL Review 81; K.W. Wedderburn (1968) 31 MLR at 690; G.R. Sullivan (1977) 93 LQR 569) is that an article in 'article 80 form' confers on the board an autonomy which is subject only to inference by *special resolution* because the word 'regulations' is used as a synonym for 'articles' and new 'articles' can be created by special resolution.

The 'problem case' for those who subscribe to this view is the *Marshall's Valve* case which, as some writers (e.g. L.C.B. Gower, *Principles of Modern Company Law* 4th ed., p.145) therefore put it, appears to lay down an exception to the rule when it comes to the power of instituting corporate litigation – the power in issue in this case. One justification which might be advanced for making an exception of the power to institute litigation on the company's behalf is that the board may have a vested interest in not suing (e.g. where they are the likely defendant). This featured in *Marshall's Valve* itself, where the three directors who carried the resolution had interests in the potential defendant.

In *Marshall's Valve* the relevant article was in old Table A form. The company's board decided, by three votes to one, not to sue Manning Wardle & Co. for the alleged infringement of Marshall's Valve's patent. The outvoted director, who held a majority of the shares, himself instituted proceedings in the company's name (it was admitted that it would have been otiose to insist that a meeting be held). Mr Justice Neville held that on a proper construction of the article (effectively article 80 Table A) a bare majority (51 per cent) of shareholders had the power to control the action of the directors 'so long as they do not affect to control it in a direction contrary to any of the provisions of the articles which bind the company'. Dr Sealy opines (*op. cit.* at p.193) that the article before the court in *Marshall's Valve* was not materially distinguishable from those considered in other cases, for example, *John Shaw & Sons Salford Ltd* v. *Shaw* [1935] 2 KB 113 and *Salmon* v. *Quin & Axtens Ltd* [1909] 1 Ch 311, CA (affirmed by the House of Lords [1909] AC 442) where a special resolution was deemed necessary for intervention.

Shaw v. *Shaw* itself concerned control over corporate litigation and it is a difficult question whether, and how far, *Marshall's* case can be reconciled with these decisions. The writer is inclined to suggest that *Marshall's Valve* is distinguishable from *Shaw* v. *Shaw* and *Salmon* v. *Quin & Axtens*. The relevant articles in *Shaw* v. *Shaw* were quite explicit, so explicit as to amount to special articles. General meeting authority was expressly excluded. Article 86A provided that the defendant 'ordinary' directors should 'have no control over, and no right to deal with on behalf of the company, any of the debts due from them or any of them mentioned in the said Terms of Settlement and shall have no rights as shareholders to vote on any matter connected with such debts ...' Article 87 of the company's articles expressly excluded those directors from control over the financial affairs of the company and only allowed them such rights of voting, or such control, over management as should be conferred on them by the permanent directors. There was no evidence of such power having been conferred upon them. In these circumstances, and on a proper construction of these quite specific articles, it is hardly surprising that Lord Justice Greer held that the ordinary directors could not as shareholders interfere with the proceedings instituted against them by the permanent directors. That would have defeated the whole purpose of the company's articles in the particular case. Such 'special articles' would need to be altered or abrogated by special resolution before the power of decision of the permanent directors ceased to be absolute. We shall return to this question in [3.9] below.

The second academic position, typified by Goldberg (1970) 33 MLR 177, was that *Marshall's Valve* correctly stated *the rule*. The other cases could be explained on the basis that, besides there being an 'article 80' to contend with, the company's articles contained other 'special articles' which brought into play Mr Justice Neville's *caveat* in the *Marshall's Valve* case itself and precluded interference by anything short of a special resolution. It will be remembered that Mr Justice Neville, while allowing a bare majority of shareholders to intervene, had said that the majority in general meeting have the right to control the action of the directors *'so long as they do not affect to control it in a direction contrary to any of the provisions of the articles which bind the company'*.

The 'problem case' for *this* view is *Scott* v. *Scott* [1943] 1 All ER 582. In this case, the company had articles in Table A (1948 Act) form. These included article 80 and article 115, the latter of which vested the power to declare interim dividends in the board. The shareholders passed an ordinary resolution to the effect that weekly sums calculated on the paid-up capital in preference shares be paid to each preference shareholder as interest-free advances until the payment of the dividend for the current year, that such sums be deducted from the dividend when this was declared, and that if the dividend was insufficient, the deficiency should be repaid by the company. The effect was that the general meeting was declaring an interim dividend. The significance of this first instance judgment is that Lord Clauson did not content himself simply with pointing out that article 115 expressly vested the power in the board. He also invoked article 80 itself as a separate ground for setting the resolution aside. His Lordship held:

'...[the] thing which is to be managed by the directors and with which the company may interfere only by removing the directors or by having an investigation under the statutory provisions is the management of the business of the company ... How can you manage a business without managing its finance, how can things be carried out if at any moment the company can interfere and say to the directors, 'You must not keep a balance at the bank although you have demands coming forward in a week or two; you must let out that money on loan because that will bring in more interest.'... How the directors can manage the business if they are to be interfered with in such an ordinary financial matter as to how to deal temporarily with balances which are *for the moment* not required for the purpose of the business I confess I cannot conceive. It seems to me quite clear that this resolution if it is not aimed at declaring an interim dividend is aimed at interfering with the management of the business by the directors and, as such, it is wholly inoperative and the general meeting had no power to pass it ... I do not take the view that those limiting words 'subject nevertheless' and so forth (in s.80), have anything to do with the duty cast upon the directors in the first two lines of the article to manage the business of the company. However that may be and if I am wrong in that and if I ought to treat the duty cast upon them to manage the business as being 'subject to any regulation of these articles' – which of course it must necessarily be – 'to the provisions of the said Act' – which it must necessarily be – 'and to such regulations being not inconsistent with the aforesaid regulations or provisions as may be prescribed by the company in general meeting' the question is whether the company by prescribing this ... regulation if it be a regulation are prescribing something which is inconsistent with the aforesaid regulations or aforesaid regulations or provisions. One of the aforesaid regulations or provisions is that provision about the business of the company being managed by the directors and I find the greatest difficulty in seeing how any resolution of the company in general meeting, controlling the directors in the management of the business, can possibly be justified under the terms of this article.'

Goldberg seeks to limit the damage which the first part of this passage could be seen as doing to his theory by arguing that 'management of the business' must be limited to matters of 'day to day control' (and also by pointing out that Lord Clauson avowedly did not refer to the authorities in support of his view). This would mean that the majority could by ordinary resolution tell directors how to invest funds which have been taken out of the current account of its business. It is submitted that this would come as a surprise to most shareholders as well as to most boards. Surely, the power to 'manage the business' is wider than this – it certainly embraces 'direction' (hence 'directors') as well as 'day to day' control. Indeed Lord Clauson was concerned that to allow general meeting interference in such an ordinary financial matter as to how to deal *temporarily* with balances which are *for the moment* not required for the purposes of the business' would be to hamstring the board in their long-term task of managing the business.

In 1985, against this background, the legislator changed the wording of the relevant article (now article 70 of the new Table A) so as to require 'interference' to be by special resolution. The big unsettled question is the impact of this change on the courts' future interpretation of the old (but still used) article 80. Will 'regulations' now be interpreted as meaning 'special resolution'? In other words, is the legislator's action 'declaratory' (i.e. does it vindicate Wedderburn's view) or constitutive (i.e. an admission that Goldberg's view was correct)? Companies are advised to alter their articles by special resolution to say precisely whether they intend that there be 'interference' by ordinary resolution or only by special resolution, rather than argue after the event, for the court's decision could go either way. In any event, article 70 only applies unless expressly excluded or modified on incorporation. Also, the company may by special resolution alter the terms of article 70 (or the particular company's equivalent). The autonomy argument is therefore essentially settled in each case by an interpretation of each company's articles.

3.4 *The return of power to the general meeting*

One manifestation of the autonomy argument gave rise to considerable litigation over the exercise by directors of their power to issue shares. In a line of cases the courts have had to decide whether directors could lawfully issue shares, under a power given them by the articles, with the immediate view of creating a 'new majority' of shareholders and sometimes with the ulterior purpose of defeating an unwelcome take-over bid or some other such purpose (see generally, *Hirshe* v. *Sims [1894] AC 654; Punt* v. *Symons & Co. Ltd [1903]* 2 Ch 506;

Piercy v. *Mills & Co. Ltd* [1920] Ch 77; *Ngurli* v. *McCann* (1954) 90 CLR 425; *Hogg* v. *Gramphorn Ltd* [1967] Ch 254; *Bamford* v. *Bamford* [1970] Ch 212). The English courts held this exercise of power to be in breach of a duty incumbent upon directors to exercise a power for its proper purpose, on the assumption that each power has its own particular purpose and that defeating a take-over bid, for example, did not fall within the purpose of the power to issue shares – even though the directors might *bona fide* (honestly) and on reasonable grounds believe that what they were doing was in the best interests of the company.

A different line was taken in other Commonwealth jurisdictions, which refused to apply a 'collateral purpose' duty separate from the general primary fiduciary duty owed by directors to their company to act *'bona fide* in what they consider to be the best interests of the company' (*Re Smith & Fawcett Ltd* [1942] Ch 304). (For Canada see *Teck Corporation Ltd* v. *Millar* (1972) 33 DLR 3d 288 and for Australia see *Harlowe's Nominees Pty Ltd* v. *Woodside (Lakes Entrance) Oil Co.* (1971) 45 ALJR 162.)

What concerned the British courts was that it was, in their opinion, really a matter for the shareholders to decide whether to accept an, or any particular, offer by a bidder for their shares, and the board had no business pre-empting that decision by creating new shareholders. However, the most recent position taken by an English court (the Privy Council, in *Howard Smith Ltd* v. *Ampol Petroleum Ltd* [1974] AC 821, PC) appeared to grope for a compromise solution. The directors will apparently be acting properly, provided their dominant motive in issuing the shares is referable to 'considerations of management'. Issuing shares primarily in order to maintain their offices and control would appear to fall outside the power, but acting primarily in order to prevent a 'looter' from taking control would appear to fall within it. On this view, the Privy Council was able to support the Canadian and Australian cases cited above because in the one case the directors' primary purpose was that of obtaining the protection of a major international company in the company interest while in the other it was that of securing the financial stability of the company.

After *Howard* v. *Ampol* it seems clear that the court will undertake a limited inquiry into the facts in order to ascertain whether the directors' 'substantial' or 'primary' purpose was a proper one in the sense indicated above. More recent cases which bear on the courts' general approach include the Canadian case of *Olson* v. *Phoenix Industrial Supply Ltd* (1984) DLR (4th) 451 and the English case of *Mutual Life Assurance* v. *The Rank Organisation* [1985] BCLC 11. It has been suggested that the 'proper purpose' cases are essentially concerned with the division of power between the board and the general meeting (see L.S.

Sealy, *op. cit.* p.278). The conclusion which the writer draws from *Howard* v. *Ampol* is that provided the board's action can be justified by reference to 'management considerations' (e.g. a need for further capital for the company's enterprise) then the directors act within the scope of their powers. In this way the interests of the company (or enterprise), tested objectively, provide the limits beyond which the directors may not stray without exceeding their 'powers'.

This review of some case law on the power to issue shares illustrates the general problem of drawing a dividing line between the respective spheres of authority of the board and the general meeting, and in particular that of deciding what are proper 'management considerations'.

It highlights the conflicts which can and do arise within the company when a block of shareholders is faced with an irresistible offer for their shares. The shareholders are by law allowed and entitled to 'take their profit and run', without any obligation even to consider the long-term interests of the company as an enterprise. On the other hand, the board must act in what they perceive to be the best interests of the company as a whole, balancing long-term against short-term interests (see, for example, Xuereb (1988) 51 MLR 156). Traditional company law theory, which regards the share as an item of property, is on the shareholders' side (but it may be noted here that in USA, for example, shareholders selling a controlling block are placed under fiduciary duties akin to those owed by directors: see generally, Henn and Alexander, *Law of Corporations*, 3rd ed. 1983 pp.653 *et seq.*; *Jones* v. *Ahmanson & Co.* (1969) 1 Cal 3d 93). However, the national interest, as well as other specific interests such as those of the employees or of the consumers or community served by the company, may conceivably dictate that this shareholder freedom be limited. Currently, the shareholder is for the most part free to deal with his shares, and the votes which go with them, as he deems fit in his own interests (see Chapter 4).

As far as the power to issue shares is concerned, section 80 of the 1985 Act now squarely provides that directors may not issue 'relevant securities' (including most shares) unless they are authorised so to do by the articles or by the company in general meeting. It is not clear whether article 70 suffices for this purpose, i.e. whether the issue of shares falls within the general power to manage the business, although since the enactment of what is now section 80 this can be regarded as unlikely. Authority to issue shares may be given for a particular exercise of the power or for its exercise generally, and may be unconditional or subject to conditions (section 80(3)). If given generally and unconditionally the issues just discussed will continue to arise. The general meeting can retain full control by withholding such authority and granting only particular and conditional authority. In any case, the general meeting may nevertheless revoke authority to issue shares by ordinary resolution although this may be to alter the articles (section 80(8), 1985 Act). A specific article authorising the board to issue shares is alterable in the same way. Clearly, the legislator was anxious to 'restore' overall control over the issue of shares to the general meeting. Section 80 is only one example of a drive by the legislator to 'restore' overall general meeting control in certain crucial areas where a clash might arise between board and shareholders. (Other examples will be found in the list of statutory general meeting powers in [3.5] below.) As the law now stands, the courts will, subject to the 'proper purpose cases' where general authority is conferred, recognise the board's 'provisional' full autonomy when the power to issue shares has been conferred upon it; that is, the board may act independently of the views of the general meeting.

In general, the general meeting may revoke the power (by altering the articles by special resolution or, as in the case of the power to issue shares, by passing an ordinary resolution) or intervene to give directions (by special resolution if article 70 is adopted) or dismiss the board or one or more directors (by ordinary resolution under section 303). An overriding limit on the general meeting's power to intervene to exercise a power would be where that power was expressly vested in the board by law. Potential common law restraints on the directors' power to issue shares are of course represented by their duty towards the company to exercise the power *bona fide* in what they consider to be the best interests of the company and not for any collateral purpose (see [3.4] above).

Moreover, the law may vest powers of overall control in the general meeting while allowing that the articles may vest in the board the power of initiating certain proposals (notably under article 70).

3.5   General meeting powers

3.5.1   (1)   Statutory powers of control

(References are to the Companies Act 1985, unless otherwise stated.)
    The general meeting has overall power over:

(1) the allotment of shares or the grant of options to subscribe for shares or the issue of convertible securities (section 80(1));
(2) the variation of share capital (section 121(4));

(3) the market purchase by a company of its own shares (section 166);

(4) the approval of compensation to directors on loss of office (sections 312, 313);

(5) the approval of directors' service contracts for periods in excess of five years, where the contracts make no provision for termination by notice or provide for such termination only in specified circumstances (section 319);

(6) the approval of loans to directors to meet expenditure on company business (section 337);

(7) the approval of substantial (currently £50,000 or over in value) property transactions with directors (section 320);

(8) in the case of a public company, the decision on measures to be taken on a serious loss of capital (section 142);

(9) in the case of a public company, the approval of an agreement by that company to acquire non-cash assets from certain founding members (section 104);

(10) alteration of the articles (section 9 – special resolution);

(11) change of objects (section 4 – special resolution);

(12) alteration of any condition contained in the memorandum which could lawfully have been included in the articles (section 17 – special resolution);

(13) change of company name (section 28(1) – special resolution);

(14) change of nature of company from private to public (section 43(1)(a) – special resolution);

(15) change of nature from unlimited to private limited (section 51(1) – special resolution);

(16) change of nature from public to private (section 53(1)(a));

(17) overriding of member's pre-emption rights to subscribe for new equity shares or on the issue of options or 'convertibles' (section 95 – special resolution);

(18) deciding that uncalled capital be called up only on a winding-up (section 120 – special resolution);

(19) reduction of share capital (section 135 – special resolution);

(20) approval of the giving of financial assistance by a private company for the acquisition of its own shares or those of its holding company (section 155 – special resolution);

(21) resolving to make the liability of directors of a limited company unlimited (section 307 – special resolution);

(22) authorisation of a proposed contract for the off-market purchase by a company of its own shares; variation, revocation or renewal of such authority; variation of any existing contract of purchase (section 164 – special resolution);

(23) authorisation of a contingent contract to purchase shares under which a company may become entitled or obliged to purchase its own shares; variation, revocation or removal of such authority; variation of any existing contingent purchase contract (section 165(2) – special resolution);

(24) authorisation of the proposed release by a company of its rights under a contract for an off-market purchase or a contingent purchase contract; variation, revocation, renewal of such authority; variation of any existing release agreement (section 167(2) – special resolution);

(25) authorisation of a payment out of capital for the redemption or purchase by a company of its own shares (section 173(2) – special resolution);

(26) approval of the assignment by a director or manager of his office to another person (section 308 – special resolution);

(27) resolving that the company be wound up by the court (section 122(1)(a), Insolvency Act 1986 – special resolution);

(28) resolving that the company be voluntarily wound up (section 84(1)(b), Insolvency Act 1986 – special resolution).

(29) approval of the acceptance by the liquidator in a members' voluntary winding-up of shares of another company to which assets of the company in liquidation are to be transferred (sections 110, 111, Insolvency Act 1986 – special resolution);

(30) variation of class rights, at class meetings (section 125(2) – extraordinary resolution);

(31) resolution to wind-up the company when, because of its liabilities, it cannot continue trading (section 84(1)(c), Insolvency Act 1986 – extraordinary resolution);

(32) entrusting the liquidator in a member's voluntary winding up with power to pay a class of creditors in full or make a compromise or arrangement concerning any of the debts of the company or any debts owed to the company (section 165(2)(a), Insolvency Act 1986 – extraordinary resolution);

(33) increase of company's authorised capital if permitted by the articles (section 121);

(34) dismissal of a director or directors (section 303 – ordinary resolution, with special notice);

(35) appointment and removal of auditors (sections 384, 386, 388 – ordinary resolution with special notice in certain cases);

(36) the fixing of the remuneration of the company's auditors, other than those appointed by the directors (see section 384(2)) or by the Secretary of State (section 385);

(37) the election of directors aged 70 or over where the age limit applies (section 293, ordinary resolution with special notice).

Such provisions vest overriding control in the general meeting over two main areas: (a) fundamental decisions, relating mainly to the capital of the company and (b) transactions involving possible conflicts of interests for directors. They are often grouped together because they represent statutory limitations on the general power to manage the business which is normally vested in the board.

3.5.2 Powers normally vested in the general meeting by the articles

The articles will also regulate the division of power between the board and the general meeting. Table A articles vest the following main powers in the general meeting:

(1) The declaration of a dividend, if any (article 102). Note that the directors' recommended dividend may not be exceeded.
(2) Election of directors in place of those retiring (articles 73-80).
(3) Remuneration of directors (article 82).
(4) Subject to the Act and the rights attached to existing shares, the determination of the rights or restrictions with which new shares are to be issued (article 2).
(5) The power to give directions to the directors by special resolution as to the management of the business (article 70).
(6) The power to extend a member's statutory rights of inspection of the company's accounting records or other company documents (article 109).
(7) Approval of a capitalisation of profits (article 110).

3.6. *Powers vested in the board*

3.6.1 Introduction

The primary source of the board's powers is the articles. The 1985 Act in the main contents itself with reserving some powers to the general meeting. As we have just seen, the articles will specify certain other powers as vesting in the general meeting. English law does not set out a category of 'managerial powers' which are inalienable by the board. The board's powers can be broad or narrow – it is all a matter for the articles to decide, subject only to the powers reserved for the general meeting by the Act. This leaves the articles generally and article 70 in particular, as the source of board power.

3.6.2   The articles generally

The Articles will specify certain powers as lying with the scope of the board. The current Table A fails to reproduce some provisions previously found in the old Table A (1948 Act) such as the power to borrow or to issue negotiable instruments but these powers would appear to fall naturally within the scope of the general delegation of power in article 70. Table A gives the board the following main powers:

(1) The power to make calls, with incidental powers such as the forfeiture of shares (articles 12-22; see Chapter 2).
(2) The power to refuse to register a transfer of shares in certain specified cases (article 24).
(3) The power to call general meetings of the company (article 37). Note that shareholders enjoy a concurrent power to do so under statute in certain circumstances (see Chapter 2).
(4) A director may appoint (and remove) an alternate director to serve in his stead subject to board approval where the nominee is not already a director (article 65).
(5) The board may delegate any of their powers to any committee consisting of one or more directors, and may delegate to any managing director or any other executive director any power or powers which they deem appropriate (article 72).
(6) The board may fill 'casual vacancies' or appoint additional directors to hold office until the next annual general meeting (article 79).
(7) Subject to the provisions of the Act, the board may enter into service agreements with any director on behalf of the company (article 84).
(8) The board may provide benefits to directors who have held office or employment with the company, or a subsidiary or ex-subsidiary or a predecessor in business of the company or of any such subsidiary. Such benefits may also be provided to members of the family or dependants of such directors (article 87).
(9) The power to recommend a dividend (article 102) and to pay interim dividends (article 103) in accordance with the Act and the articles.
(10) The power to resolve to capitalise profits (with the authorisation of the general meeting) (article 110).

(11) The power to bind the company by authorising the use of the corporate seal (article 101).

3.6.3   Article 70, Table A

The question here is what is meant by the phrase *'the business of the company shall be managed* by the directors who may exercise all the powers of the company'. There has been no comprehensive judicial statement of what is meant by the power 'to manage the business'; nor could there be, for the powers will vary from company to company depending on a proper construction of the objects clause in the memorandum. There is a clear link between the board's powers and those of the company itself. If the company engages in commercial activities, it will have express or implied powers to do all that is incidental to the carrying on of a commercial activity in general and the carrying on of the particular commercial activities set out in the objects clause in particular. The board's powers will be co-extensive. For example, although not expressly conferred on the board by the articles the board will have power to borrow and give security for such borrowing (*Gibbs and West's case* (1870) LR 10 Eq 312), to enter into a compromise agreement (*Bath's case, Re Norwich Provident Insurance Society* (1878) 8 ChD 334), or to sue in the corporate name. The acute difficulties which the apparent simplicity of article 70 masks are illustrated by the discussion in [3.3.3], [3.4] above and in [3.7.2] below.

3.6.4   Statute

While the division or allocation of powers within the company is left largely to the memorandum and articles, statute also makes some allocation. We have seen that certain powers are reserved, and increasingly so, to the general meeting. However, statute may also vest certain powers in the board. For example, section 384(2), 1985 Act provides that the first auditors of a company may be appointed by the directors at any time before the first general meeting of the company at which accounts are laid.

3.7   *Concurrent authority*

3.7.1   The general meeting as the supreme organ

The listing of general meeting powers and board powers, above, masks one important fact which needs to be borne in mind. This is that there is no prohibition, unless statute expressly reserves the power to a particular organ, against the articles vesting the same power in the general meeting and in the board concurrently. The articles may simply vest a power in 'the company'. It might be thought that article 70 vests the power of management concurrently in the board and the general meeting *acting by special resolution*, but this is probably not an accurate analysis. The general meeting is clearly regarded as the 'supreme body'. It lies within its power to alter the articles, including article 70, by special resolution. Article 70 appears to recognise that the general meeting should be able to instruct the directors how to act in particular cases without having to alter article 70 in order to do so. Therefore, where the general meeting gives directions on a particular matter in exercise of its power in article 70 this is presumably in virtue of its higher authority, and in doing so it abstracts the power of decision from the board and returns it to itself with regard to that matter. The same analysis would apply to article 80 (although it may be that in that case the general meeting may intervene by ordinary resolution – see [3.3.3]).

3.7.2   Intervention by the general meeting

The broad question, whenever powers are vested concurrently in the two company organs, is whether the general meeting can intervene to overturn a decision already taken by the board. In other words, the linked questions are: (1) whose view is to prevail when the general meeting and the board seek to exercise the power in a conflicting way? and (2) does the answer to this first question depend entirely on which of these organs is the first to act? The question can also arise in a statutory context in those cases where the statute itself vests power concurrently in the board and in the general meeting. For example, it is provided in section 384(4), 1985 Act, that 'the directors, *or* the company in general meeting, may fill any casual vacancy in the office of auditor'.

Professor Pennington suggests that a distinction can be drawn between 'managerial powers' and other (non-managerial) powers. The distinction is of no relevance where the articles clearly vest a power in the board exclusively. But where the articles are unclear it may be that 'managerial powers' will be treated as exclusive, but not 'other powers'. These other powers, together with powers clearly vested concurrently in the general meeting and the board, will be treated as concurrent, and 'the members' decision would generally prevail over that of the directors, because the members in general meeting are a superior authority' (*Pennington's Company Law*, p.650). Pennington supports his view by reference to cases which deal with powers which are ostensibly classifiable as 'managerial' or 'non-managerial':

(a) *Powers classifiable as 'managerial' – and therefore to be treated as exclusive to the board*

(i)   The power to sell or retain the company's assets (*Quin & Axtens Ltd v. Salmon* [1909] AC 442; *Automatic Self-Cleansing Filter Syndicate* v. *Cunninghame* [1906] 2 Ch 34).

(ii)   The power to appoint one of their number to be managing director (*Thomas Logan Ltd* v. *Davis* (1911) 105 LT 419).

(iii) The power to declare interim dividends (*Scott* v. *Scott* [1943] 1 All ER 382).

(iv)   The power to sue in the company's name (*John Shaw (Salford) Ltd* v. *Shaw* [1935] 2 KB 113).

(v)   the power to borrow on the company's behalf.

(b) *Powers classifiable as 'non-managerial' – therefore concurrent*

(i)   The power to appoint additional directors and to fill casual vacancies (*Worcester Corsetry Ltd* v. *Witting* [1936] Ch 640).

(ii)   The power to fix the remuneration of the managing director (*Foster* v. *Foster* [1916] 1 Ch 532 – subject to *Thomas Logan Ltd* v. *Davis* (1911) 105 LT 419, above under (a)(ii))

Yet Pennington has to point out that if power (b)(i) is exercised by the board before the general meeting acts, the board's appointments cannot be rescinded (this would answer the second question posed above in the affirmative) and that although power (a)(iv) was held to be 'exclusive' in *Shaw* v. *Shaw*, the general meeting still appears to be able to sue despite a decision by the board not to sue (citing *Marshall's Valve Gear Co. Ltd* v. *Manning, Wardle & Co. Ltd*, *[1909] 1 Ch 267, see [3.3.3] above*).

3.7.3   A matter of interpretation

It is respectfully submitted that Professor Pennington's interesting analysis may be making too much of the cases. It is premised on a distinction ('managerial' *versus* 'non-managerial' powers) which the courts would not appear expressly to have made in the cases; and it may be asked: Is power (a)(ii) essentially different from powers (b)(i) and (b)(ii)? The truth is that each of the cases cited under (a) and (b) was based on an interpretation of the particular articles of the company involved in order to decide in whom the final say was vested, as well as on other factors. For example, in *Foster* v. *Foster* it was crucial that the board was incapacitated from acting. The question was whether the general meeting could act when the board was *incapable* of acting, i.e. it was a 'residual power' case, not a case on 'concurrent power' (see [3.8] below). It is most difficult to extract general rules from such cases. Each case must depend on its own facts and indeed each case is approached by the courts as raising an issue of interpretation of the particular sets of articles in question (see, for example, *Worcester Corsetry Ltd* v. *Witting* [1936] 1 Ch 640 at 645 *per* Lord Hanworth MR). Nevertheless, there is the unsettled hypothetical question of how the court would settle a conflict where there was clearly concurrent power and both organs were capable of acting and willing to act. The draftsman of a company's articles would be wise to avoid such 'concurrent power' clauses. Professor Pennington's suggestion that the general meeting should have its way (provided that it had not been pre-empted by the board) commends itself to reason. Perhaps the following can be tentatively suggested:

(1)   As far as powers vested in the board by the 'delegation' in article 70 are concerned, it is perhaps arguable that the will of the general meeting should prevail provided that the board has not already exercised the power. This is supported by the wording of article 70 which permits the general meeting to 'give directions'. This may be to read too much into the general wording of the first sentence of the article, but it is submitted that it is the more natural and logical interpretation of a provision which allows directors to manage the business subject to such directions as may be given. Once the directors have managed it, it would appear to be too late for the shareholders to give directions as to how they should do so. So much is expressly stated in the second sentence of the article (as also in the full version of article 80 in Table A of the First Schedule, Companies Act 1948.)

(2)   If the power appears to be vested exclusively in the board by some other article the chances are that the courts will not allow the general meeting to intervene (whether before or after the board has exercised the power) by *ordinary* resolution, since a special resolution would be required to alter such articles (the *Automatic Self-Cleansing* line of cases would support this). It would seem that the article in question would need to be abrogated or altered by special resolution before the general meeting had any chance of intervening. The *Marshall's Valve* case does not affect this as it was an 'article 80 case' pure and simple. However, it must be noted that the court will need to be convinced that it was the intention to vest a power exclusively in the board, in view of the shareholders' over-arching authority. The articles will be looked at as a whole and any

doubt will benefit the general meeting (see *Worcester Corsetry Ltd* v. *Witting* [1936] Ch 640 at 647-8 *per* Lord Hanworth MR).

(3) As far as powers vested in the board by a delegation in 'old article 80' terms are concerned, *Scott* v. *Scott* ([1943] 1 All ER 382 vies with *Marshall's Valve* [1909] 1 Ch 267 for precedence (see [3.3.3] above). In *Marshall's Valve* the board had exercised their discretion, yet the majority shareholder was allowed to overturn their decision. In *Scott* v. *Scott* the board's power to manage was held to have been wrongly usurped by the general meeting. This does not necessarily give the lie to any theory that the issue is resolved by reference to who it is who 'gets in first', as is put forward in (1) above, for the general meeting had purported to intervene by ordinary resolution.

The upshot of this difficult case law seems to be that the only reasonably certain thing is that the shareholders are in complete control *provided* they can muster the majority required to pass a special resolution and act before the board – very difficult in practice. Otherwise, the situation is very difficult indeed. An explanation of *Marshall's Valve* and a possible solution to this difficulty is put forward in [3.9] below, where the power of corporate litigation is dealt with.

The question is whether, under article 80, the general meeting may instruct the board how to exercise their powers of management in 'specific instances' (provided the proper majority is obtained). The writer would support an affirmative answer (see [3.7.1] above). Professor Pennington has come to the opposite conclusion, relying on *Scott* v. *Scott* [1943] 1 All ER 582, but as we have seen, *Scott* v. *Scott* concerned a 'special article'.

It is not yet clear what interpretation the courts will give to the new article 70, Table A, in this regard. Some of the basic difficulties which persist under the 'old' article 80 also present themselves in connection with article 70. Companies would be well advised to review their equivalent article with these difficulties in mind, and in particular with an awareness that it is not yet clear whether the effect of the old article 80 is to vest concurrent power in the board and the general meeting acting by *ordinary* resolution or to vest power in the board subject to the power of the general meeting to intervene by passing a special resolution.

3.8   Residual power

3.8.1   Board unable to act

Even where a power has clearly been vested by the articles exclusively in the board it may be that the board is unable to 'act' (i.e. to exercise its discretion one way or the other). Unwillingness to act in a particular way is, of course, to decide against exercising the power, and this is not what concerns us here. The question here is whether the general meeting can exercise the power by ordinary majority if the board is unable to do so? The courts have held that it can. Statute may also make provision to this effect. For example, section 384(3), 1985 Act provides that if the directors fail to exercise the power vested in them by section 384(2) to appoint the company's first auditors then that power may be exercised by the company in general meeting.

3.8.2 Examples

An example of the exercise of residual power by the general meeting is provided by the case of *Foster* v. *Foster* [1916] 1 Ch 532. Here the articles vested the power to appoint a managing director in the board. There were three directors, two of whom were candidates for the post. The problem was that the articles prohibited a director from voting on any matter in which he was interested. This left the board effectively reduced to one member for the purpose, and unable to act. The court held that the company in general meeting could settle the matter, i.e. the general meeting had 'residual' authority to exercise the power – otherwise the company could not act.

The same applies where the board is 'deadlocked' through dissension or otherwise, i.e. where the board is permanently and totally incapacitated through constant inability to reach a quorum or an unwillingness on the part of its members even to meet. This happened in *Barron* v. *Potter* [1914] Ch 895 where one frustrated director resorted to bundling himself into a taxi occupied by the other director in the hope of holding a meeting! The position is similar if there are no directors (*Alexander Ward & Co. Ltd* v. *Samyang Navigation Co. Ltd* [1975] 2 All ER 424). A temporary or 'partial' deadlock over some proposals, for example through equal voting power, would not suffice to cause power to revert to the general meeting (*Barron* v. *Potter; Foster* v. *Foster*, above).

3.8.3   Scope

The scope of residual power is limited to resolving the particular difficulty which is paralysing the board. Once the general meeting has resolved the difficulty, for example by appointing an additional director (as in *Barron* v. *Potter*, [3.8.2] above), or commencing proceedings (as in *Alexander Ward & Co. Ltd* v. *Samyang Navigation Ltd* [1975] 2 All ER 424), power re-vests in the board in accordance with the terms of the articles.

3.8.4 Authorisation and ratification

Sometimes, the board will act beyond its own authority but still within the scope of the objects, and therefore the legal capacity, of the company. One example of this is provided by the cases on the power to issue shares ([3.4] above) where the board allotted shares in circumstances in which they were not authorised to do so (the author is here adopting the 'excess of authority' analysis of those cases). It was held in such a case (*Bamford* v. *Bamford* [1970] Ch 212, [1969] 1 All ER 969) that an ordinary resolution subsequently passed in order to validate the board's action was a ratifying resolution, i.e. the general meeting's action amounted to *ex post facto* approval given in virtue of the meeting's inherent power to ratify a voidable act performed in excess of authority, and not the exercise by the meeting of any residual power to allot shares. At all times that power lay with the board. The same issue arose in *Irvine* v. *Union Bank of Australia* (1877) 2 App Cas 366 and in *Grant* v. *United Kingdom Switchback Rlwys Co.* (1888) 40 ChD 135, CA. In *Irvine's case*, the court held that the company in general meeting could ratify, by ordinary resolution, borrowings by directors which exceeded limits imposed by the articles.

In the light of this analysis it appears quite correct to say that 'members may authorise directors to do an act which is outside the directors' own powers, but within the company's powers, by passing an ordinary resolution *either before or after* the directors act' on the ground that 'in acting under such authority the directors act as agents for the members and not as directors of the company' (Pennington, p.655, relying also on *Re London and New York Investment Corporation* [1895] 2 Ch 860 at 869. Note, however, that in this case approval was subsequent to the act sought to be impugned and furthermore the resolutions were passed by unanimity). This does not ignore the rule that where the articles vest a power exclusively in the board, then, on the principles discussed above (see [3.7]), the general meeting may not itself exercise the power save where either it first alters the articles or where the residual power doctrine operates (e.g. because of deadlock). It is no contradiction to say that while the meeting can exercise a power vested by the articles in the directors in lieu of the directors only by altering the articles, it can ratify by ordinary resolution an improper (but ratifiable) exercise of power by the board by ordinary resolution *provided* that the power was exercisable in the first place by ordinary resolution in general meeting.

Farrar (J.H. Farrar, *Company Law*, p.298) writes that it seems 'artificial to insist that ratification does not amount to an alteration of the articles when the net result is the same, although the proper procedures have not been followed and the protection which they afford to minority shareholders has been swept aside'. Surely there would only be a contradiction and an artificiality if the power being wrongly exercised by the board were reserved to or vested in the general meeting acting by *special* resolution. If it is exercisable by *ordinary* resolution, surely such a resolution may authorise in advance the board to exercise it, or ratify the board's unauthorised exercise of it.

On the other hand, if the power is initially only reserved to or vested in the general meeting acting by *special* resolution, then prior authorisation or subsequent ratification should be allowed, if at all, only by special resolution. This is because the articles are in the first instance 'adopted' by all the shareholders (subscribers) and thereafter can only be varied by special majority (under section 9, 1985 Act). Furthermore, it is established law that the articles may only be varied prospectively (for the future) and not retrospectively. Therefore, it should follow that a breach of those articles should be ratifiable, if at all, only by special majority and the law may develop in this direction. Nor does this necessarily have implications generally for the power of ratification by ordinary majority, for example in the context of a mere 'internal irregularity' (*MacDougall* v. *Gardiner*, [2.6]). There 'simple majority rule' operates, and can be allowed to operate because what is in issue is not a re-drawing of articles of real substance but the power to decide whether the company should waive (i.e. decide not to take remedial action against) a breach of its 'merely procedural' rules. On the other hand it is well established that the breach of articles which require a special majority to be obtained cannot be ratified by ordinary majority and a single shareholder is entitled to sue to have that article observed (*Edwards* v. *Halliwell* [1950] 2 All ER 1064; see [8.3.2.2]). To allow ratification by ordinary resolution in this case could clearly deprive the minority of the protection which the requirement of a special majority afforded them. This power, on current authority, vests in the general meeting acting by ordinary resolution (see Chapter 2). Of course, one can argue that the company's waiver of 'mere internal irregularities' ought not to imply waiver by a minority shareholder personally aggrieved by the breach of the articles, but this is a separate question which we have mentioned above (see [2.8]). The point here is that if ratification is to be allowed at all in the present context, it should be by special resolution, for the breach is not of a mere procedural rule.

Bamford v. *Bamford* (above), *Irvine's case* and *Grant's case* are supportable because the board's excess of authority encroached on the general meeting's power to act in the matters at issue by *ordinary* resolution. The *Automatic Self-Cleansing* line of cases is not in conflict with this position for, to take one example, in authorising directors in advance to borrow in excess of a borrowing limit imposed on the board's borrowing powers by the articles (as in *Irvine's case*) the general meeting does not thereby 'alter the articles'. It simply delegates its own inherent borrowing powers to the board – something it may do by ordinary resolution. It is only logical that it should be able to ratify an unauthorised borrowing in the same way (see *Boschoeck Pty. Co. Ltd* v. *Fuke* [1906] 1 Ch 148).

3.9   *Control over corporate litigation*

At this point it is appropriate to return to this particular issue (we referred to it in [3.3.3]). It is generally accepted that the power of decision over whether to sue on the company's behalf in a business matter falls within the general mandate given to the board by article 70 (or article 80) to 'manage the business of the company' (*Shaw* v. *Shaw* [1935] 2 KB 113). Yet, it is often said, on the authority of *Marshall's Valve*, and despite *Shaw* v. *Shaw*, that the general meeting may by ordinary resolution reverse the board's decision in such cases. Professor Pennington has sought to reconcile *Marshall's case* with *Shaw's case* ([3.3] and [3.7.2] above) by saying that 'it seems that the directors' power to sue in the company's name is exclusive *only if they choose to exercise it'* (as had been done in *Shaw's case*), and that 'their power really amounts to nothing more than the right to continue litigation which they have begun despite the members' wishes to the contrary' (Pennington, *op. cit.*, p.650). The real explanation of *Shaw* v. *Shaw* is difficult to state, as effectively three different judgments were given, but one of the judgments in the majority (that of Lord Greer) is clearly based on the fact that a special article existed vesting the power to sue the 'ordinary directors', who owed the company money, in the 'permanent directors' to the exclusion of the other (debtor) directors whether as directors or as shareholders. Another article vested all powers of management also in the permanent directors. The case can therefore be explained on the basis that there was a special article dealing with the power of suit and relating to the action in question (see also *Kraus* v. *J.G. Lloyd Pty Ltd* [1965] V.R. 232).

Where the question 'should the company sue or not?' arises *other than* in the context of managing the business, it seems that it is for the company acting by ordinary resolution to decide the question. As Lord Russell said in *Bamford* v. *Bamford* [1970] Ch 212, 'it would be for the company by ordinary resolution to decide whether or not to proceed against the directors for compensation for misfeasance' or whether to institute proceedings to avoid a voidable allotment of shares made by the directors.

As Dr Sealy puts it (*op. cit.* p.446), where what is involved is an internal, or intra-corporate, dispute (for example, where the board is implicated in the irregularity which is being complained of) it is consistent with *Foster* v. *Foster* that the shareholders should have the power to decide whether the company should sue or not. Indeed, Articles 94 and 95 of Table A prohibit directors from voting at directors' meetings where they have, directly or indirectly, an interest or duty which is material and which conflicts or may conflict with the interests of the company. So also does the common law. This would cover the *Marshall's Valve* situation, where the directors had interests in the potential defendant company. Where the directors are not so disenfranchised, the board can properly decide on company action even against wrongdoing directors. It seems that it would be going too far to say that such an issue is not a 'management' issue, so that the inherent power of the general meeting to decide by ordinary resolution whether to sue or not is not comprised in the article 70 or article 80 delegation of power at all. Seen in this light *Marshall's Valve* is correctly decided. Perhaps the litigation in question there was not 'simply a business matter' (again using Dr Sealy's words). The board had interests in the potential defendant company. Although the case was technically decided on a particular interpretation of the 'article 80' provision in the articles, as we saw above (in [3.3]), it could arguably have been decided in the same way – but possibly more satisfactorily – by the court holding that the power of decision *on the particular issue* could not be exercised by the board at all, even on general principles which prohibit directors from putting themselves in a position where their interests may conflict with their duties. Nevertheless, as it stands, *Marshall's Valve* cannot be easily dismissed (i.e. 'distinguished') as a case which did not involve a management issue. Boards sue their members all the time, without reference to the general meeting. Directors and shareholders would be surprised to learn that this power had never been delegated at all by articles 70 or 80. If this is right, we are left with the difficulty, therefore, of interpreting the word 'regulations' in article 80.

Chapter 4

The Right to Attend and Vote in General Meeting

4.1 Introduction

The rules as to attendance and voting at general meetings of the company are usually set out in the company's articles of association. Very unusually, the rights attached to shares, including voting rights, may be set out in the memorandum of association. In the most abnormal case where both the memorandum and articles are silent, the relevant provisions in the model form of articles in Table A apply, since these apply unless expressly or impliedly excluded and silence does not amount to implied exclusion. In this case, article 54 provides that:

'Subject to any rights or restrictions attached to any shares, on a show of hands every member who (being an individual) is present in person or (being a corporation) is present by a duly authorised representative, not being himself a member entitled to vote, shall have one vote and on a poll every member shall have one vote for every share of which he is the holder.'

This embodies two rules: (1) in principle, each shareholder has one vote; (2) (modifying rule (1)) voting power is in principle to be proportional to shareholding on a poll. This latter rule 'weights' voting power by reference to the number of shares held.

Section 370(6) of the 1985 Act backs this up by providing that when the articles make no provision in the matter then every member of a company having a share capital shall have one vote per share, or one vote for every £10 of stock held by him. As far as companies not having a share capital are concerned, every member is entitled to one vote unless the articles make different provision.

In general, provisions regarding voting in the articles and in the memorandum are alterable in the manner discussed above (Chapter 2). However, if there are different classes of shares, provisions as to voting may only be altered in pursuance of the procedure for the variation of class rights laid down by law (see Chapter 7).

As has been said it is usual for the articles to provide for voting (e.g. articles 54 to 63, Table A). Furthermore, it is common to find provision in the articles going to the extreme of denying voting rights to one or more classes of share issued by a company (non-voting shares) or to the other extreme of conferring multiple voting rights on certain members or classes of shares at the other extreme. Either of these alternatives may be adopted generally, irrespective of the subject matter of the resolution, or they may be limited to particular resolutions. Some companies have complicated voting structures, often vesting voting control in the holders of a particular class of shares although those shareholders may constitute a minority in number or even in value of the members of the company (see *Rights and Issues Investment Ltd* v. *Stylo Shoes Ltd* [1965] Ch 250).

This restriction or amplification is rendered permissible by the opening words of article 54, viz. 'subject to any rights or restrictions attached to any shares'. An example of a restriction on voting is that which is very often imposed on preference shareholders. Preference shares are commonly issued on terms that the holders enjoy a right to vote only when the dividends which are due to them under the terms of issue remain unpaid but not otherwise. Such provisions need to be very carefully drafted (see for example, *Coulson* v. *Austin Motor Co.* [1927] 43 TLR 493). Again, the articles commonly provide that no member may vote in respect of any share held by him unless all moneys currently payable by him in respect of *that* share have been paid up (article 57). At the other extreme, the law does not prohibit multiple voting rights, so that it is perfectly lawful for articles to create a class of shares with permanent multiple voting rights (*Rights and Issues Investment Trust Ltd* v. *Stylo Shoes Ltd* [1965] Ch 250) as well as to provide that certain members will enjoy multiple voting rights on any particular matter. In *Bushell* v. *Faith* [1970] 1 All ER 53 an article which conferred multiple voting rights on a shareholding director on a resolution to dismiss him from office as director was held to be valid although the result was that he could not be removed.

4.2   By whom is the vote exercisable?

This question may baffle some at first sight. We have just seen that, subject to the articles, a member has the right to vote. However, it is common for shares to be sold, or to be charged as security for loans. The member may be bankrupt, may suffer from mental disorder or may die. Shares may be owned jointly by two or more persons, or they may be owned by companies. The question here is who is entitled to attend and vote at general or class meetings in such circumstances.

4.2.1 The register of members

The principle is that every person (this includes corporations) whose name appears on the register of members is, *prima facie*, a member of the company and may vote accordingly (section 352, 361, 1985 Act). The register of members provides evidence of membership and the articles may provide that the register be sole evidence of membership and (subject to rectification of the register by the court) of the right to vote (*Pender* v. *Lushington* (1877) 6 ChD 70). Article 38 of Table A provides that, subject to the provisions of the articles and to any restrictions imposed on any shares, notice of meetings shall be given (as well as to the directors and auditors) to all the members and to all persons entitled to a share in consequence of the death or bankruptcy of a member. This does not entitle personal representatives or trustees in bankruptcy to vote; they must be registered as the holders of the shares before they can do so (see [4.2.5] and [4.2.6] below).

4.2.2 Mental disorder

Article 56 Table A provides that a member who is incapable of managing his affairs by reason of mental disorder may vote by his receiver, *curator bonis* or other person authorised in that behalf appointed by a competent court (whether in the United Kingdom or elsewhere).

4.2.3 Joint holders

In the case of joint holders of a share, who jointly enjoy the right to vote, only one vote per share is allowed. Therefore, the articles commonly provide that the vote of the senior joint holder will be accepted to the exclusion of the votes, if any, tendered by the other joint holders. Seniority is determined by the order in which the names of the holders stand in the register of members (see article 55, Table A).

4.2.4 Corporate numbers

The vote of a member which is a corporation (whether a company or not) may, of course, be given by its duly authorised representative (section 375, 1985 Act, and article 54, Table A), under the same conditions as would apply to the corporation had it been an 'individual' member.

4.2.5 Deceased members

The personal representative of a deceased shareholder can at common law (and under the usual form of articles, – see articles 29, 30 and 31, Table A) demand to be entered on the register of members in place of the deceased member subject to any power of veto contained in the articles (*Scott* v. *Frank F. Scott (London) Ltd* [1940] Ch 794). The executor or administrator of a deceased member, after entry on the register, is entitled to vote in respect of the shares of which he is now the registered owner.

4.2.6 Bankrupt members

The trustee of a bankrupt shareholder is likewise entitled to be registered as the owner of the shares of the bankrupt in place of the latter, whereupon the trustee acquires the right to exercise the votes attached to those shares (*Re Bentham Mills Spinning Co.* (1879) 11 ChD 900; and see articles 30 and 31, Table A). Until this happens, the bankrupt remains entitled to attend and vote at company meetings, although he will be obliged to vote as directed by the trustee (*Morgan* v. *Gray* [1953] Ch 83).

4.2.7 Creditors

Where shares are charged by a member in favour of his creditors but no transfer of the shares is effected so that the debtor remains the registered owner, it is the debtor alone who is entitled to vote at meetings. This is the position as far as the company is concerned. As between the member and his creditors, the member will normally be obliged to vote as directed by his creditors (*Wise* v. *Lansdell* [1921] 1 Ch 420).

4.2.8 Trustees

Shares may be held 'on trust', that is, the legal ownership may be vested in one person who is obliged to hold the shares for the benefit of another. As legal owner, the former (the trustee) will be the registered owner. Section 360 of the 1985 Act expressly provides that no notice of any trust (whether express, implied or constructive – all different types of trust) is to appear on the register of members. Again, therefore, as far as the company is concerned it is the registered owner alone who is entitled to attend and vote at company meetings. Should there be more than one trustee the rule as to joint owners applies (see

[4.2.3]) if more than one are registered as owners of the same share(s). It is not for the company to inquire into the beneficial ownership of shares. As far as the company is concerned the beneficiaries are not members, and the company is perfectly entitled to accept the votes of the trustee even where he may be acting in breach of trust; the breach of trust is a matter for the trustee and the beneficiaries (see *Pender* v. *Lushington* (1877) 6 ChD 70).

4.2.9 Objections to qualifications

Article 58 provides that no objection may be raised to the qualification of any voter except at the meeting or adjourned meeting at which the vote objected to is tendered, and every vote not disallowed at the meeting shall be valid. Any objection made in due time shall be referred to the chairman whose decision shall be final and conclusive.

4.3 Suspension of the right to vote

The individual member's right to vote may be lost (or more precisely, suspended) in certain circumstances. The reasons are most often not expressly declared by the law and the question arises whether some of these cases are the reflection of an evolving awareness that some limit must be put on the exercise of the right (i.e. the manner in which the vote may be exercised). This point is developed later (see [4.5] below).

4.3.1 Wartime

The right is suspended during time of war in relation to shares held by enemy aliens. So also is the right to receive notice of company meetings and other company communications (e.g. company accounts). This disability lasts as long as hostilities continue (*Robson* v. *Premier Oil Co.* [1915] 2 Ch 124; *Re Anglo International Bank* [1943] Ch 233). If the shares held by enemy aliens are vested in the Public Trustee, he may exercise the voting rights attached to those shares (Re *Pharaon et fils* [1916] 1 Ch 1). Clearly, the higher interest which justifies the suspension of the right to vote is that of maintaining national security (see, also, Trading with the Enemy Act 1939, section 7).

4.3.2 Suspension under the Companies Act 1985

The 1985 Act itself provides for the suspension of the right to vote in clearly defined circumstances. The effect is to deny certain shareholders the right to vote in specific situations. After detailing these rules, the question will be asked what the philosophy or principle behind the rules might be and particularly whether the courts ought not to feel bound to follow the legislature's lead.

4.3.2.1   Secretary of State

Under section 445, 1985 Act, the Secretary of State for Trade and Industry may direct that voting rights be not exercisable in respect of certain shares by way of sanction. The purpose of this power (enshrined in section 454, Part XV of the Act) is to facilitate the gathering of relevant information about the shares in connection with a Departmental investigation into company ownership (under section 442) or as to interests in shares (under section 444). Similar restrictions may be imposed by the Secretary of State under section 210 where a person is convicted of an offence under that section through a failure to fulfil the obligation to notify interests in shares. They may also be imposed by the court under section 216 in the event of a failure to provide information to the company relating to interests in shares at the company's request (see section 212; see also [5.4.3.2]).

4.3.2.2   The court

The court has wide powers under section 461 to make any order it thinks fit in order to give relief to any member or members from unfairly prejudicial acts or omissions on the part of those conducting the company's affairs (see section 459, 1985 Act, and Chapter 8 below). This would include the power to disenfranchise shares, although the most commonly applied remedy can be expected to be that of ordering that the complaining member be 'bought out' by the controllers at a fair price (See Chapter 8).

4.3.2.3   Other statutory provision

We now come to some particularly interesting provisions in the 1985 Act. They are of special interest because they effectively suspend the right to vote not by way of sanction or as a means of compulsion but as a means of allowing a certain corporate operation to be embarked on by the company in a proper manner. This raises interesting questions regarding the legislator's unspoken hierarchisation of interests within the company.

First, section 164 provides, in connection with the power of a company limited by shares (or limited by guarantee and having a share capital) to make an 'off-market purchase' of its own shares, that such a purchase and its terms require the general meeting's prior authorisation by special resolution. An 'off-market' purchase is a purchase by a company of its own shares either (a) otherwise than on a recognised investment exchange, or (b) on a recognised investment exchange but where the shares are not subject to a marketing arrangement on that exchange (section 163, 1985 Act). The point of interest here is that by section 164(5):

'A special resolution to confer, vary, revoke or renew authority is not effective if any member of the company holding shares to which the resolution relates exercises the voting rights carried by any of those shares in voting on the resolution and the resolution would not have been passed if he had not done so.'

Second, section 165(2) makes section 164(5) applicable to the case where a company proposes to enter into a 'contingent purchase contract' (defined in section 165(1)). Third, section 174(2) sets out an identical restriction in relation to the passing of a special resolution authorising a private company to make a payment out of capital for the purpose of redeeming or purchasing its own shares.

Whatever one's views of the general implication, and the degree, of legislative encroachment on established principle, these provisions represent a clear statutory encroachment on the previously (pre-1981) unmitigated principle that a shareholder is free to cast his vote as he pleases in his personal interests, even where these interests conflict with those of the company (see [4.5] below). The effect is that where the member has a personal interest in these resolutions his right to vote is suspended entirely on a show of hands (i.e. he may not vote at all, even though he holds other shares which are themselves not the subject of the resolution), while on a poll his right to cast the votes attached to the shares which are the subject of the resolution (but not those attached to other shares which he may hold) are suspended for the purposes of that resolution.

These provisions were first enacted in the Companies Act 1981. The philosophy behind allowing the company to purchase its own shares was that provided that the interests of creditors were safeguarded there was no intrinsic objection to allowing the company to do so. The 1981 Act, now consolidated in the 1985 Act, set out the company's power to undertake these operations and set out the necessary safeguards of which sections 164, 165(2) and 174(2) of the 1985 Act are an example. The other safeguards are beyond the scope of this book. The question which is of interest here is the nature and degree of encroachment on established principle which the statutory provisions under consideration may represent. In accordance with these provisions the special resolution is rendered ineffective not merely because the interested member votes but only if it would not have been passed without the interested member's votes. Otherwise, there can be no point in declaring it invalid, for the only result would be that another meeting would have to be held at which he would refrain from voting and the resolution would be carried. This much of a concession is made to the 'vexatious litigation' rationale of *Foss* v. *Harbottle* (see Chapter 8). Also, the disenfranchisement does not depend on the member's being the holder of the required majority, that is three-quarters of the votes cast. It might be argued that while not absolutely depriving him of his voting rights (i.e. he can still demand to have his votes recorded, *Pender* v. *Lushington* (1877) 6 ChD 70) the purpose of the law is to annul any influence which his votes might have on the result. This is done not by disenfranchising him or declaring his votes invalid but by declaring the ensuing resolution to be ineffective. Technically, his voting rights are not abrogated or suspended, but in substance the law achieves the same result.

An alternative view may be that having regard to the policy of the Act, which is that of allowing a company to engage in these operations subject to safeguards, these provisions actually go so far as to disenfranchise the interested member to the extent of his direct interest at least. Thus, as far as relevant shares are concerned, he may not vote, and may not insist on a right to have his vote recorded. The chairman would be entitled to refuse to accept the votes attached to the relevant shares. Logic would have required total disenfranchisement of an interested shareholder if the adoption of a 'personal interest no vote' rule were at the root of these provisions. However, it must be emphasised that on a poll, the interested shareholder is allowed to cast the votes attached to other shares which he may hold. This militates against the 'direct disenfranchisement' view, for if the legislator had wanted to eliminate the influence of an interested party he would have imposed total disenfranchisement. In this state of uncertainty the chairman would be well advised to accept *all* the interested party's votes. This latter view is favoured by commentators and will in practice most likely appeal to chairmen and interested shareholders alike.

However, one point needs to be emphasised. Even accepting that these provisions 'directly' disenfranchise the interested shareholder they do so only in relation to the votes attached to shares which are the subject of the particular resolution. This casts doubt on the idea that the provisions reflect a fundamental change in principle and that the way is now open to the argument that shareholders ought not any longer to be allowed to vote where their interests might possibly conflict with those of the company (see also [4.5] below).

4.4 The manifestation of the vote

4.4.1 At common law

The common law method of voting at meetings is by show of hands, i.e. 'one man one vote'. This is the method of voting adopted at company meetings, at least in the first instance. Of course, if this rule were not varied by the articles (as it can be: *Re Horbury Bridge Coal, Iron & Waggon Co.* (1879) 11 ChD 109) the holder of a majority of the shares would have as much (or as little) power or control over the general meeting as the holder of a single share. Clearly, however, he has a greater stake in the company and a greater interest in the management of the company. The articles and the 1985 Companies Act (section 375) reflect this.

4.4.2 Table A

As we have seen ([4.1] above) article 54, Table A adopts the 'one man one vote' rule on a show of hands but the 'weighted or proportional vote' rule on a poll. Article 46, Table A provides that:

'A resolution put to the vote of a meeting shall be decided on a show of hands unless before, or on the declaration of the result of, the show of hands a poll is duly demanded.'

It is therefore important to ascertain in which circumstances a poll may be demanded. Again, this will depend on the articles which may make any provision deemed desirable, subject to one limitation imposed by section 373 of the 1985 Act (see [2.13.3] above). Article 46 in effect echoes section 373 by providing that:

'Subject to the provisions of the Act, a poll may be demanded –

(a) by the chairman; or
(b) by at least two members having the right to vote at the meeting; or
(d) by a member or members representing not less than one-tenth

of the total voting rights of all the members having the right to vote at the meeting; or

(d) by a member or members holding shares conferring a right to vote at the meeting being shares on which an aggregate sum has been paid up equal to not less than one-tenth of the total sum paid up on all the shares conferring that right;

and a demand by a person as proxy for a member shall be the same as a demand by the member.'

Article 46 is more liberal than it needs to be under section 373, in that under section 373 a provision in the articles remains valid although it requires five members to join in demanding a poll or excludes the right completely on the question of the election of the chairman of the meeting or the adjournment of the meeting. Article 51 impliedly allows a poll to be taken on the questions just referred to. It merely provides that a poll on these questions must be taken 'forthwith', – that is, at the meeting – while a poll demanded on any other question may be taken forthwith or within thirty days at such time and place as the chairman may direct. The reason for the distinction is obvious.

Also, article 46 goes beyond section 373 in allowing the chairman to demand a poll. It has been held that he is under an obligation as chairman to demand a poll if necessary in the interests that the resolution passed give effect to the sense of the meeting. Otherwise, the resolution is invalid (*Second Consolidated Trust Ltd* v. *Ceylon Amalgamated Tea and Rubber Estates Ltd* [1943] 2 All ER 567).

4.4.3 Chairman: deadlock

Whichever method of voting is adopted, a tied vote may result. In order to break the deadlock, the articles commonly provide that:

'In the case of an equality of votes, whether on a show of hands or on a poll, the chairman shall be entitled to a casting vote in addition to any other vote he may have.' (Article 50, Table A.)

One unresolved difficulty about such a provision refers to the manner in which the chairman may exercise this right. We shall see that a shareholder may in principle vote as he pleases even if this be in his own personal interests and these conflict with those of the company. However, the chairman exercising his casting vote does so not as shareholder but as chairman. As chairman, his overriding duty is to ensure that a resolution reflects the sense of the meeting. But, by definition, deadlock implies that there is no clear 'sense of the meeting'. The dilemma seems insoluble. There would seem to be no case on this point, and it is arguable that the chairman should act as a fiduciary in the same way as the directors. If this is correct, he is obliged to use his casting vote (if not his votes *qua* shareholder) *bona fide* in what he considers to be the best interests of the company as a whole (by analogy with the directors' primary fiduciary duty, see Re *Smith & Fawcett Co. Ltd* [1942] Ch 304)

In the first instance, voting is by show of hands. While the notice of the meeting must inform every member entitled to attend and vote of his right to appoint a proxy (section 372, 1985 Act), a proxy may not vote on a show of hands unless the articles expressly allow him to do so. Table A does not so allow; article 54 speaks of the member being present in person. This is why corporate members prefer to appoint a representative under section 375 than to appoint a proxy. However, article 58 allows votes to be given in person or by proxy on *a poll*.

4.4.4 Chairman: declarations

The articles usually provide (see article 47, Table A) that:

'Unless a poll is duly demanded, a declaration by the chairman that a resolution has been carried or carried unanimously, or by a particular majority, or lost, or not carried by a particular majority, or lost, or not carried by a particular majority and an entry to that effect in the minutes of the meeting shall be conclusive evidence of the fact without proof of the number or proportion of the votes recorded in favour of or against the resolution.'

In most cases the fact that the chairman gets it wrong will not matter, since a poll can usually be demanded if there is real doubt on the point. In any case, the chairman's declaration is not conclusive if he does give the number or proportion of the votes in favour or against the resolution and his figures are inconsistent with the record (*Re Caratal (New) Mines Ltd* [1902] 2 Ch 498).

Article 47 supplements section 378(4), 1985 Act. This section provides that:

'At any meeting at which an extraordinary resolution or a special resolution is submitted to be passed, a declaration by the chairman that the resolution is carried is, unless a poll is demanded, conclusive evidence of the fact without proof of the number or proportion of the votes recorded in favour of or against the resolution.'

Where the chairman at an extraordinary general meeting declared that a special resolution had been carried by the required majority and no poll was demanded the Scottish Court held that the declaration could not be reviewed despite an allegation that it was carried by the votes of members who were not qualified to vote (*Re Graham's Morocco Co.* (1932) SC 269).

4.4.5   The poll

It is said that the poll is the device whereby the views of those who individually or collectively have most at stake are enabled to win the day. Of course, it follows from what we have said about the company's freedom to attach different voting rights to different shares that it is possible for a shareholder with a comparatively low investment to have disproportionate voting power (see *Bushell* v. *Faith*, [4.1] above). Besides the possibility of some shares carrying multiple voting rights, there is the possibility of issuing shares of different nominal value but all carrying equal votes. These possibilities aside, the 'one vote per share' rule which the poll effects instils fairness into the voting process by matching voting power to investment interest. On a poll, every member usually has one vote for each share of which he is the holder (article 54, Table A) and this may be given in person or by proxy (article 59, Table A).

We have noted the effect of article 46 (see [4.4.2]). It is usual for the articles of private companies (whose membership can be quite small) to be even more liberal and to allow a single member, in person or by proxy, to demand a poll.

The poll is taken in such manner, at such place and time as the chairman directs and the result of the poll is deemed to be the resolution of the meeting at which the poll was demanded (article 49, Table A) although it may be held up to thirty days later (article 51, Table A). The chairman's freedom to determine the 'manner' in which the poll may be taken (article 49) does not permit voting on a poll to be otherwise than in person or by proxy, as required by article 59 (*McMillan* v. *Le Roi Mining Co. Ltd* [1906] 1 Ch 331). The right to demand a poll in person or by proxy applies in the context of class meetings held to vary class rights as it does to general meetings (section 125(6)(b), 1985 Act).

The mechanics of the poll involve the verification of the right to vote and the counting of the votes. Therefore, it is usually impossible for the result of a poll to be declared at the meeting at which the poll is demanded and taken. This is another reason why the law allows the articles to exclude the right to demand a poll on the questions of the election of a chairman and the adjournment of the meeting.

4.5 The exercise of the right to vote

4.5.1 The traditional position

In *Pender* v. *Lushington* the chairman at a general meeting, in breach of the articles, rejected certain votes as invalid. Lord Jessel MR held:

> '(Pender) is a member of the company, and whether he votes with the majority or with the minority he is entitled to have his vote recorded, an individual right in respect of which he has a right to sue. That has nothing to do with the question like that raised in *Foss* v. *Harbottle* and that line of cases.'

Again, in *Carruth* v. *Imperial Chemical Industries Ltd* [1937] AC 707, Lord Maugham said:

> 'The shareholder's vote is a right of property, and *prima facie* may be exercised by a shareholder as he thinks fit in his own interest.'

Therefore, not only is the right to vote stated to be a right of property but there is no *a priori* obligation to exercise it for any reason other than self-interest. This principle was regarded as firmly established by the Privy Council in *Burland* v. *Earle* [1902] A.C. 83, where Lord Davey held that it was a principle of law that:

> 'unless otherwise provided by the regulations of the company, a shareholder is not debarred from voting or using his voting power to carry a resolution by the circumstances of his having a particular interest in the subject matter of the vote.'

The Privy Council cited with approval *North-West Transportation Co. Ltd* v. *Beatty* (1887) 12 App Cas 589, where Sir Richard Baggallay had held that:

> 'unless some provision to the contrary is to be found in the charter or the instrument by which the company is incorporated, the resolution of a majority of the shareholders, duly convened, upon any question with which the company is legally competent to deal, is binding upon the minority ..., and every shareholder has a perfect right to vote upon any such question, although he may have a

personal interest in the subject-matter opposed to, or different from, the general or particular interests of the company ...'

In *Northern Counties Securities Ltd* v. *Jackson and Steeple Ltd* [1974] 1 WLR 1133, Mr Justice Walton said:

'when a shareholder is voting for or against a particular resolution he is voting as a person owing no fiduciary duty to the company and who is exercising his own right of property to vote as he thinks fit. The fact that the result of the voting at the meeting (or at a subsequent poll) will bind the company cannot affect the position that, in voting, he is voting simply in exercise of his own property rights ... his act therefore in voting as he pleases cannot in any way be regarded as an act of the company.'

Lord Cozens Hardy stated the law succinctly in *Phillips* v. *Manufacturers' Securities Ltd* (1917) 116 LT 290 thus:

'... (M)embers of a company voting at a general meeting properly convened have no fiduciary obligation either to the company or to the other shareholders.'

The above principle applies also to directors when they vote as shareholders even though in so voting they further their personal interests, possibly even to the detriment of the company and the other shareholders. One such instance would be where the directors use their voting power as shareholders to ratify their own (ratifiable) breaches of duty (see Chapter 8). The only safeguard insisted upon by the courts in recent years has occurred where the breach of duty to be ratified was one which increased the voting power as shareholders of the directors. Here, the courts have precluded them from exercising their newly acquired votes (*Hogg* v. *Cramphorn* [1967] Ch 254; *Bamford* v. *Bamford* [1970] Ch 212). A totally independent majority vote, in the sense that the directors' original shares (i.e. shares other than those in question) were also disenfranchised, has never been insisted upon by the courts. This is in line with the statutory approach which we considered in [4.3] above.

While not all breaches of their duties by the directors are ratifiable, English law is clearly far less strict than other systems of law, which prohibit the directors from voting *qua* shareholders even in respect of their original votes whenever the resolution concerns the performance by them of their duties as directors. The Draft 5th EEC Directive on Company Law will follow this latter approach (see [4.6] below).

4.5.2   Is English law changing?

This section deals with the possible effect on the traditional position in English law of two relatively recent judgments. The first of these is *Clemens* v. *Clemens Bros Ltd and another* [1976] 2 All ER 268. In a 'family company', plaintiff held 45 per cent and her aunt 55 per cent of the issued share capital. The capital of the company consisted of 200 preference shares, of which plaintiff and her aunt each held 100, and 1,800 ordinary shares of £1 each fully paid, of which plaintiff held 800 and her aunt 1000. Under the articles, members had a right of pre-emption if another member wished to transfer his/her shares. All this meant that the niece could expect to acquire total control of the company if the aunt ever parted with her interest and also that the niece could expect to block special resolutions with which she disagreed (her 45 per cent stake giving her 'negative control'). The aunt was one of five directors, the niece was not. The directors proposed to increase the company's share capital from £2,000 to £3,650 by creating a further 1650 ordinary shares all of which were to carry voting rights. The directors other than the aunt would receive 200 shares each, and the remaining 850 shares would be placed in trust for long service employees of the company. An extraordinary general meeting was called to approve the setting up of the trust, increase the company's capital and provide for the proposed allotments. The three resolutions were passed despite objections by plaintiff. Plaintiff then sued the company and the aunt seeking (a) a declaration that the resolutions were oppressive because they resulted in her losing her 'right' to veto a special or extraordinary resolution and greatly watered down her existing right of pre-emption under the articles, and (b) an order setting them aside.

Mr Justice Foster first referred to *North-West Transportation* v. *Beatty* (above) where Sir Richard Baggallay decided that a shareholder could vote always in his own personal interests. He then turned to *Allen* v. *Gold Reefs of West Africa Ltd* [1900] 1 Ch 656, where Lord Lindley MR laid down the rule restricting *majority power with regard to alteration of the articles* in the following terms:

'wide ... as the language in (section 9, 1985 Act) is, the power conferred must, like all other powers, be exercised subject to those general principles of law and equity which are applicable to all powers conferred on majorities and enabling them to bind minorities. It must be exercised not only in the manner required by law, but also *bona fide* for the benefit of the company as a whole and it must not be exceeded.' (See also [4.5.3] below.)

From this judgment, Mr Justice Foster went on to *Greenhalgh* v. *Arderne Cinemas Ltd* [1951] Ch 286, CA and Lord Evershed's famous passage. In that passage Lord Evershed MR took the criterion laid down for controlling majority power in relation to alteration of the articles, *viz.* 'that those who passed it did so in good faith and for the benefit of the company as a whole' and then, in the face of all the authorities quoted above to the effect that a shareholder may not vote in his own personal interests even where these conflict with those of the company, he immediately 'interpreted' that criterion to mean that 'the *shareholder* must proceed on what, in his honest opinion, is for the benefit of the company as a whole'.

Mr Justice Foster, without commenting on Lord Evershed's apparent *faux pas* in reading the duty as one incumbent on each individual shareholder, proceeded to rely on Lord Evershed's judgment to reduce the question raised in the Clemens case to this: Did Miss Clemens (the aunt), when voting for the resolutions, honestly believe that these resolutions, when passed, would be for the benefit of the plaintiff? Unfortunately, due to Lord Evershed MR's use of language it is not clear whether Mr Justice Foster saw the duty to act '*bona fide* for the benefit of the company as a whole' as incumbent on the aunt as an individual shareholder or as a majority shareholder. The judgment is replete with *dicta* which support either view. Perhaps Mr Justice Foster's reference to *Meyer* v. *Scottish Textile and Manufacturing Co. Ltd, Scottish Co-operative Wholesale Society Ltd* 1954 SC 381 *per* Lord Cooper at 382 – a case dealing with the affairs of the company being conducted in an oppressive manner under section 210 of the 1948 Act (now section 459, 1985 Act, see Chapter 8) – might be of some significance, since it is only the board of directors or the majority in general meeting which really 'conduct the company's affairs'. Again, after quoting Lord Wilberforce in *Ebrahimi* v. *Westbourne Galleries Ltd* [1973] AC 360, Mr Justice Foster held that

> 'in such a case as the present Miss Clemens is not entitled to exercise her majority vote in any way she pleases. The difficulty is finding a principle, and obviously expressions such as '*bona fide*' for the benefit of the company as a whole, 'fraud on a minority' and 'oppressive' do not assist in formulating a principle.'

The reference to 'majority vote' in the same breath as references to criteria evolved to restrain the use of majority power, might be considered evidence of Mr Justice Foster's intention not so much to control the exercise by Miss Clemens of her votes as an individual shareholder, but rather to apply a restriction on the use of *majority* power. This, however, seems to be contradicted by his subsequent statement that the right (to exercise one's votes as an ordinary shareholder) is subject to equitable considerations which may make it unjust to exercise it in a particular way. He proceeded to find that such equitable considerations existed in the case before him.

In the light of such conflicting statements it is quite impossible to say exactly what *Clemens* v. *Clemens* did decide as far as the individual shareholder's freedom to vote as he pleases is concerned. Since, however, the court made no reference to the strong authority in favour of unrestricted freedom, except for *North West Transportation Co. Ltd* v. *Beatty* (above) which the court seemed to dismiss as of no further use after deciding that it concerned the individual shareholder's right to vote to ratify a voidable contract to which he was a party, the writer tends to view the case as a special case possibly best confined to the question of the area of application of equitable considerations between shareholders in the case of family or 'quasi-partnership' companies (see Chapter 8).

The second case is *Estmanco (Kilner House) Ltd* v. *Greater London Council* [1982] 1 WLR 2. In this case the court was mainly concerned with the rule in *Foss* v. *Harbottle* and also with the question of there being any limits on the power of the majority. However, Sir Robert Megarry VC did say (at p.16):

'No right of a shareholder to vote in his own selfish interests or to ignore the interests of the company entitle him with impunity to injure his voteless fellow shareholders by depriving the company of a cause of action and by stultifying the purpose for which the company was formed.'

However, as in the case of *Clemens* v. *Clemens* the judgment does not offer clear support for a change in the traditional law, for the wrongdoing voter was the majority shareholder, and there are other *dicta* which indicate that the issue in the court's mind was essentially one of the abuse of majority power, and in particular a question of 'fraud on the minority' so that it is doubtful whether the English courts will extend the principles stated in the *Estmanco* case to the situation of the individual minority vote, for example, where a minority blocks a special resolution for (extra-company) personal reasons.

4.5.3 Limits on the exercise of majority power

It has for long been established law that when exercising the power to alter the articles – a power vested in the general meeting by section 9,

1985 Act – the general meeting must act 'bona fide for the benefit of the company as a whole' (see below). It is difficult for the reasons given above in [4.5.2] to see Clemens v. Clemens as a case which extends the application of this principle outside the narrow sphere of alteration of the articles, but it is arguable that Estmanco v. GLC has done just that. If so, the implications are far-reaching. The question is whether the courts have, albeit very tentatively, taken the first steps towards extending the sphere of operation of this limitation outside the narrow sphere of alteration of the articles. Clemens concerned an ordinary resolution purporting to allot shares. Estmanco concerned an ordinary resolution ordering directors to discontinue proceedings brought by them on behalf of the company. Although the courts have affirmatively held that shareholders owe no duty of care to the company or to other shareholders (Multinational Gas and Petrochemical Co. v. Multinational Gas and Petrochemical Services Ltd [1983] Ch 258) and have traditionally defended the free exercise of the individual right to vote, the dawning realisation appears to be that the general meeting is an organ of the company and must act as such. In other words, its powers are vested in it for the benefit of the company as a whole and not for that of the majority. Considering that the general meeting wields the most crucial powers in the company (e.g. alteration of memorandum and articles, variation of class rights, changes in capital structure, and even the power to wind up the company) it would not be surprising if the courts built on the 'alteration of the articles' cases (below) and the 'extending cases' like Estmanco to formulate a general limitation on the exercise of all majority power in general meeting. Some more recent support for this trend is to be found in Smith v. Croft (No.3) (1987) 3 BCC 218, where the court deferred to the wishes of the independent majority on the question whether a derivative action brought on behalf of the company ought to be allowed to proceed (see [8.3.2.3]).

We have said that it is well established that when altering the articles of association, the majority must act 'bona fide for the benefit of the company as a whole'. Essentially, this means that the majority may not use their power in such a way as to discriminate unfairly against the minority. It would seem that the majority acts properly, and the alteration will be upheld by the court, if there are reasonable grounds for saying that the prejudice inflicted on the minority is justifiable by reference to the interests of the 'hypothetical member' – whose interests are in turn divined by reference to those of the company as a going concern (see generally, Allen v. Gold Reefs of West Africa Ltd [1900] 1 Ch 656; Greenhalgh v. Arderne Cinemas Ltd [1951] Ch 286, CA and [4.5.2.] above; Shuttleworth v. Cox Bros. & Co. Ltd [1920] 1 Ch 154 (CA); Brown v. British Abrasive Wheel Co. [1919] 1 Ch 290; Dafen Tinplate Co. Ltd

v. *Llanelly Steel Co.* (1907) Ltd [1920] 2 Ch 124; *Sidebottom* v. *Kershaw, Leese & Co. Ltd* [1920] 1 Ch 154; and see generally P.G. Xuereb (1985) 6 Co. Law 119, and F.G. Rixon (1986) 49 MLR 446).

The courts will intervene if the alteration 'is so oppressive as to cast suspicion on the honesty of the persons responsible for it, or so extravagant that no reasonable man could really consider it for the benefit of the company' (*per* Lord Bankes in *Shuttleworth* v. *Cox*, above). The principles are well illustrated by the *Sidebottom* case (above). There the majority proposed to alter the articles in order to permit the company to compulsorily purchase the shares, at a fair price, of any shareholder who might be competing with the company. It was held that this was a valid exercise of the power to alter the articles. Generally speaking, an alteration of the articles to provide for the compulsory expropriation will be upheld provided it is for a fair price and there is some valid commercial ground for inserting such a power. However, the need to extend these principles to the actual *exercise* of the power by the general meeting (assuming it to be vested in the general meeting) is obvious. It is in this area where the general meeting is acting by ordinary majority that cases like *Clemens* and *Estmanco* are of significance for they concerned ordinary resolutions, and not the exercise of the power to alter the articles.

In *Estmanco*, Lord Megarry VC was concerned that it was not enough to say that the majority must act *bona fide* for the benefit of the company. He said:

'Plainly there must be some limit to the power of the majority to pass resolutions which they believe to be in the interests of the company and yet remain immune from interference by the courts. It may be in the interests of the company to deprive the minority of some of their rights or some of their property, yet I do not think that this gives the majority an unrestricted right to do this however unjust it may be, and however much it may harm shareholders whose rights as a class differ from those of the majority.'

This can be met by saying that the majority do not act '*bona fide* for the benefit of the company as a whole' if no reasonable man would say that the prejudice inflicted on the minority was *reasonably required* in the interests of the company (see Xuereb (1985) 6 Co. Law 119).

The courts have always restrained the worst abuses by the majority even when acting by ordinary resolution, for example where the majority in effect seek to expropriate company property (*Cook* v. *Deeks* [1916] 1 AC 554; *Ngurli* v. *McCann* (1954) 90 CLR 425). In *Menier* v. *Hooper's Telegraph Works* (1874) LR 9 Ch App 350 the majority compromised a company action and sought to put the company into liquidation in such circumstances as to leave themselves in possession of the company's assets to the exclusion of the minority. The court allowed a derivative action to be brought on the company's behalf (see Chapter 8).

It may be that it is still true to say that the courts have stopped short of recognising that majority shareholders owe fiduciary duties akin to those owed by directors, but the sum of the above cases indicates that that day is not too far off. When it happens it should not be seen as the final nail in the coffin of shareholder voting power but rather as a vindication of the legitimacy of the interests and expectations of each and every shareholder, so that the interests of the majority and those of the minority are fairly balanced. It has been said in the context of directors' duties that 'the interests of the company' is not always a useful test because in some cases the company has no interest in the dispute between majority and minority. The test then becomes one of 'fairness' (*Mills* v. *Mills* (1938) 60 CLR 164). The writer has suggested elsewhere that the fact that the company has no interest may itself afford good reason for saying that the majority are acting purely in their own selfish interest in prejudicing the minority in those circumstances. If the articles do not give them a right to the benefit which they are seeking, the mere fact that they have the power to confer it upon themselves should not of itself make it 'fair' that they receive it (Xuereb (1988) 51 MLR 156).

It is clear that the same principles as apply to the alteration of the articles in general meeting also apply to the exercise of majority power in class meetings (i.e. meetings of a particular class of shareholders). The majority must act *bona fide* for the benefit of the class as a whole (*Re Holders Investment Trust Ltd* [1971] 1 WLR 583, and Chapter 7 below).

4.6   EEC proposals

The Draft 5th EEC Directive on Company Law (O.J. 1983, C.240 2-38) makes important provision for harmonising the law on shareholder voting rights as applicable to public companies in the various EEC Member States. Assuming that the current Draft Directive is adopted in its current form English law will need to be brought into line with the following provisions.

4.6.1   Conflicts of interests

Article 34 of the Directive provides that neither a shareholder nor his representative shall exercise the right to vote attached to his shares or to shares belonging to third persons where the subject matter of the resolution relates to:

(a) discharge of that shareholder (i.e. from liability);
(b) rights which the company may exercise against that shareholder;
(c) the release of that shareholder from his obligations to the company;
(d) approval of contracts made between the company and that shareholder.

This provision clearly embraces the principle that a shareholder may not vote if he has a personal interest in the subject matter of the vote which conflicts or may possibly conflict with the interests of the company. Whether this is in turn premised on a general obligation to vote in the interests of the company cannot be stated with certainty. No such principle is set out in the Directive. However, various continental systems of company law apply concepts analogous to the 'fraud on a power' concept (see *per* Lord Megarry VC in *Estmanco* [1982] 1 WLR 2 at 11-15) in order to restrain 'illegitimate' action by the majority in general meeting. France has *abus de droit*, Italy has *abuso di diritto* or *eccesso di potere*. Many European laws already suspend voting rights in general terms in cases of conflict of interest (e.g. Italian Civil Code, article 2373).

If a shareholder were to vote in breach of article 34, the resolution would be void or voidable insofar as 'the outcome of the vote was decisively affected' by reason of his votes. Any shareholder who was excluded from voting or who disputes the right to vote of some other shareholder will be entitled to bring nullity proceedings (for breach of article 34) under article 42 (without prejudice, however, to rights acquired in good faith by third parties).

4.6.2   General review

The Draft Fifth Directive contains other important provisions relating to voting. In particular:

(1) In principle, every shareholder is entitled to attend the general meeting (article 26).
(2) Every shareholder will be entitled to appoint a proxy (article 27).
(3) A qualified minority may request the company to convene a general meeting (articles 23 and 16).
(4) Every shareholder who so requests at a general meeting shall be

entitled to obtain correct information concerning the affairs of the company if such information is necessary to enable an objective assessment to be made of the items on the agenda (article 31(1)). This is subject to safeguards in the interests of the company (Article 31(3)). Disputes are to be settled by the court, i.e. the shareholders will have a right to institute nullity proceedings under articles 42 and 43 in the event of a failure by the management organ to comply with its duty to provide information under article 31.

(5) Every shareholder is entitled to adequate notice of meetings and the content of business (article 32).

(6) In principle, a shareholder's right to vote shall be proportionate to the fraction of the subscribed capital which the shares represent (Article 33(1)). However, the laws of Member States will be permitted to allow companies (if authorised by their memorandum and articles) (a) to restrict or exclude the right to vote in respect of shares which carry special advantages, and (b) to restrict votes in respect of shares allotted to the same shareholder, provided the restriction applies at least to all shareholders of the same class (article 33(2)). Of course this will continue to permit the current practice of the restriction of voting rights in relation to preference shares. Article 42 applies also in the context of a breach of such restrictions as may be imposed in consequence of these provisions.

(7) A shareholder who, at the date of the general meeting, has not paid up calls made by the company at least one month earlier, will be debarred from exercising his right to vote (article 33(3)). It is not clear whether he will lose all voting rights or only those attached to shares to which the call relates. This needs to be clarified in view of the fact that article 42 applies in this context.

(8) Certain shareholder agreements which fetter a shareholder's vote are avoided (article 35). Article 35 as currently worded provides that agreements whereby a shareholder undertakes to vote in any of the following ways shall be void: (a) that he will always follow the instructions of the company or of one of its organs; (b) that he will always approve proposals made by the company or by one of its organs; (c) that he will vote in a specified manner, or abstain, in consideration of special advantages.

4.7　Voting agreements

We have just seen that voting agreements between shareholders, whereby they agree in advance always to vote in a particular interest or as directed by some party will be prohibited by the Fifth EEC Directive. This prohibition is based on the continental view that the right to vote is at the same time a 'power' or 'function' which shareholders enjoy as much (or even primarily) in the interests of the company as in their own interest. In general, English law adheres steadfastly to the notion that the right to vote is a right of property. Voting agreements are therefore a valid exercise of property rights and are enforceable in the courts provided they do not contravene the general law (*Greenwell* v. *Porter* [1902] 1 Ch 530; *Puddephatt* v. *Leith* [1916] 1 Ch 200).

If all the trends in the law which have been referred to in this chapter are indicative of an appreciation that the right to vote is not an unfettered right but also a power with corresponding responsibility, it can be expected that the development of the law on voting agreements will also be informed by the same spirit.

Already, it can be said that voting agreements are most probably invalid if they (a) provide for a pecuniary benefit to a shareholder for voting as directed; (b) purport to oblige members to vote in a certain way *as directors*; (c) purport to fetter the company's power to alter its articles (see J.H. Farrar, *Company Law*, 1985, Chapter 11, p.116; H.R. Hahlo and J.H. Farrar, *Hahlo's Cases and Materials on Company Law*, 3rd ed., Chapters 12 and 15). Also, if the effect of a voting agreement entered into by some shareholders is to work a 'fraud' or 'unfair prejudice' on the minority, the law on minority shareholder protection considered in Chapter 8 may come into play.

Voting agreements are only one kind of shareholder agreement. Shareholder agreements can cover proxy or pooling agreements, agreements limiting the transferability of shares, or can relate generally to the activity of the company. In the American case of *Mason* v. *Curtis* (223 NY 313) it was said:

'It is not illegal or against public policy for two or more (share-holders) ... to unite upon a course of corporate policy or action, or upon the officers whom they will elect ... shareholders have the right to combine their interests and voting powers to secure such control of the corporation and the adoption of and adhesion by it to a specific policy and course of business. Agreements upon a sufficient consideration between them, of such intendment and effect, are valid and binding, if they do not contravene any express charter or statutory provision or contemplate any fraud, oppression or wrong against other (shareholders) or other illegal object.'

Chapter 5

The Right to Information about Corporate Affairs

5.1 Introduction

In company law circles it is customary to refer to the 'disclosure philosophy' – that is, the idea that provided sufficient transparency or disclosure by company management of the right sort of information is ensured a multitude of problems will disappear. In particular, current shareholders will be in a position to exercise their powers in general meeting effectively; potential investors and creditors will make sufficiently informed decisions; other interests, including employee interests and the national interest itself, will be adequately protected (see generally, J.H. Farrar, *Company Law*, Chapter 28).

In this chapter we shall outline the rights of the existing shareholder to information about the company's affairs. Detailed statutory rules exist on disclosure to members, and these are supplemented by stringent Stock Exchange requirements for listed companies. We shall deal with the topic in three parts: (1) The Annual Report and Accounts; (2) the seeking of information in general meeting; (3) the seeking of information outside general meeting. The position of the potential investor is outlined in Chapter 10.

5.2 The Annual Report and Accounts

5.2.1 Introduction

The Annual Reports and Accounts provide the shareholder with an overview of the company's financial position. They must comply with the Companies Act 1985. Company accounts must also be drawn up in accordance with Statements of Standard Accounting Practice (SSAPs), issued by the Accounting Standard Steering Committee; any significant departure from these SSAPs must be disclosed by the company or its auditors and the latter must 'qualify' (i.e. 'make a reservation to') their report on the accounts unless they justify the departure. Listed companies must comply with the requirements of the Yellow Book (i.e. the Stock Exchange's terms for the Admission of Securities to Listing) which they ignore at the peril of losing their listing.

5.2.2 The shareholder's right in general

5.2.2.1 *The company's obligation*

At the end of each 'financial year' (see section 742(1)(c), 1985 Act) every company must draw up a set of accounts for that financial year (or 'accounting reference period', sections 224(4) and 227(1)). The 'accounts' comprise (a) the balance sheet, (b) the profit and loss account, (c) the directors' report, and (d) the auditor's report (section 239, 1985 Act). Where the company has subsidiaries at the end of its financial year and none of the exemptions set out in section 229 apply, the company must in addition to drawing up the above four documents also prepare 'group accounts' (usually in 'consolidated' form; see sections 229(5) and (6)), i.e. accounts or statements which deal with the state of affairs and profit or loss of the company and its subsidiaries (section 239, 1985 Act). Just as the Fourth EEC Directive (No. 78/660, O.J. 1978 L.222/11), which was implemented in the UK by the Companies Act of 1981, sought to harmonise 'individual company' accounts legislation throughout the European Economic Community, the Seventh Directive (No. 83/349, O.J. 1983 L 193/1) will harmonise the law on group accounts throughout the EEC. The form and content of group accounts are governed by section 230, 1985 Act. The overriding requirement is that group accounts should give a 'true and fair view of the state of affairs and profit or loss of the company and the subsidiaries dealt with by those accounts as a whole, so far as concerns members of the company' (section 230(2), 1985 Act).

5.2.2.2 *Delivery to members*

In the case of every company, a copy of the company's accounts for the financial year must be sent to every member of the company whether or not he be entitled to receive notice of general meetings. This must be done not less than 21 days before the date of the meeting at which they are to be laid (section 240, 1985 Act). Copies need not be sent: (a) to a member of the company who is not entitled to receive notices of general meetings and of whose address the company is unaware, (b) to more than one of the joint holders of any shares none of whom are entitled to receive notices of general meetings, or (c) in the case of joint holders of shares some of whom are, and some not, entitled to receive such notices, to those who are not so entitled (section 240(3), 1985 Act). A fourth exception to the rule is made in the case of members of a company which does not have a share capital who are not entitled to receive notices of general meetings (section 240(2), 1985 Act). The company's obligation under section 240 is supplemented by section 246 which provides that any member of the company, whether or not he is entitled to have sent to him copies of the accounts is entitled to be furnished (on demand and without charge) with a copy of its last accounts.

5.2.2.3   Laying of accounts before general meeting and delivery to Registrar

As indicated above, the accounts in respect of each financial year must be laid before the company in general meeting (section 241(1), 1985 Act). A copy must be sent by all limited companies to the registrar of companies (section 241(3)), but unlimited companies are exempt from this obligation, thus enjoying 'privacy', except in certain cases (see section 241(4)). The exemption whereby directors of an unlimited company need not deliver accounts to the registrar applies only if:

(a) at no time during the accounting reference period has the company been, to its knowledge, the subsidiary of a company that was then limited and at no such time, to its knowledge, have there been held or been exercisable, by or on behalf of two or more companies that were then limited, shares or powers which, if they had been held or been exercisable by one of them, would have made the company its subsidiary; *and*
(b) at no such time has the company been the holding company of a company which was then limited, *and*
(c) at no such time has the company been carrying on business as the promoter of a trading stamp scheme within the Trading Stamps Act 1964.

By 'limited company' here is meant a body corporate, under whatever law incorporated, the liability of whose members was limited at the relevant time.

The periods allowed by law for the laying of the accounts before the company and their delivery to the registrar are set out in section 242, 1985 Act. The periods, in general, are ten and seven months from the end of the accounting reference period for private and public companies respectively. Listed companies are obliged by the Yellow

Book to comply within six months of that date (section 5, para. 20, Admission of Securities to Listing).

5.2.3 Outline of contents of accounts

5.2.3.1 *Balance sheet and profit and loss account*

The directors of every company are obliged to prepare a balance sheet as at the last day of the financial year (section 227(3), 1985 Act) and a profit and loss account or, if the company does not trade for profit, an income and expenditure account in respect of each 'accounting reference period' (as to 'accounting reference period' see sections 224-226, 1985 Act). By section 228 the accounts must comply with Schedule 4 to the 1985 Act ('so far as applicable') with respect to form and content of balance sheet and profit and loss account *and* any additional information to be provided by way of notes to the accounts (see sections 228(4), (5), (6); section 231 and Schedule 5, 1985 Act).

However, the overriding criteria are (1) that the balance sheet shall give a *true and fair view* of the state of affairs of the company as at the end of the financial year and (2) that the profit and loss account shall give a true and fair view of the profit or loss of the company for the financial year (section 228(2) and (3)). This means that the statutory requirements as to content must, if necessary, be ignored (and, for example, additional information be supplied) in the pursuit of disclosure which gives a true and fair view. Schedule 4 sets out the general Rules and Formats (Part I), Accounting Principles and Rules (Part II), matters requiring a note to the accounts (Part III), Special Provisions dealing with particular problems or sets of circumstances (Parts IV, V, VI). Group accounts are regulated separately by the Act (sections 229, 230, 1985 Act), and certain 'special category companies' which fell outside the scope of the Fourth EEC Directive (i.e. banking, insurance and shipping companies) are regulated by their own provisions (sections 257, 258 and Schedule 9, 1985 Act). An EEC draft proposal is under discussion for a Directive on the annual accounts of insurance undertakings.

5.2.3.2 *Auditors' Report*

The law goes to great pains to ensure that independent and expert auditors report to members of the company on the accounts. The auditors' report is circulated to members and read out in annual general meeting. The auditors' duty is to examine the accounts prepared by the directors and to report: (1) whether the balance sheet and profit and loss account (and, if it be a holding company submitting group accounts, the group accounts) have been properly prepared in accordance with the 1985 Act and (2) whether, in their opinion, a true and fair view is given (i) in the balance sheet, of the state of the company's affairs at the end of the financial year; (ii) in the profit and loss account (if not framed as a consolidated account) of the company's profit or loss for the financial year, and (iii) in the case of group accounts, of the state of affairs and profit or loss of the company and its subsidiaries dealt with by the accounts, so far as concerns members of the company (section 236, 1985 Act). Section 237 elaborates on this duty: for example, although the directors' report is not subject to audit, it is the auditors' duty to consider whether the information given in the directors' report for the financial year for which the accounts were prepared is consistent with those accounts; and if they are of the opinion that it is not, they must state that fact in their report (section 237).

Statute vests auditors with strong powers of access to information (sections 237, 392, 1985 Act), and ensures their independence of, in particular, the board of directors (section 389, 1985 Act). Indeed, Chapter V, Part XI of the 1985 Act is devoted to ensuring that auditors are properly qualified and independent and provides, *inter alia*, that (i) auditors are to be appointed as a rule by the members in general meeting (except for the first auditors; casual vacancies may be filled by the board: section 384, 1985 Act); (ii) auditors are removable only by the general meeting by ordinary resolution (section 386); (iii) auditors have protected rights of attendance at general meetings including, if they are removed, that at which their term of office would otherwise have expired and any general meeting at which it is proposed to fill the vacancy caused by their removal (section 387); (iv) auditors who resign have power, subject to limited exceptions, to requisition an extraordinary general meeting for the purpose of presenting their explanation of the circumstances of their resignation to members (section 391).

Auditors do not simply have statutory functions, duties or powers. They are experts on whom reliance is placed (as to their required qualifications, see section 389). As such they owe a common law duty of care and skill i.e. they must exhibit the care and skill of the ordinary, reasonable auditor (*Re London and General Bank* [1895] 2 Ch 673 at 682; *Whiteoak* v. *Walker* (1988) 4 BCC 122 – a share valuation case). In reviewing the accounts, they are watchdogs, not bloodhounds (*per* Lord Lopes in *Re Kingston Cotton Mill (No.2)* [1896] 2 Ch 279 at 288), or as Lord Denning put it in *Fomento (Sterling Area) Ltd* v. *Selsdon Fountain Pen Co.* [1958] 1 All ER 11 at 23:

'(An auditor must approach his task) with an inquiring mind – not suspicious of dishonesty, I agree – but suspecting that someone may have made a mistake somewhere and that a check must be made to ensure that there has been none.'

With all due respect, it must be said that the investing public can be forgiven for expecting rather more of the auditor in the way of fox-hunting and that the standard of care is pitched too low – although beleaguered auditors will not agree.

In any case this duty is owed by auditors as a matter of contract to the company itself and if the company suffers loss it can sue the negligent or fraudulent auditor in contract (as well as in tort). But under the law of tort (and more specifically the law of negligence) the auditor also owes all persons who might foreseeably be harmed by his negligence a duty of care the extent of which has not yet been clearly defined (*Hedley Byrne & Co. Ltd* v. *Heller & Partners Ltd* [1964] AC 465). It is unclear whether a shareholder who suffers indirect loss (e.g. the diminution in value of his shares) may sue negligent auditors in a personal action, or whether a company action is the only available remedy. Individual members might be able to claim that they were induced by the auditors to act to their own detriment by voting for a particular scheme on the basis of the auditors' report and that they fall with the class of persons who might forseeably have been injured. At least as far as potential investors who invest on the basis of a negligent report are concerned it is clear that although their loss is 'pure economic loss' – to which type of loss recovery on a tort basis usually does not extend – they can recover damages. Whether a duty of care is owed at all depends on how 'proximate' the relationship between the auditors (and their act or omission) and the investor (and his loss) is. If 'sufficiently' proximate – and this is a difficult issue of tort law – recovery lies (see *Hedley Byrne* v. Heller, above).

The test would appear to be whether the auditor knows or ought to have known that the accounts were likely to be relied on by persons of a certain class (e.g. potential investors) of which plaintiff is one. It has been held in New Zealand that a duty of care is owed by the auditors to a take-over bidder when the take-over bid was reasonably forseeable, albeit unknown to the auditors (*Scott Group* v. *McFarlane* [1975] NZLR 582).

In a recent case in England in similar circumstances (*Capara Industries plc* v. *Dickman & Ors* (1988) 4 BCC 144) it was held that in determining the auditors' liability for negligent misstatement (beyond their clear liability in contract to the company which had engaged them) three questions arose:

(1) whether there was forseeability on the auditors' part of economic loss arising from their lack of due care;
(2) whether the negligent misstatement was made where there was a 'close and direct' relationship between the maker and the recipient of the statement, and where the recipient was known or ought to have been known to the maker as a person (or a member of a limited class of persons) likely to rely on the statement; and
(3) whether in all the circumstances the imposition of liability for economic loss flowing from the misstatement would be fair, reasonable and just.

It was said by Sir Neil Lawson that

> 'in any event, it would not be fair, reasonable or just to impose a duty on the auditors of a public company which would create a liability for an indefinite period to any member of the public who chose to rely on the auditors' report to invest in the company, or to lend to the company or to give credit to the company; (or) to decide to take over the company.'

He came to the same conclusion on the question whether plaintiff could recover in the capacity of shareholder. The chances of individual investors and members getting relief against negligent auditors seem slim after this judgment.

It may be mentioned that as part of a general review of the law by the Department of Trade with a view to relieving the burden on small business, the Department has looked into possible alternatives to the statutory audit requirement. The Institute of Chartered Accountants in England and Wales have expressed the view that, where all the shareholders agree, a small company should be free to choose not to have an audit, substituting the audit with a directors' declaration on the accounts.

5.2.3.3   The directors' report

The modern law on the directors' report reflects the increasing concern of company law with other interests besides the traditional shareholder and creditor interests. In particular, the 'directors' report, the main purpose of which is to review the progress of the company's business, is a valuable source of information for potential investors and their advisers as well as for employees and their representatives.

By section 235(1), 1985 Act, the directors' report must (a) contain a fair view of the development of the business of the company and its subsidiaries during the financial year and their position at the end of it and (b) state the amount (if any) which they recommend should be paid as dividend and the amount (if any) which they propose to carry to reserves. It must state the principal activities of the company and its subsidiaries (and any significant change) as well as the names of those persons who were directors at any time during the financial year (section 235(2)) and give detailed information about the latter's shareholdings and other interests (section 235(3) and Schedule 7, Part I). Sections 235(3)(4) and (5) require the application of Parts I to V of Schedule 7 to the Act. Part I deals with information on 'general matters' including directors' interests (para. 2); changes in asset values (para. 1); political and charitable gifts (paras. 3-5); important events affecting the company or any subsidiary and occurring since the *end* of the financial year, likely future developments in the company's business, and research and development activities (if any) (para. 6). Part II details information to be given in the event of the acquisition by a company of its own shares or of a permitted charge on them. Parts III, IV and V relate respectively to the employment, training and advancement of disabled persons; the health, safety and welfare at work of the company's employees; and the involvement of employees in the affairs, policy and performance of the company.

5.2.3.4 *Modified accounts*

We have already mentioned that banking, insurance and shipping companies receive separate treatment as regards accounting requirements (see 1985 Act, Part VII, Chapter II and Schedules 9 and 10).

Besides the treatment of these 'special category' companies, the law also speaks of 'modified accounts', allowing the company to file with the Registrar accounts with modifications applied by reference to company size. The relevant rules are to be found in sections 247 to 251 and Schedule 8, 1985 Act. Whether directors are able to deliver modified accounts in respect of any particular financial year depends on whether the company qualifies, in that financial year, as a 'small' or 'medium-sized' company (section 247(1)). 'Large' private companies remain subject to the full rigour of the law, as also do *all* public companies, all 'special category' companies (above), and companies (other than 'dormant' companies – see section 252) which are members of a group which is ineligible to submit modified accounts (section 247(2), (3) and (4)). 'Small' and 'medium-sized' companies are defined in sections 248(1) and (2) respectively. A 'small' company may file an abbreviated balance sheet, it need not file a profit and loss account nor a directors' report, and it is exempt from most of the rules on notes to the accounts (Schedule 8, Part I, paras. 2-6). A 'medium-sized' company may file a modified profit and loss account and need not disclose disaggregated figures for turnover (Schedule 8, Part I, paras. 7 and 8).

Listed companies have to comply with the stringent disclosure rules of the Stock Exchange (Requirements for the Admission of Securities to Listing). Since these are more onerous than the statutory rules it has been suggested that listed companies should be allowed to issue shareholders with 'abridged' accounts unless the shareholder expressly requests the full accounts. A new Act of Parliament will be introduced in 1988-89 to this effect. In Australia, the reverse solution to the disclosure 'burden' on business has been adopted, so that companies must issue full accounts to members unless the latter elects to receive the abridged version. The Department of Trade and Industry (DTI) has issued a consultative document in search of the minimum requirements for such abridged accounts. The British proposal would not only go against the trend towards greater disclosure and disclosure of wider scope but might create two 'classes' of shareholder – the informed institutional shareholder who opted for the full accounts and the rather less well informed individual shareholder.

5.3   *Information connected to the general meeting*

5.3.1   Introduction

The shareholder performs his role as such, namely, that of exercising general meeting powers and monitoring management, at periodic general meetings and particularly at the annual general meeting. We adverted in Chapter 2 to the recent trend to 'return power to the general meeting'. Increasingly, the shareholders' approval is required by statute before certain transactions can be proceeded with by the board (e.g. the approval of directors' service contracts or of substantial property transactions between the company and its directors: see sections 319 and 320, 1985 Act). In such cases, provision is made for adequate disclosure to shareholders in advance of their voting in general meeting.

5.3.2   General requirements

In a more general way, it is the aim of the law that shareholders be in possession of sufficient information to enable them to decide whether or not to attend a general meeting (whether in person or by proxy) and to vote in an informed manner. Statute is supplemented by Table A articles, or a company's own articles of association, and by the Yellow Book in the case of listed companies. It is not possible here to detail the law of meetings and we shall confine ourselves to the main rules which touch on the issue of information.

5.3.3 Notice of general meetings

5.3.3.1 Periods of notice

The annual general meeting is in theory the forum for shareholder review of management and the best opportunity for a member to voice his opinion on company policy or to ask direct questions of management. In practice, these meetings are all too often rubber-stamping sessions, due in the case of large companies to the wide dispersal of shareholdings. Nevertheless, each member must be sent 21 clear days' notice of each annual general meeting and 14 days' notice of each extraordinary general meeting. The period is varied to 21 days in the latter case where it is proposed to pass a special resolution (sections 369 and 378, 1985 Act). These periods, or such longer periods as may be set out in the company's articles, may be waived if the requisite majorities so agree (sections 369 and 378, 1985 Act). Unless the articles otherwise provide, and subject to any restrictions imposed on any shares (e.g. non-voting preference shares: see *Re Mackenzie & Co. Ltd* [1916] 2 Ch 450) notice must be given to every member (section 370; Table A, article 38). In default, the meeting is invalid at common law (*Smyth* v. *Darley* (1849) 2 HL Cas 789; *Musslewhite* v. *C.H. Musslewhite & Son Ltd* [1962] Ch 964) but the articles usually provide that the accidental omission to give notice or its non-receipt shall not invalidate proceedings (Table A, article 39).

5.3.3.2 Contents of notice

The notice must indicate the time and place of the meeting and give members such sufficient information about the business to be transacted as will enable them to decide whether to attend or not (*MacConnell* v. *E.Prill & Co. Ltd* [1916] 2 Ch 57). In *Henderson* v. *Bank of Australasia* (1890) 45 ChD 330, Mr Justice Chitty put the principle thus:

'The notice which specifies ... the objects of the meeting is to be a fair one, intelligible to the minds of ordinary men, the class of men who are shareholders in the company, and to whom it is addressed.'

Table A will sometimes require that specific information be given; for example, article 77 provides that where a person is to be appointed or re-appointed director (unless retiring by rotation) a notice including the person's name, address, nationality and other directorships must be given to all those entitled to notice of the meeting between 7 and 28 days before the meeting. While it is usually sufficient for the notice to indicate the general nature of the business to be transacted at the meeting (Table A, article 38), proposed extraordinary or special resolutions, which require a three-quarters majority, must be specified as such and the notice must set out either the text or the entire substance of the resolution (section 378, 1985 Act; *McConnell* v. *Prill*, above; *Re Moorgate Mercantile Holdings Ltd* [1980] 1 All ER 40). Again, the precise text of any resolution proposed as a result of a shareholder requisition must be set out in full (section 376, 1985 Act). Also, any benefit which the directors stand to gain from the passing of any resolution must be fully disclosed if the resolution is to be validly passed (*Kaye* v. *Croydon Tramways Co.* (1898) 1 Ch 358, CA; *Tiessen* v. *Henderson* (1899) 1 Ch 561; *Baillie* v. *Oriental Telephone and Electric Co. Ltd* [1915] 1 Ch 503 – the 'tricky notice cases').

5.3.3.3   *Laying of documents before the general meeting*

The return of power (and therefore of control over the board) to the general meeting has meant that the law increasingly stipulates what information must be available to the shareholders, and when. For example:

(1) Regarding a proposed contract for an off-market purchase by a company of its own shares, a special resolution conferring, varying, revoking or renewing authority for such a contract is ineffective unless the contract (or a memorandum of its terms, if it is not in writing) is available for inspection at the meeting at which it is passed and is made available for inspection at the company's registered office for at least 15 days before the meeting (section 164(6), 1985 Act). The same applies to 'contingent purchase contracts' (section 165(2), 1985 Act).

(2) A special resolution approving the giving by a private company of financial assistance for the acquisition of its own shares is ineffective unless the required directors' statutory declaration and auditors' report are available for inspection at the meeting at which the resolution is passed (section 157(4), 1985 Act).

(3) A term in a director's employment contract whereby the employment is to continue for more than 5 years, during which time there is a prohibition or restriction on the company's capacity to terminate it by notice, is void unless approved at a general meeting at which a written memorandum setting out the proposed agreement is available for inspection and has been so available at the company's registered office for at least 15 days ending with the date of the meeting (section 319(5), 1985 Act).

5.3.3.4 *Special notice*

'Special notice' is required in six cases: (i) A resolution to remove a director by ordinary resolution under section 303 (section 303(2), 1985 Act); (ii) a resolution to allow a director to serve beyond retiring age (section 293(5), 1985 Act); (iii) a resolution to remove an auditor before the expiry of his term of office (section 388(1)(d), 1985 Act); (iv) a resolution appointing as auditor a person other than a retiring auditor (section 388(1)(a), 1985 Act); (v) a resolution filling a casual vacancy in the office of auditor (section 388(1)(b), 1985 Act); (vi) a resolution reappointing as auditor a retiring auditor who was appointed by the directors to fill a casual vacancy (section 388(1)(c), 1985 Act).

In these cases, the resolution is not effective unless notice of the intention to move it has been given to the company at least 28 days before the meeting. The company must then give notice of such a resolution to the members at the same time and in the same manner as it gives notice of the meeting. If this is not practicable, the company must give members notice either by advertisement in newspapers having an appropriate circulation, or in any other mode allowed by the articles, at least 21 days before the meeting (section 379, 1985 Act).

5.3.4 Circulars

The directors owe a duty at common law to give members such explanations and additional information as may be necessary for the latter to understand the implications of any proposed transactions. This is commonly done by the issue of a circular to accompany the notice of the meeting. A failure to fulfil the general obligation may result in the relevant resolution being set aside (*Baillie* v. *Oriental Telephone & Electric Co. Ltd* [1915] Ch 503, CA; *Re Moorgate Mercantile Holdings Ltd* [1980] 1 All ER 40; *Tiessen* v. *Henderson* [1899] 1 Ch. 861; *Jessel Trust* [1985] BCLC 119; *In re Minster Assets plc* [1985] BCLC 200).

Yet it has recently been held that while in principle the facts stated in company circulars should not be otherwise than completely reliable yet the court could, and did in this case, confirm a company resolution passed on the strength of an inaccurate company circular where it appeared that the mistake would not have influenced the voting, and the creditors were not prejudiced. The case concerned a resolution cancelling a company's share premium account and the references to confirmation and creditors' interests arise in that context (*In re Home Products plc, The Times*, 14 April 1988).

Statute may also require the issue of a circular. Thus, a directors' statement containing stipulated information is required with regard to a resolution disapplying pre-emption rights (section 95, 1985 Act). By section 426, 1985 Act, notices convening a meeting under section 425 (schemes of compromise or arrangement; see Chapter 9) must be accompanied by an explanatory statement, or an indication of the place at which copies of such a statement may be obtained (see *In Re Dorman Long & Co. Ltd* [1934] Ch 635 at 657 *per* Maughan J). The circulation of statements, or their reading out at the meeting, is also required in connection with the removal of a director or auditor (sections 304 and 388, 1985 Act). Table A, in article 77, requires that particulars of a person proposed for election as director (other than an existing director due to retire by rotation) be notified to all persons entitled to receive notice of the relevant meeting. For listed companies, Stock Exchange requirements on explanatory circulars need to be complied with (e.g. Yellow Book, section 5, Chapter 2, paras. 31, 32 which require an explanatory circular to be sent out with the notice of an annual general meeting at which it is proposed to deal with business which is other than usual for the annual general meeting). The Stock Exchange requires circulars and notices to be submitted to its Quotations Department for approval before publication (Yellow Book, section 5, Chapter 2, paras. 31, 35).

A qualified minority of shareholders may require the company to give members notice of a resolution which they propose to move at the annual general meeting and to circulate a statement of up to 1,000 words (section 376 and 377, 1985 Act).

5.3.5   Right to speak at meetings

The chairman's obligation is to ensure that a resolution reflects the sense of the meeting (e.g. *Second Consolidated Trust Ltd* v. *Ceylon Amalgamated Tea & Rubber Estates Ltd* [1943] 2 All ER 567). He must therefore treat the minority fairly by allowing them a fair hearing. This may not mean that each single member is entitled to have his say, but, as it has been put, '(T)he members ... have a positive and substantial right to demand that the proceedings should be conducted with due regard to their respective interests' (Sebag Shaw & Smith, *The Law of Meetings*, 5th ed., p.60). Unless the *MacDougall* v. *Gardiner* 'internal irregularity' concept (see Chapter 2) precludes a member from complaining about the irregular conduct of a meeting at which opposing views were not allowed to be aired, an individual shareholder would be able to sue to have the resolution set aside. There appears to be no clear authority on this point. In a private company, proxies have the same rights as the member who appoints them to speak and vote (section 372(1), 1985 Act). The Jenkins Committee recommendation that the statutory right to speak be extended to proxies attending general meetings of public companies has not yet been implemented (Report of the Company Law Committee, Cmnd. 1749 para. 468). Clearly, the right to speak implies the right to ask questions of the board, thus eliciting further valuable information or explanation.

5.4   Information outside general meeting

5.4.1   Registers

The law requires all companies to keep various books of record. Besides accounting records, which can only be inspected by company officers (sections 221 and 222, 1985 Act), these include various registers and reports, many of them also available to the general public:

(1) Minute Books of General Meeting – there is a right to inspect these free of charge and a right to copies at a stipulated rate. No similar rights extend to the minutes of board meetings or managers' meetings (sections 382 and 383, 1985 Act).

(2) Register of directors' interests in the company of which they are directors (section 325(1), 1985 Act). All companies must keep this record. Inspection is free of charge while copies are available on payment.

(3) Register of directors and secretaries (section 288, 1985 Act). All companies must keep it. Members may inspect it without charge.

(4) Register of Members (section 352(1), 1985 Act). Members may inspect it without charge and request copies on payment.

(5) Register of substantial shareholdings (section 211, 1985 Act). Only a public company need keep this register. Again there is no fee for inspection and copies are available against payment.

(6) Reports on an investigation by a public company into interests in its shares (section 215, 1985 Act). This must be kept for six years.

There is no inspection fee and copies are available on payment.

(7) Register of debenture holders. This is not compulsory, but if kept there is a right of inspection (section 191, 1985 Act). No inspection fee can be charged to members (or debenture holders) and copies are available to members for a charge.

(8) Register of charges – every limited company must keep this (section 407, 1985 Act). In addition, there is a right to inspect copies of instruments which create registrable charges (section 408, 1985 Act). No inspection fee can be charged and copies can be made.

(9) The directors' statutory declaration and the auditors' report required in connection with a payment by a company out of capital for the redemption or purchase of its own shares must be kept at the registered office for 5 weeks after the resolution is passed. They can be inspected there free of charge and copies can be made (section 175, 1985 Act).

(10) Copies of every contract of service which a director or shadow director has with the company, or any of its subsidiaries or, if such contract be not in writing, a written memorandum of its terms (section 318, 1985 Act). There is no inspection fee and copies can be made.

5.4.2 The annual return

Every company (with limited exceptions in certain cases for newly incorporated companies) must complete an 'annual return' in the prescribed form within 42 days of the date of its annual general meeting (section 365(1), 1985 Act). On its completion, a copy, signed by the secretary and a director, must be sent forthwith to the Registrar of Companies (section 365(2), 1985 Act). The required contents of the annual return are set out in Schedule 15, 1985 Act and together with the annual accounts, this document provides all the essential information about a company as at the date of its completion. Schedule 15 details the information required to be disclosed regarding:

(1) the place of the company's registered office;
(2) the place where the register of members and the register of debenture holders are kept or may be inspected, if they are not available at the company's registered office (see sections 353(2) and (3));
(3) the company's share capital, specifying amount and structure of share capital, number of shares taken, calls on shares, concessions and discounts on shares and debentures, the number of shares

forfeited, information on share warrants;

(4) the total amount of the company's indebtedness in respect of all registrable mortgages and charges (see section 396(1), 1985 Act);

(5) membership, shareholdings and changes in membership (this information may be 'abbreviated' on certain conditions: section 363(5), 1985 Act);

(6) the directors and secretary of the company at the date of the return.

5.4.3   Department of Trade inspections and investigations

5.4.3.1   The power to inspect books and papers

Section 447, 1985 Act gives the Secretary of State for Trade and Industry power to require companies (including overseas companies which are carrying on, or have at any time carried on, business in Great Britain) to produce books and papers if he thinks that 'there is good reason' for him to do so. This is a wide-ranging power which can be extended to rights of entry and search (section 448) although there are safeguards for solicitors' privilege and a bank's confidentiality. The inspection falls short of a full-scale investigation in that it is conducted discreetly and expeditiously but is often in practice a preliminary step leading to an investigation.

'Good reason', in practice, includes grounds for suspecting fraud, misconduct, misfeasance or minority oppression and it seems would include a failure to give shareholders the information which they might reasonably expect. Any member of the public can alert the DTI to these suspicions. However, before we claim that section 447 enshrines an individual membership right to such information as might reasonably be expected, enforceable through the DTI, two points must be made. First, the DTI is only likely to be interested if there is a 'public interest' element involved. Second, and this is linked to the first point, there are strict constraints on the use to which information obtained under section 447 can lawfully be put without company consent (see section 449). Such information may not, without the company's consent be published or disclosed – except to a 'competent body' – unless this is required in connection with criminal proceedings, other investigations and the exercise of statutory functions or powers (section 449). Nowhere are minority shareholder actions mentioned, although the potential utility of such inspections for companies which are able and willing to sue is undeniable and a company decision not to institute proceedings may amount to a 'fraud on the minority' justifying a derivative action (see Chapter 8).

5.4.3.2 Department of Trade and Industry (DTI) investigations (Part XIV, 1985 Act)

These are potentially of more direct use to the minority shareholder than the inspection but have been notoriously difficult to mount because of the publicity and attendant damage to the company which accompanies an investigation. The DTI is wary of embarking on this course without very good reason. This can put a heavy onus on the 'complainant' who may feel that he is in the 'catch-22' situation of requiring DTI help to secure evidence but of having to produce sufficient evidence to the DTI to convince the Department to act (see section 431(3)).

The DTI completed a review of its investigation powers and procedures in May 1988. One result is that the practice of publicly announcing investigations will only be made in connection with major investigations of public interest, for example under sections 432 and 442 (below). Enquiries of a more limited nature (e.g. under sections 447 or 105) will not require public announcement. Nor will investigations into suspected insider dealing under section 177 of the Financial Services Act 1986 (below and Chapter 10) be publicly announced unless to do so is in the public interest. The scope and flexibility of the DTI's powers are to be extended, especially with regard to the obtaining and use of information, and DTI resources are to be increased. The general powers of company investigation under section 432 are to be extended to cases of suspected fraud, misfeasance or misconduct when the prime purpose is to consider the case for prosecution or regulatory action and there is no intention to publish a report. Various powers will be strengthened, including the powers of search, the power to recover the costs of investigations and the power to appoint 'outsiders' to undertake inquiries under section 447, 1985 Act. The DTI is constantly seeking to improve cooperation with overseas regulatory organisations and considering the taking of suitable powers to facilitate this.

(1) Investigations into the affairs of a company
The Secretary of State *must* appoint inspectors to investigate the company's affairs and report on them to the Secretary of State if the court by order declares that its affairs ought to be investigated (section 432(1), 1985 Act). For example, the court may so order under Section 461, 1985 Act, as part of a package of remedies for 'unfair prejudice' suffered by a shareholder (see section 459, 1985 Act and also Chapter 8 below). More usually, a section 459 petition will follow the disclosure of information through an investigation.

The Secretary of State also has a *discretion* to appoint inspectors. By section 431(1), he may appoint inspectors to investigate the affairs of the company on the application (section 431(2)):

(a) in the case of a company having a share capital, of not less than 200 members or of members holding not less than one-tenth of the issued shares; or
(b) in the case of a company *not* having a share capital, of not less than one-fifth in number of the persons on the company's register of members; or
(c) of the company.

The qualified minority requirements, coupled with the provision that an applicant under section 431 is liable for the expenses of, and incidental to, the investigation to the extent determined by the Secretary of State, could well discourage members who cannot make an allegation with a 'public interest' element from considering making a section 431 application. Section 431 is a wide-ranging provision, but the applicant(s) must convince the Department that there is 'good reason for requiring the investigation' (section 431(3)).

Without prejudice to the width of section 431, section 432(2) allows the Secretary of State to order an investigation if 'it appears to him' (evidence can be produced to him by any person) that there are circumstances suggesting:

(a) that the company's affairs are being or have been conducted with intent to defraud its creditors or the creditors of any other person or otherwise for any fraudulent or unlawful purpose; or
(b) that the company's affairs are being, or have been conducted in a manner which is unfairly prejudicial to some part of its members; or
(c) that any actual proposed act or omission of the company (including an act or omission on its behalf) is or would be so prejudicial; or
(d) that the company was formed for any fraudulent or unlawful purpose; or
(e) that persons concerned with the company's formation or the management of its affairs have in connection therewith been guilty of fraud, misfeasance or other misconduct towards it or towards its members; or
(f) that the company's members have not been given all the information with respect to its affairs which they might reasonably expect.

'Members' in paragraph (b) above is expressly declared to include persons who are not members (i.e. because not registered as such) but to whom shares in the company have been transferred or transmitted by operation of law (section 432(4)). It is unclear why the same was not stipulated for case (c), or for that matter, for case (e). Paragraphs (b) and (c) mimic the 'unfair prejudice' provision (section 459, 1985 Act: see also Chapter 8). Paragraph (f) speaks of the member's legitimate expectations as to information and would seem to have provided the DTI with one of its grounds for inspecting books and papers under section 447. Paragraph (a) mimics the wording of the provisions on 'fraudulent trading' (section 458, 1985 Act; section 213, Insolvency Act 1986). Section 432 also applies, as a rule, to all bodies corporate incorporated outside Great Britain which are carrying on, or have at any time carried on, business in Great Britain (section 453).

The expenses of an investigation into a company's affairs are borne in the first instance by the Secretary of State. However, he may recoup some or all of these from:

(a) a person convicted on a prosecution instituted as a result of an investigation (section 439(2)).
(b) a person ordered to pay the costs of any civil proceedings brought by the Secretary of State on a company's behalf under section 438 (see 3(ii) below) (section 439(3)). Also, a body corporate in whose name proceedings are instituted is liable to make repayment to the extent of any money or property recovered by it as a result of the proceedings (section 439(3)).
(c) a body corporate dealt with by the inspector's report, in the case where the inspectors were appointed otherwise than on the motion of the Secretary of State, which is liable except when it was the applicant for the investigation, and except so far as the Secretary of State otherwise directs (section 439(4)).
(d) the applicant(s) for the investigation, where the inspector was appointed under section 431 (see above), which is (are) liable to such extent as the Secretary of State may direct (section 439(5)).

(2)   Investigation of ownership and control
Similar (but not identical) provisions to the above exist (sections 442-445, 1985 Act) for the purpose of determining 'the true persons who are or have been financially interested in the success or failure (real or apparent) of the company or able to control or materially influence its policy' (section 442(1), 1985 Act). If the number of applicants, or the number of shares held by them, is not less than that required for the appointment of inspectors under

sections 431(2)(a) and (b) (see above), the Secretary of State *must* appoint inspectors unless satisfied that the application is vexatious.

The expenses of a section 442 investigation are borne by the Secretary of State [section 443(4)].

We have already had occasion to refer to the Secretary of State's power to impose restrictions on shares (see [4.3.2.1]). Section 445 vests this power in the Secretary of State as a measure for compelling the disclosure of information. Restriction orders can prevent the issue of, transfer of, or agreement to transfer, shares which are the subject of an order; the exercise of voting rights attached to such shares; the issue of further shares in right of shares which are the subject of a restriction order or in pursuance of any offer made to their holder; except in a liquidation, the payment of any sums due from the company on the shares, whether in respect of capital or otherwise (e.g. dividends). The effect of an order can therefore be devastating – practically nullifying any immediate benefit deriving from the holding of the shares subject to the order.

The attempted evasion of the restrictions is an offence (section 455), though provision is made for the relaxation and removal of restrictions on application to the court by any aggrieved person (section 456). The detail of these provisions is to be found in Part XV of the 1985 Act (sections 454-457). It may be noted here that restrictions on shares may be imposed by the court where a public company requires assistance in pursuit of a company investigation into interests in its shares under section 212, 1985 Act (section 216(1), 1985 Act). They may also be imposed by the Secretary of State in the event of a failure to disclose notifiable interests in shares in accordance with Part VI of the 1985 Act (see section 210 and below in [9.4.3]). These provisions are constantly under review with a view to their improvement (see DTI Press Release, 11 May 1987, para.12). Also the court may impose restrictions in virtue of the unrestricted power to relieve minority shareholders from unfair prejudice (sections 459 and 461, 1985 Act; see Chapter 8).

(3)   Investigation into share dealings
If 'it appears' to the Secretary of State that there are circumstances suggesting a contravention of sections 323, 324 or 328(3) and (5), 1985 Act (which prohibit directors and their families from engaging in certain dealings in the director's company's securities and require the notification of interests in certain securities) he may appoint inspectors to establish whether or not any such

contravention has occurred and to report to him accordingly (section 446(1), 1985 Act).

(4)   Investigations into insider dealing; section 177 Financial Services Act 1986
By section 177, Financial Services Act 1986 (see also Chapter 10), if it appears to the Secretary of State for Trade and Industry that there are circumstances suggesting that there may have been a contravention of sections 1, 2, 4 or 5 of the Company Securities (Insider Dealing) Act 1985, he may appoint inspectors to investigate and submit a report. The inspectors have wide powers of investigation (see generally Part VII, Financial Services Act 1986 and Chapter 10 below).

(5)   Remedies
Information obtained as a result of Department of Trade and Industry investigations may well prove to be vital evidence in legal proceedings consequent upon such investigation. These can be instituted by minority shareholders, the company itself or, indeed, by the Secretary of State. However, the latter is only likely to be motivated to act in this way if the public interest so requires. It may therefore be left to the minority shareholder(s) to take matters further (see Chapter 8). Where the Secretary of State does decide to take the matter further:

(i)   If he thinks it expedient in the public interest that the company should be wound up (and the company is not already being wound up by the court), he may present a petition for it to be so wound up if the court thinks it just and equitable for it to be so (section 440, 1985 Act; see further, Chapter 8).

(ii)   If he thinks it expedient in the public interest, he may bring civil proceedings in the name and on behalf of the company.

Minority shareholders faced with the decision whether or not to bring such an action – called a 'derivative action' – themselves (see further, Chapter 8) may find it useful to refer the whole matter to the DTI, where there is an element of public interest involved, thus relieving themselves of the burden. Presumably, in this case, the company cannot lawfully prevent or obstruct the action (even if an independent majority of members so desire – see Chapter 8, [8.3.2.1] and [8.3.2.3]) but the Secretary of State in any event bears all costs and expenses associated with such proceedings (section 438(2), 1985 Act; but see also section 439(3)).

(iii)   In appropriate circumstances, he may present a petition under section 459, 1985 Act (see Chapter 8), either in addition to or instead of a winding-up petition under (i) above.

(iv) If he thinks it expedient in the public interest that an order should be made disqualifying any person who is or has been a director or shadow director of any company from acting as director, liquidator, or administrator of a company or from being a receiver or manager of company property or in any way taking part in the promotion, formation or management of a company, the Secretary of State may apply to the court for such a disqualification order (section 8, Company Directors Disqualification Act 1986).

This power is exercisable also in connection with investigations into insider dealing offences under wide powers set out in section 177 of the Financial Services Act 1986.

5.5 Pending EEC legislation

The Draft Eleventh EEC Council Directive (COM(86)397 final) proposes to harmonise the disclosure requirements in respect of branches opened in a Member state. This Directive represents an important extension of the general harmonisation programme to branches, as opposed to subsidiaries. It will go some way to reducing the existing disparity of treatment of shareholders and third parties whose treatment currently depends on whether companies of one Member state which operate in another Member state do so through a branch or through a legally distinct subsidiary company. The aim is an equivalent level of protection for these interest groups and the elimination of obstacles to freedom of establishment.

The Directive is a comprehensive measure, which in general seeks to ensure that national laws as to disclosure in respect of branches, which vary from the stringent to the liberal, are largely harmonised. It relies heavily on the system of disclosure already established within the community in respect of limited liability companies. It extends to branches of companies (of a similar nature to those operating in Member states and covered by the Directive) in non-Member countries. The disclosure requirements relate both to the branch itself and to 'the company as such'.

Another proposal exists for a Directive harmonising the law on the annual accounts of the branches of credit institutions.

Chapter 6

The Transfer of Shares and Acquisition of Shares Generally

6.1 Introduction

This chapter seeks to explain the nature of, and possible limits on, the right of a member to transfer his shares as well as the acquisition of title to (ownership of) shares in general. Of course, if he transfers all his shares in a company he ceases to remain a member of that company.

The other side of the coin relates to a member's being forced to sell his shares. We have seen that this can happen, for example in circumstances where his continued presence is damaging to the company (see [4.5.3]). In such cases, the articles can, if necessary, be validly altered to provide for the compulsory purchase, at fair value, of his shares. Second, the court may order the compulsory sale of shares by way of relief from unfairly prejudicial conduct on the part of those conducting the affairs of the company (section 461, 1985 Act) – a particularly useful remedy for a minority shareholder locked into a company by transfer clauses, or for whose shares there is no ready market (see Chapter 8). Third, there is the possibility of the forfeiture of shares under the articles (Chapter 2).

In this chapter we shall concentrate on the nature of the right to transfer one's shares and on those limits upon it which may be imposed by the articles of association (namely, restrictive transfer clauses) or by statute (for example, the statutory right of pre-emption).

6.2 Nature of the right

In *Re Smith & Fawcett Ltd* [1942] Ch 304, Lord Greene MR said:

'One of the normal rights of a shareholder is the right to deal freely with his property and to transfer it to whomsoever he pleases ... (t)he shareholder has such a *prima facie* right, and that right is not to be cut down by uncertain language. The right, if it is to be cut down, must be cut down with satisfactory clarity.'

The right is a *prima facie* right. All depends on the memorandum and articles. In practice, it is common for the articles of private companies to restrict the *prima facie* freedom of transfer by (a) pre-emption clauses or (b) transfer agreement clauses. Both types come under the generic description 'restrictive transfer clauses'. A statutory right of pre-emption was introduced by the Companies Act 1980 (and is now regulated by the 1985 Act). The reader is reminded that statute also makes provision for the restriction of the right to transfer shares in connection with certain company investigations (see [5.4.3.2.2]).

6.3   The statutory right of pre-emption

6.3.1   General

The Companies Act 1985 makes important provision for pre-emption rights in the context of a new issue of shares by the company.

Sections 89-96 of the Companies Act 1985 contain important provisions designed to ensure that equity shareholders have rights of pre-emption over new issues of equity shares. The result is that a public or private company proposing to issue equity shares (or rights to subscribe for or to convert to equity shares) for cash must first offer them – on terms identical to or more favourable than the terms on which it proposes to offer those securities to persons other than the existing shareholders – to existing equity shareholders (including those who held shares 28 days before the offer made) in proportion to the nominal value of the shares held by them. If the company constitution provides that equity securities of a particular class must first be offered to the equity shareholders of that class, they must be offered on a *pro rata* basis. Shares not taken up on this basis must then be offered to the equity shareholders generally.

6.3.2   Scope

The statutory right of pre-emption does not apply to the holders of shares which carry limited rights of participation as respects dividends and capital (i.e. preference shares), or to equity shares which are to be wholly or partly paid up otherwise than in cash, or shares to be held under an employees' share scheme.

6.3.3   Private companies

However, a private company may exclude the right of pre-emption in its memorandum or articles (section 91, 1985 Act). The power of alteration of the articles (if it be necessary to exercise this to 'disapply' the statutory right) must be exercised *bona fide* for the benefit of the company as a whole. Though much depends on the interpretation of this test, it should provide significant protection against the abusive disapplication of the right of pre-emption.

6.3.4   Disapplication: general

Section 95 makes provision for the qualification or withdrawal ('disapplication) of pre-emption rights by both public and private companies. It provides that where the directors are 'generally authorised' to allot relevant securities in accordance with section 80 of the 1985 Act (see [3.4]), power may be given to the directors expressly by the articles or by a special resolution to modify or disapply the pre-emption rights accorded by section 89. This power lasts as long as the authority conferred under section 80 lasts (to be reviewed at least once every five years by the general meeting). Where the company seeks to 'disapply' section 89 by special resolution in relation to a specific allotment the resolution must have been recommended by the directors (as also must be a special resolution renewing such a resolution), and a written statement must have been circulated with the notice of the meeting at which the resolution is proposed. The statement must set out the reasons for making the recommendation and the amount (justified by the directors) to be paid to the company for the equity shares to be allotted.

6.3.5   Class rights

Unless the company has provided for class rights of pre-emption in accordance with section 89(2) and (3), section 89(1) also has the effect that each new issue of shares of whatever class must be offered to all the company's shareholders. In other words, the Act preserves rights of pre-emption conferred by the company constitution on any class of shareholders and permits a new issue of securities to be offered to members of the class concerned, but applies the general statutory right of pre-emption to any shares not taken up by the original offerees or by persons in whose favour the offerees have renounced their rights.

6.3.6 Disapplication. Challenge by minority shareholders

In so far as the general meeting may confer power on the directors to allot shares without regard to the right of pre-emption or with qualification of this right, or may itself exclude or modify the right in connection with a specific allotment, the question arises whether the general meeting resolution may be challenged by a minority share- holder. Although the resolution needs must be a special resolution, it may not actually involve an alteration of the articles so that the principle that the general meeting must act *bona fide* for the benefit of the company as a whole could not apply on that basis. Therefore, the question whether this principle is extendable to powers other than that of altering the articles acquires crucial importance (see [4.5.3]).

6.3.7 Board action

We have said that the right of pre-emption may thus be excluded or qualified by the board of directors, or by the general meeting itself on the recommendation of the directors. Although the application of section 95 depends on the directors having been given authority to allot shares by the general meeting, action is always required of the directors who may exclude the right of pre-emption, allow it to apply with such modifications as they may determine, or recommend (giving reasons) that the right be excluded or modified by the general meeting in regard to any particular allotment. The directors, as fiduciaries, must exercise all these powers 'bona fide in what they consider to be the best interests of the company and not for any collateral purpose'. An individual shareholder who can prove the breach or proposed breach of the above duties may in appropriate circumstances be able to sue the directors by way of derivative action to restrain them from acting in breach of their duty towards the company (see Chapter 8). The shareholders' rights and interests are further protected by the provisions creating offences regarding the directors' recommendation to the general meeting (see below).

The shareholders' protection would of course be complete if the general meeting itself, when conferring power on the directors under section 95(1) or when exercising its power to accept or reject the directors' recommendations under section 95(2), were placed under certain limited objective restraints akin to those ensuring fair play in certain continental laws (e.g. Article 2441(5) of the Italian Civil Code provides that the disapplication must be required in the interests of the company). Moreover, the general meeting is not always independent of the board of directors and the fact that on present authority the general meeting may ratify breaches by the directors of their duty to exercise powers for their proper purpose, as well as the court's unwillingness to interfere, however limitedly, in directors' (or indeed general meeting) decisions leads one to conclude that the right of pre-emption is in English law, a rather vulnerable membership right.

As far as listed companies are concerned, a working party was set up by the Stock Exchange to look into the whole question of disapplication of rights of pre-emption. The resulting guidelines (published October 1987) are designed to provide companies with some flexibility in capital limits on the amount of share capital which may be issued for cash on a non-pre-emptive basis, as well as restrictions on the discount and cost of such issues. These guidelines do not have the force of law. The Yellow Book continues to require general meeting approval of any issue for cash of equity capital other than on a *pro rata* basis to existing equity shareholders (Stock Exchange Rules for the Admission of Securities to Listing (1984) Section 5, Chapter 2, para. 38).

6.3.8   Breach of statutory rights: remedies

The statutory rights of pre-emption are not enforced by criminal penalties save with regard to misleading, false or deceptive statements made under section 95(5). However, the Act does lay down a specific civil remedy. Where securities are allotted in contravention of the provisions of section 89(1) (in respect of the statutory right of pre-emption), or of section 90 (in respect of service and duration of offers – 21 days – made to persons enjoying rights or pre-emption), or of any provisions conferring class rights of pre-emption to which section 89(3) applies, any person to whom an offer should have been made under the statutory pre-emption rights (or, as the case may be, the 'class' pre-emption rights conferred by the memorandum or articles) may claim compensation from the company and any company officer who knowingly authorised or permitted the contravention. The liability of the company and any such officer to such a person is joint and several, and extends to any loss, damage, costs or expenses which that person has sustained or incurred by reason of the contravention.

6.3.9   Stock exchange requirements

It has been noted that with regard to listed companies the Stock Exchange rules continue to require general meeting approval of any issue for cash of equity capital other than on a *pro rata* basis to existing equity shareholders. Also, it must be noted that section 445 of the Companies Act 1985 empowers the Department of Trade, in connection with its investigations under sections 442 to 444, to exclude the right to transfer shares and the right of pre-emption with regard to the specific shares which are the subject of investigation (see [5.4.3.2]).

6.4 Pre-emption clauses

The statutory right of pre-emption does not obviate the need for pre-emption clauses in the memorandum or articles. The statutory right only applies to new issues of shares; it does not apply to transfers. A pre-emption clause will be required if it is desired to maintain the *status quo* as to control while at the same time allowing transfers. Table A contains no such provision, but it is common for the articles of private companies to provide that a member may not sell his shares without first offering them to existing members for sale at a price to be determined by independent valuation, or according to some formula set out in the articles. The courts will not set aside such a valuation unless there is fraud or manifest error (*Dean* v. *Prince* [1953] Ch 590).

This preserves the *status quo* in terms of shareholder identity provided that the other shareholders are in a position to buy. If not, the only way of preserving such identity is for the company itself to purchase the shares, in which case this will be subject to the conditions laid down by law for the purchase by a company of its own shares (sections 162-181, 1985 Act). If a member ignores a pre-emption clause and sells his shares without offering them first to existing members, and the articles give the board of directors the power to refuse to register transfers (see [6.5] below) it is the board's duty to refuse to register the transfer (*Tett* v. *Phoenix Property & Investment Co. Ltd* [1984] BCLC 149, CA). However, a transfer in breach of pre-emptive rights given by the articles to a person who has paid for the shares does operate to transfer the beneficial interest in the shares to the buyer (*Hawks* v. *McArthur* [1951] 1 All ER 22; *Tett* v. *Phoenix Property & Investment Co. Ltd*, above). The court will issue an injunction to restrain a transfer of shares in breach of the articles (*Curtis* v. *J.J. Curtis & Co. Ltd* [1986] BCLC 86, NZ).

There is a *prima facie* right to transfer one's shares. Therefore, the courts will interpret pre-emption clauses narrowly so as to admit maximum freedom of transfer (*Safeguard Industrial Investments Ltd* v. *National Westminster Bank Ltd* [1982] 1 All ER 449; *Theakston* v. *London Trust plc* [1984] BCLC 390). In the *Safeguard* case, it was held that a pre-emption clause did not apply to a bank executor who was registered as a shareholder and was transferring the shares to a beneficiary. The article spoke of shareholders being 'desirous of transferring their shares' and 'desire' played no part in the execution of his duty by the executor. This has been compared (by Farrar, *Company Law*, p.199) with *Rayfield* v. *Hands* ([1960] Ch 1) where the court adopted an unusually liberal interpretation of the pre-emption clause.

6.5   Transfer agreement clauses

It is also common for the articles of a private company to provide that the board shall have the power to refuse registration of a transfer. Table A contains no such provision. Again, the courts will interpret such clauses strictly in favour of freedom of transfer. However, again it is a question of construction of the particular article. If the power to refuse registration is vested in the board, the board must exercise it properly, i.e. in accordance with their duties as directors. Like all powers, it must be exercised '*bona fide* in what the board may consider – not what a court may consider – to be in the interests of the company, and not for any collateral purpose'. This was laid down clearly in *Re Smith & Fawcett Ltd* [1942] Ch 304, where it was held that this duty exists even where the power is conferred in absolute terms, for example, where it is provided that the directors may refuse to register a transfer in their absolute discretion. As Lord Greene MR put it in *Re Smith & Fawcett* (above):

> 'The question ... simply is whether on the true construction of the particular article the directors are limited by anything except their *bona fide* view as to the interests of the company.'

It being a question of construction, with a bias in favour of transfer, careful wording is required if court enquiry is to be avoided other than on the fiduciary duty point. With proper extensive wording, the court will not oblige the directors to divulge their grounds for refusing registration, but if the article only permits refusal on specified grounds and the directors give their reasons (but not otherwise) the court will set the refusal aside if the board exceed the terms of their power (*Re Smith & Fawcett Ltd* above; *Re Bede S.S. Co. Ltd* [1917] 1 Ch 123, CA; *Berry and Stewart* v. *Tottenham Hotspur Football Athletic Co. Ltd* [1935] Ch 718). In *Tett* v. *Phoenix Property & Investment Co. Ltd* [1984] BCLC 599 at 621, Mr Justice Vinelott summarised the position as regards the extent of the court's enquiry. He said:

> '[T]he court will not interfere with the exercise by directors of a

discretion not to register a transfer if their decision was one which a reasonable board of directors could *bona fide* believe to be in the interests of the company. If the discretion is an unfettered one and not limited to specific grounds of refusal the court will not compel the directors to give their reasons for their refusal. If their decision was one which a reasonable board could consider to be in the interests of the company then the court presumes that they acted *bona fide* and had good grounds for their decision. However, if the directors once give their reasons the court can consider how far those reasons did justify their decision.'

Where the articles provide that registration may be refused if the board do not approve of the transferee (see, for example, article 24, Table A), the disapproval must be on grounds personal to the transferee. However, it seems that in exercising the general power of refusal the board is entitled to act on such considerations as the fact that 'the transferee would obtain too great a weight in the councils of the company or might even obtain control' (*Re Smith & Fawcett Ltd* above). Article 24, Table A, besides allowing the board to refuse to register a transfer of a share which is not fully paid to a person of whom they do not approve (see above) also empowers them to refuse to register the transfer of a share on which the company has a lien (see Chapter 2). Article 24 stipulates further discretion. Under the article, the directors *may* refuse to register a transfer *unless* (a) it is lodged at the office or at such other place as the directors may appoint and is accompanied by the certificate for the shares to which it relates and such other evidence as the directors may reasonably require to show the right of the transferor to make the transfer; (b) it is in respect of only one class of shares; and (c) it is in favour of not more than four transferees. It would seem that 'and' should read 'or'.

If the directors refuse to register a transfer, article 25 of Table A provides that they must within two months after the date on which the transfer was lodged with the company send to the transferee notice of the refusal. This is also the time limit laid down by statute (section 183(5), 1985 Act). In default, the company and every officer in default are liable to a fine (section 183(6)). By article 6, the registration of transfers of shares, or of transfers of any class of shares, may be suspended at such times and for such periods (not exceeding 30 days in any year) as the directors may determine.

A formal active exercise of the power of refusal to register is required. Therefore if the directors cannot agree on whether or not to register a transfer, as where no quorum can be mustered or where they are equally divided on the issue, the transfer must be registered

(*Shepherd's Trustees* v. *Shepherd* (1950) SC(HL)60; *Re Hackney Pavilion Ltd* [1924] 1 Ch 276; *Re Copal Varnish Co. Ltd* [1917] 2 Ch 349). If there are no properly appointed directors and a quorum can therefore not be obtained to decide whether to refuse registration or not, the right to registration arises on the expiry of the two-month period mentioned above but not before (*Re Zinotty Properties Ltd* [1984] 1 WLR 1249).

If registration of a transfer is wrongfully refused, the transferor's and transferee's remedy is to apply to the court for 'rectification' of the register of members by the substitution of the transferee's name for that of the transferor [sections 183(4), 359, 1985 Act: and see *Charles Forte Investments Ltd* v. *Amanda* [1964] Ch 240, CA, and *Property Investment Co. of Scotland Ltd* v. *Duncan* (1887) 14 R 299]].

6.6 Transfer procedure

6.6.1 General

Section 183(1), 1985 Act provides that it is not lawful for a company to register a transfer of shares in (or debentures of) a company unless a proper instrument of transfer has been delivered to it, or the transfer is an exempt transfer within the Stock Transfer Act 1982. This applies notwithstanding anything in the company's articles (see, for example, article 23, Table A which provides that the instrument of transfer may be in the usual form or in any other form which the directors may approve).

By 'proper instrument of transfer' is meant an instrument such as will attract stamp duty (*Re Paradise Motor Co. Ltd* [1968] 1 WLR 1125 CA). Most transfers will come under the regulation of the Stock Transfer Act 1963. By section 1(1) of this Act, fully paid shares or stock (in any company within the meaning of the 1985 Act except unlimited companies and companies limited by guarantee) are transferable by the execution of a transfer document in one of the forms set out in Schedule 1 of the Act. The execution of a stock transfer need not be attested or executed under seal. It need be signed only by the transferor. Where the Stock Transfer Act does not apply (e.g. the transfer of partly paid shares) the articles may require the signature of the transferee (see article 23, Table A). The articles will govern 'non-Stock Transfer Act' transfers. Section 183 only rules out oral transfers.

Schedule 1 of the Stock Transfer Act 1963 sets out (a) the Stock Transfer form and (b) the Sold Transfer and Bought Transfer forms (see the Stock Transfer (Addition of Forms) Order 1979, SI 1979 No.

277). The former is used for transfers which do not take place on the Stock Exchange. The latter are used in Stock Exchange transactions.

Ad valorem (by value) stamp duty is payable on share transfers. Hence, the statutory requirement that transfers be in writing. The directors must refuse to register a transfer which is not properly stamped (*Maynard* v. *Consolidated Kent Collieries Corporation* [1903] 2 KB 121; Stamp Act 1891, section 17). The penalty is a fine.

6.6.2 Non-exchange transfer procedure

The transferor will complete and execute a stock transfer form. This contains the following information: the name of the company whose shares are being transferred; the number, nominal value and class of those shares; the consideration (usually price) being paid; the transferor's name and address; the transferee's name and address.

The second stage procedure depends on whether all the shares represented on the transferor's share certificate(s) are being transferred or whether only a certain number of those shares comprised in a share certificate are being transferred. In the first case, the stock transfer form and the share certificate(s) are handed over to the transferee, who proceeds to pay the stamp duty and then to forward these documents to the company for registration. In the second case, the transferor does not hand over his certificate(s) to the transferee. He will send the executed stock transfer form and the share certificate(s) directly to the company whereupon the company will 'certify' receipt of these documents by stamping the stock transfer form (usually with the words 'certificate lodged'). This is known as 'certification of transfer'. The certificate is retained by the company while the 'certificated' transfer form is returned to the transferor who in turn sends it on to the transferee. The transferee then proceeds to pay the duty and to resubmit the transfer form to the company for registration. The certification is a representation (i.e. a statement intended to be relied upon) made by the company to the effect that the company has received documents which provide *prima facie* evidence of the transferor's title – that is that he is entitled to sell the shares (section 184(1), 1985 Act).

The company does not guarantee that the transferor actually has good title to the shares, but the company will be liable to an innocent transferee if it issues an erroneous certification fraudulently or negligently (section 184(2), 1985 Act). This second type of second stage procedure protects the transferor of only a part of the shareholding indicated on his certificate(s) by avoiding the giving to the proposed 'partial' transferee possession of the valuable share certificate. On registration of the transfer in this second case the company will issue two new certificates, one for the transferor and relating to shares retained and the other to the transferee and relating to the shares transferred. The old certificate is cancelled. The same procedure will be employed where the transferor proposes to sell the shares comprised in one share certificate to two or more transferees separately. (For example, A sells 500 shares comprised in one certificate, 250 being sold to B and 250 being sold to C. In this case, two new certificates will be issued, one to B and one to C each for 250 shares.)

Article 27 of Table A provides that no fee shall be charged for registration of any instrument of transfer or other document relating to, or affecting, the title to (ownership of) any share. This is a Stock Exchange requirement for companies listed on the Exchange (Admission of Securities to Listing (Yellow Book) section 5, Chapter 2, para. 27).

6.6.3 Stock Exchange transfer

Stock Exchange transfers are transfers of shares listed on the Stock Exchange (listed securities). The Stock Exchange's Yellow Book (Admission of Securities to Listing) lays down specific requirements for such transfers. We have just referred to one of these (above). A fundamental Yellow Book rule is that listed securities must be fully transferable, so that listed companies may not (as a rule) make provision in their memoranda or articles for restrictive transfer clauses (e.g. transfer agreement clauses) or for pre-emption rights (section 9, Chapter 1, para. 1.2). Certain exceptions can be made whenever independence (and freedom from take-overs) is important in the public interest. The Yellow Book also stipulates that no charge may be made for the issue of share certificates (section 5, Chapter 2, para 28(b)) or for the registration of a transfer (section 5, Chapter 2, para. 27). A time-limit of 14 days, from the date when the transfer is lodged, is stipulated for the issue of share certificates.

The bulk of Stock Exchange transfers are processed by the Talisman system. This involves the transfer of shares by the seller to Sepon Ltd (Stock Exchange Pool Nominees), a company owned by the Stock Exchange. This company owns a 'pool' of listed shares; sellers sell to and buyers buy from Sepon Ltd. A 'trading period' usually lasts for two weeks (it is proposed to move to a shorter period, probably a five-day rolling settlement), during which time the relevant listed companies register Sepon Ltd as the holder of the shares held by it at the start of the trading period. At the end of the 'trading period', a final reckoning is made and the relevant shares are transferred to the 'final buyer' at that time. Meanwhile, share certificates need not be issued in Sepon Ltd's name (section 185(4), 1985 Act). A special transfer form is completed by the seller (a 'sold transfer', see [6.6.1] above) whereby the shares are transferred to Sepon Ltd. No stamp duty is payable (Finance Act 1976, section 127(1)). If the seller is only selling a part of his holding, he must send the share certificate and sold transfer to the Stock Exchange Certification Office which will 'certificate' the Transfer (see [6.6.2] above), sending the share certificate on to the company. An interim certificate ('balance ticket') will be supplied to the transferor. If he is selling his entire holding, the share certificate and the sold transfer are sent to the Stock Exchange Settlement Department, which in turn forwards them to the relevant company so that Sepon Ltd can be registered as the holder.

The buyer is allocated shares from Sepon Ltd's pool. Sepon Ltd here sends a 'bought transfer' form (see [6.6.1] above) to the relevant company, giving the buyer's name and asking that the shares be registered in his name and that a certificate be issued to him. Stamp duty is payable on this transaction, and is collected by the Stock Exchange for the account of the Inland Revenue. The certificate is dispatched to the buyer *via* the Stock Exchange Settlement Department.

This system came in for severe criticism in the quite disastrous circumstances of the 'October Crash' of 1987. The demand to sell (and buy) was such that the system came close to breaking down. Brokers had great difficulty in processing the documentation and only increased computerisation can prevent a recurrence. The new SAEF system (SEAQ Automatic Execution Facility) is an example of this increased computerisation.

The Deputy Chairman of the Stock Exchange has gone on record in opposition to an idea intended to prevent the sharp fluctuations (i.e. falls) in share prices witnessed on 'Black Monday' in October 1987, namely the idea of introducing the 'circuit-breaker' whereby dealing in shares would be suspended when the index fell below a certain bottom figure – thus artificially (and possibly only temporarily) stabilising the market. Some exchanges, such as Tokyo, operate such a 'time-buying' system but the Stock Exchange's line is that this is only a temporary and artificial device which is unacceptably in conflict with the 'free marketability' quality (i.e. liquidity) of listed securities. Liquidity, which must be maintained at all costs, is the byword.

6.7   *The legal effect of a transfer as between transferor, transferee and the company*

6.7.1   The transfer of ownership

The transferor, in selling his shares, promises the transferee that he shall give the latter a valid transfer and that he shall do all that is required to enable (and refrain from doing anything which might prevent) the purchaser to be registered by the company as a member (*Skinner* v. *City of London Marine Insurance Corp.* (1885) 14 QBD 882, CA; *London Founders' Association Ltd and Palmer* v. *Clarke* (1888) 20 QBD 576). If the 'transferor' does not already own the shares which he is selling (this operation is called 'arbitrage') his obligation is to purchase such shares or procure the transfer of the shares to the buyer from a registered holder (who will in the latter case be the transferor).

The question of remedies arises in practice as a problem when the directors of the company in question then refuse to register a transfer under some transfer agreement clause (above). Buyers may, and often do, protect themselves from this possibility by expressly stipulating in advance with the seller that they purchase only on condition that registration as a member is forthcoming (the usual form of words is 'with registration guaranteed'). In this case, the purchaser can sue for damages and/or repudiate the contract and recover the price paid for the shares if he is not registered as a member. Unless he protects himself in this way, the purchaser cannot release himself from the contract and, provided the seller has fulfilled his side of the bargain, will have to remain content with the 'beneficial interest' in the shares. That is, the seller (or transferor) remains the registered and legal owner (a company registered in England and Wales will not take notice of any trust – section 360, 1985 Act) but will hold the shares 'in trust' for the benefit of the purchaser (*Hooper* v. *Herts* [1906] 1 Ch 549). This means that to all intents and purposes it is the seller who is the member and who, as such, is entitled to receive notice of meetings, receive dividends, vote and so on but that he must exercise 'his' rights as member for the benefit of the purchaser (see, for example, *Morrison* v. *Harrison* (1876) 3 R 406; *Tennant's Trustees* v. *Tennant* (1946) SC 420), although it may be that the seller may vote entirely as he sees fit until full payment of the purchase price has been made (*Musslewhite* v. *C.H. Musslewhite & Son Ltd* [1962] Ch 964).

This state of affairs is hardly satisfactory for either party to the sale. As a rule, the seller remains primarily liable for calls made on the shares after the date of the contract (albeit with a right to be indemnified by the purchaser, *Stray* v. *Russell* (1859) 1 E & E 888). Also, he must look to the interests of the purchaser, and vote in general meeting as directed by the latter. With this in mind, it is hard to see why a term to the effect of 'with registration guaranteed should not be implied by the courts into every contract for the sale of shares. Both parties would presumably wish it to be so.

6.7.2 The share certificate

It will be apparent from what has already been said that the share certificate plays an important role as evidence of title to the shares comprised in it. Article 6 of Table A is typical. It provides that:

> 'Every member, upon becoming the holder of any shares, shall be entitled without payment to one certificate for all the shares of each class held by him (and, upon transferring a part of his holding of shares of any class, to a certificate for the balance of such holding) or several certificates each for one or more of his shares upon payment for every certificate after the first of such reasonable sum as the directors may determine. Every certificate shall be sealed with the seal and shall specify the number class and distinguishing numbers (if any) of the shares to which it relates and the amount or respective amounts paid up thereon. The company shall not be bound to issue more than one certificate for shares held jointly by several persons and delivery of a certificate to one joint holder shall be a sufficient delivery to all of them.'

Article 7, Table A, provides for the issue of duplicate certificates in the event of loss, destruction, defacing or wearing-out of a certificate. This is required of listed companies by the Yellow Book (Admission of Securities to Listing, Section 9, Chapter 1, para. 2.2).

The share certificate is not a document of title to shares, but a certificate under the common seal or securities seal (see section 40, 1985 Act) of the company is *prima facie* (i.e. rebuttable) evidence of the named person's title to the shares comprised in it (section 186, 1985 Act). The company is therefore able to contest the statements contained in it as against the person named as holder, but is totally estopped (i.e. precluded) from denying (1) that the named person is the holder or (2) that the sum indicated as paid up is so paid up, as against any other person who acts without knowledge of the true facts in reliance on those statements. This means, for example, that a company which refuses to register a transfer to a person on the basis that the transferor named as holder in the certificate was not the true owner will be liable to compensate such person (*Re Bahia and San*

Francisco Rly Co. (1868) LR 3 QB 584). The same applies where the reliance is on the statement as to the amount paid up on the shares in question (*Burkinshaw* v. *Nicholls* (1878) 3 App Cas 1004, HL; *Bloomenthal* v. *Ford* [1897] AC 156). If the holder himself, unaware that his title is defective, purports to sell his shares and then finds that the company will not register the 'purchaser' as a member because of his (the seller's) defective title, so that the seller is forced to buy shares in order to fulfil his contract, the company is liable to compensate the seller (*The Balkis Consolidated Co. Ltd* v. *Tomkinson* [1893] AC 396 HL; see also *Dixon* v. *Kennaway & Co. Ltd* [1900] 1 Ch 833 where the shareholder was himself held entitled to hold the company to its statements in the incorrectly completed share certificate).

Estoppel can only arise against the company if the statements are made by the company – that is, by someone with authority to make them for the company. On this basis, a third party acting in good faith (*bona fide*) is not protected if he relies on a certificate issued by someone who has no authority to do so. It is thought that this is the correct principle underlying the classic case on the point, namely *Ruben* v. *Great Fingall Consolidated* [1906] AC 439, HL, although the case is sometimes cited as authority for the proposition that the company will not be liable upon a forgery (see also *South London Greyhound Racecourses Ltd* v. *Wake* [1931] 1 Ch 496). In this case, the company secretary had forged the directors' signatures on a share certificate. Lord Macnaghten held in clear terms that 'the secretary of the company ... may be the proper hand to deliver out certificates ... but he can have no authority to guarantee the genuineness or validity of a document which is not the deed of the company'. In other words, the clear basis is lack of authority to represent a document as genuine. (See, in a different context but to the same effect, *Lloyd* v. *Grace Smith & Co.* [1912] AC 716 at 738 again *per* Lord Macnaghten.) One can argue, however, that the company secretary should be regarded as just the person who does have at least apparent authority to represent a document as genuine, and that the company should be bound in such circumstances.

6.7.3   Certification of transfers

Similar considerations arise in the context of the certification of a transfer (see [6.6.2]). If the transfer is returned 'certificated' by a duly authorised company officer, the company is estopped from denying, as against any person acting in good faith on the certification, that there have been produced to the company documents (i.e. a share certificate) which show a *prima facie* title to the shares in the transferor named in the instrument of transfer. Note, however, that the certification is not to be taken as a representation by the company that the transferor *actually has* any title to the shares in question (section 184(1), 1985 Act). Section 184(3) spells out that the certification is deemed made by the company if (1) the person issuing the certificated instrument of transfer is authorised to issue certificated instruments of transfer on the company's behalf, and (2) the certification is signed by the person authorised to certificate transfers on the company's behalf or by an officer or servant either of the company or of a body corporate so authorised. A person who takes and relies on the certificated transfer may, therefore, hold the company liable if either the company never received the documents referred to above (i.e. the share certificate) or if it negligently parts with the original share certificate by, for example, returning it to the transferor (who then proceeds to 're-transfer' the shares already 'sold' to this first person to a second buyer).

The problem arises because a second buyer who manages to secure registration as a member before the first buyer and without knowledge of the latter's equitable claim may not be ousted from his membership. He has the legal title to the shares and takes priority (see *Coleman* v. *London County and Westminster Bank Ltd* [1916] 2 Ch 353). By the same token the second 'buyer' may find that the first buyer, armed with his certificated transfer, has secured registration first. In this case, the second buyer has no remedy against the company. He will not have a certificated transfer and, while he will be in possession of the share certificate, the company owes no duty to the general public as far as the custody of the certificate is concerned (*Longman* v. *Bath Electric Tramways Ltd* [1905] 1 Ch 646). It may be noted here that if a company fraudulently or negligently makes a false certification it will be liable in damages to any person who acts to his detriment on the faith of the certification (section 184(2), 1985 Act). If neither buyer has yet been registered as a member, the buyer whose equitable title is first in order of time has priority.

Directors should refuse to register a transfer if they receive notice of a prior equitable claim to the shares in question (*Ireland* v. *Hart* [1902] 1 Ch 522 at 529 *per* Joyce J). Once a transferee has been registered as a member, the effect of section 360, 1985 Act ([6.7.1] above) is that the company is entitled to ignore all other claims to the shares. A person who stands to lose his right to registration as a member by virtue of the above rules may protect himself by applying to the court for a 'stop notice' (Charging Orders Act 1979, section 5; Rules of the Supreme Court Order 50, rules 11-15). This requires a company to refrain from registering a transfer of the shares in question and from paying any dividends before sending a notice by first class post to the successful applicant for the stop notice and giving the latter eight days within which to take action – for example, apply for an injunction.

6.7.4   Forged instruments of transfer

A forged instrument of transfer (as where the holder's signature is forged) is a nullity and the holder cannot be deprived of his title in this way. If the true owner has been removed from the register as a result the company must restore his name to the register and pay him any dividends which he has 'missed'. The company is likely to have issued a share certificate on the basis of the forged transfer and anyone acting to his detriment, in good faith, on the share certificate may seek compensation from the company (*The Balkis Consolidated Co. Ltd* v. *Tomkinson*, above). However, this remedy does not extend to the transferee under the forged transfer, even if he is totally innocent and as much a victim as anyone else, because in submitting the instrument of transfer to the company he warrants, under an implied contract, that it is genuine (*Sheffield Corpn.* v. *Barclay* [1905] AC 392 HL). Indeed, he is liable to indemnify the company for any compensation which it has had to make to any person who acted to his detriment on a certificate issued as a result of the forgery. The original transferee's remedy lies against the forger, although there is the theoretical possibility (but a remote one in practice) of the company being unable to recover a full indemnity if it acted negligently in registering a forged transfer (under section 2(1) of the Civil Liability (Contribution) Act 1978; *Stanley Yeung* v. *The Hong Kong & Shanghai Banking Corpn.* [1980] 2 All ER 599, PC)). Since most transfer instruments do not need to be signed by transferees, companies do not have records of most members' signatures, and it would be most difficult to show negligence in failing to detect a forged member's signature.

6.8   Other ways of acquiring shares

Besides acquiring shares by transfer (whether by way of purchase or gift) a person may acquire title to shares and proceed to membership of the relevant company in other ways. These are (a) subscription of the memorandum; (b) application, allotment and registration; (c) transmission; (d) delivery of a share warrant.

6.8.1   Subscription of the memorandum

The memorandum of association is the principal document of registration (See Chapter 2). It is a pre-requisite to company registration. Every subscriber to the memorandum (i.e. every 'first share-holder') must take at least one share (section 2(5)(b), 1985 Act). On registration of the company every subscriber must be entered on the register of members (section 22(1), 1985 Act), but a subscriber is a member of the company in the sense of being bound by the statutory contract (see Chapter 2) even before registration, and is therefore liable, for example to pay calls on his shares, (*Re Esparto Trading Co.* (1879) 12 ChD 191; *Re London, Hamburgh and Continental Exchange Bank, Evan's case* (1867) 2 Ch App 427). By section 1, 1985 Act, the memorandum must contain an 'association clause' whereby the subscribers to the memorandum (of which there must be at least two) declare that they desire to be formed into a company and agree to take the subscription shares indicated opposite to their respective names. Each subscriber signs his name in the presence of at least one witness and the signatures must be attested (section 2, 1985 Act). Although English law does not as yet formally admit of the French or Belgian possibility of one person forming a company by unilateral declaration, the subscribers need not be 'independent', i.e. they may be nominees, or one of two subscribers may be a trustee for the other subscriber. Work is in progress in the EEC on a Twelfth Council Directive which will make provision for single-member private limited companies (Com (88) 101 final; O.J. 1988 No. C.173/10 of 2.7.88).

6.8.2   Application, allotment and registration

A person may apply to a public company which is issuing shares, for an allotment to him of such shares, either directly or indirectly. He applies directly by responding to a public issue. He applies 'indirectly' where the company is making a rights issue or a bonus issue to its existing members on terms that these may renounce their rights in favour of other persons, i.e. where the company issues renounceable letters of allotment to existing member applicants who then renounce their rights in favour of other persons. Whether the application is direct or indirect, section 22(2), 1985 Act provides that every person (other than a subscriber to the memorandum, in whose case registration is not necessary for him to become a member; see [6.8.1] above) who agrees to become a member and whose name is entered in its register of members, shall be a member of the company. This means that an allottee must be registered before he can be regarded as a member (*Re Florence Land and Public Works Co., Nicol's case, Tufnell and Ponsonby's case* (1885) 29 ChD 421 at 447 *per* Fry LJ; *Musslewhite* v. *C.H. Musslewhite & Sons Ltd* [1962] Ch 964).

Apart from transfers of shares (above) the more usual way for a person to become a shareholder is by contracting with the company. This will arise most often as a result of that person's direct application for shares to the company in response to the issue by the company of an advertisement or prospectus. The ordinary law of contract applies. The applicant makes an offer to purchase shares, represented by his application. The allotment of a number of shares to the applicant by way of a 'letter of allotment' represents the company's acceptance of that offer (*Nicol's case* (1885) 29 ChD 421). The applicant can withdraw his offer at any time up to notification to him of the allotment. The terms of the contract between the applicant and the company depend upon the conditions in the form of application.

The 1985 Act places restrictions on allotment. Some apply to all companies, others only to public companies. The purpose is the maintenance of the integrity of the company's capital. The main rule applying to all companies is that shares may not be allotted at a discount. If shares are allotted at a discount the allottee is liable to pay the company an amount equal to the amount of the discount with interest (section 100).

Section 84(1) prohibits a public company from making an allotment of any share capital offered for subscription unless either (a) that capital is subscribed in full, or (b) the offer states that even if the capital is not subscribed in full, the amount of that capital subscribed for may be allotted in any event or in the event of the conditions being specified in the offer being satisfied. If shares are not allotted because of the application of this provision and 40 days have elapsed after the first issue of the prospectus, all moneys paid by applicants for shares must be returned to them without interest (section 84(2)), but if any such moneys are not repaid within 48 days of the date of the issue of the prospectus the directors are jointly and severally liable to repay them *with* interest at 5 per cent *per annum*, interest to run from the 48th day (section 84(3)). A director is not so liable if he proves that the default in repayment was not due to misconduct or negligence on his part (section 84(3)).

Section 85(1) provides that where an allotment is made in breach of section 83 (which deals with the 'minimum subscription' required by the directors, and stated in the prospectus, before any allotment can be made and prohibits any allotment if that is not obtained) and section 84, the allotment is voidable (i.e. can be avoided) by the applicant within one month after the sale of the allotment, and remains so notwithstanding that the company is being wound up. This means that the allottee must give the company notice of avoidance within the month; he need not have started legal proceedings (*Re National Motor Mail Co. Ltd* [1908] 2 Ch 228). Any director who knowingly contravenes, or permits or authorises, the contravention of sections 83 or 84 is liable to compensate the allottee and the company for any loss, damage or costs which results respectively to them from the contravention (section 85(2)).

While in principle shares allotted by a company, and any premium on them may be paid up in money or money's worth (including goodwill and know-how) (section 99(1)) a public company may not accept in payment an undertaking given by any person that he or another should do work or perform services for the company or any other person (section 99(2)). If it does, the holder of the shares (defined in section 99(5)) remains liable to pay an amount equal to the nominal value of the shares and any premium (or such proportion of that amount as is treated as paid up by the undertaking) with interest (section 99(3)). This section does not prevent a company from allotting bonus shares or from paying up, with sums available for the purpose, any amounts for the time being unpaid on any of its shares (section 99(4)).

Under section 101(1), 1985 Act, no share in a public company (other than shares alloted in pursuance of an employees' share scheme – section 101(2)) may be allotted unless one quarter of the nominal value and the whole of any premium thereon has been paid up. If this provision is breached, the allottee *and* any subsequent holder will be liable to pay that amount *with interest*, but this does not apply to the allotment of bonus shares (i.e. shares issued to existing members, at least initially, in proportion to their dividend entitlements on a capitalisation of profits or revenue reserves) unless the allottee knew or ought to have known that the shares were allotted in contravention of section 101(1) (section 101(5)).

By section 102(1), a public company may not allot shares as fully or partly paid up otherwise than in cash if the consideration for the allotment is or includes an undertaking which is to be, or may be, performed more than five years after the date of the allotment. The allottee remains liable to pay the nominal value and the whole of any premium (section 102(2)). Non-cash considerations must be valued before allotment (sections 103 and 108-111). Furthermore, section 104 prohibits, except under specified conditions, a public company formed as such from entering into agreements with a subscriber for the transfer by him to the company within the 'initial period' (two years from the issue of the certificate of entitlement to do business under section 117) of a non-cash asset.

The liability of subsequent holders of shares allotted in violation of sections 99, 100, 101, 103, 104 is dealt with in sections 112 to 116. These lay down important exemptions for purchasers for value without notice of the contravention concerned or persons claiming through such persons (section 112(3)). Section 113 permits persons liable to a company under sections 99, 102, 103, 105, 112 to apply to the court for exemption at its discretion on grounds of justice and equity. The overriding principles to which the court will have regard in exercising this discretion are (1) that a company which has allotted shares should receive money or money's worth at least equal in value to the aggregate of the nominal value of those shares and the whole of any premium (or, if the case so requires, such portion of it as is treated as paid up) and (2) subject to the above, that where such a company would, if the court did not grant the exemption, have more than one remedy against a particular person, it should be for the company to decide which remedy it should remain entitled to pursue (section 113(5)). Undertakings to do work or perform services or to do any other thing do not become unenforceable by the company simply because there is a contravention of sections 99, 102, 103 or 104 (s.115).

6.8.3   Transmission

Transmission is the transfer of title by operation of law and takes effect on the death, bankruptcy ('legal death') or liquidation of a member. The articles of association will commonly deal with transmission in some detail (articles 29 to 31, Table A). Article 30 lays down that a person becoming entitled to a share in consequence of the death or bankruptcy of a member may, upon such evidence being produced as the directors may properly require, elect either to become the holder of the share or to have some person nominated by him registered as the transferee. However, it must be noted that while shares are transmitted to a member's personal representative on the latter's death, the question whether a personal representative can be registered as a member is a matter for the articles of association. Therefore, by section 183(3), a personal representative may transfer the shares in question even though he be not registered as a member. Also the personal representative is entitled to petition for relief from unfairly prejudicial conduct under section 459 (see Chapter 8).

Article 31, Table A, provides that a person becoming entitled to a share in consequence of the death or bankruptcy of a member shall have the same rights to which he would be entitled if he were the holder of the share, except that before he is registered as a member he may not in respect of it attend or vote at any general or class meeting of the company. In the event of the bankruptcy (or liquidation) of a member, the share remains in the legal ownership of the bankrupt (or company in liquidation) but the beneficial interest vests in the trustee in bankruptcy or liquidator. Section 183(3) (above) also applies in these contexts.

6.8.4   Delivery of a share warrant

If so authorised by its articles, a company limited by shares may, with respect to fully paid-up shares, issue under its common seal, a warrant stating that the bearer of the warrant is entitled to the shares specified in it (section 188, 1985 Act). Table A does not so provide. The importance of this is that the shares comprised in the warrant can be transferred by simple delivery of the warrant (section 188(2)). In other words, share warrants are negotiable instruments (*Webb, Hale & Co.* v. *The Alexandria Water Co. Ltd* (1905) 21 TLR 572). They are not common, largely because of the inherent dangers of forgery and theft.

6.9   Restrictions on membership

Subject to the articles of association, minors (i.e. persons under 18 years of age) may be members of a company but the contract of membership is voidable by the minor before, or within a reasonable time after, his attaining the age of majority. Again, subject to the articles, bankrupts may be members, as we have seen. There are no statutory nationality or residence restrictions in operation at present.

A company cannot be a member of itself or of its holding company (section 23, 1985 Act). In certain circumstances a company is empowered to purchase its own shares but these must then be quickly disposed of. The subsidiary/holding company relationship is defined for the purposes of the above prohibition in section 736, 1985 Act.

6.10   Statutory restrictions on transfer

The reader is referred to the treatment of this topic in Chapter 5 (see [5.4.3.2.(2)]).

Chapter 7

The Variation of Shareholder Rights

7.1 Introduction

This chapter deals with the variation of the rights of shareholders. This variation can come about in one of two ways, depending on whether the capital of the company is divided into different classes of shares or not. If authorised by its memorandum or articles, a company may issue different classes of shares.

If there is only one class of shares and it is proposed to alter the rights or obligations of all or a part of the shareholders as conferred or imposed on these members by the articles, the articles will need to be altered by special resolution. On the other hand, if there are different classes of shares and the rights of one class are being varied, the statutory rules on the variation of class rights will need to be followed.

We have already mentioned the power to alter the articles and the restriction on that power, namely that the power must be exercised 'bona fide for the benefit of the company as a whole' (Chapter 4). This chapter will concentrate on class rights and their variation. In this context, it is crucial to distinguish between rights and interests. In general, 'interests' do not appear to receive a considerable amount of protection under the statutory variation of class rights regime (see [7.2.3.1] below) although section 459 of the 1985 Act may provide a supplementary remedy (see [7.2.3.2] below).

7.2 Classes of shares

Before proceeding to the procedure for varying class rights it is important to clarify two concepts, namely (1) the concept of a 'class' of shares and (2) the concept of a class 'right' as opposed to an 'interest' or the 'enjoyment' of a right.

Mr Justice Farwell gave the classic definition of a share in *Borland's Trustee* v. *Steel Bros. Ltd* [1901] 1 Ch 279. He said:

'A share is the interest of a shareholder in the company measured by
a sum of money, for the purpose of liability in the first place, and of
interest in the second, but also consisting of a series of mutual
covenants entered into by all the shareholders *inter se* in accordance
with (s.14, 1985 Act). The contract contained in the articles of
association is one of the original incidents of the share. A share
is...an interest measured by a sum of money and made up of various
rights contained in the contract.'

Therefore, a share is a proprietary interest in the company and not in
its assets. It is in the nature of personal property, constituting what
lawyer's call a 'chose in action' [section 182(1)(a), 1985 Act).

The rights attached to any particular share are therefore a matter of
contract. They are part of the 'terms of issue'. These terms may be set
out in the memorandum or articles or elsewhere, such as in a
resolution increasing capital for the purpose of a share issue under
section 121, 1985 Act. A company is free to create and issue shares
with such rights or restrictions as the company may determine by
ordinary resolution (article 2, Table A). This is subject, of course, to the
provisions of the Act and without prejudice to any rights attached to
any existing shares (article 2, Table A). Where a company issues shares
with rights which are not set out in its memorandum or articles, or in
any resolution or agreement which requires to be delivered to the
registrar for registration under section 380 (see section 380(4)), section
128 obliges the company to deliver particulars to the Registrar within
one month from allotment unless the shares are in all respects
uniform with shares previously allotted.

7.2.1   Some examples

(A)   Redeemable shares

One example of a separate class of shares is given by article 3 of Table
A, namely:

'Subject to the provisions of the Act shares may be issued which are
to be redeemed or are to be liable to be redeemed at the option of the
company or the holder on such terms and in such manner as may be
provided by the articles.'

In keeping with the aim of this book to give an overview in terms of
principle it is not proposed to give detailed treatment to the statutory

rules on redeemable shares. These are to be found in Chapter VII of the 1985 Act.

(B)   'Deferred' or 'founders'' shares

These are shares which by the terms of issue confer on their holders (usually the company 'founders') rights of participation in the profits (i.e. dividend rights) or in the assets on a winding-up, which are postponed (hence 'deferred') to the claims of preference shareholders, if any, and of ordinary shareholders.

(C)   'Non-voting' shares or 'limited voting' shares

Unlike some continental company law systems, English law allows the issue of non-voting shares. The articles of association commonly deprive preference shareholders of the right to vote unless the dividend payable is in arrears. However, even where there are no preference shares (see (E) below) some shares may be issued which do not carry the right to vote, the obvious reason being to raise capital without parting with, or diluting, existing control. Whether buyers can be found for such shares will, of course, depend on security and anticipated investment return.

(D)   'Multiple voting' shares: weighted voting

Shares vesting multiple voting rights are likewise permitted, whether the shareholder is to enjoy multiple votes generally or only in specified circumstances. *Bushell* v. *Faith* [1970] AC 1099 is an example of the latter type. There, article 9 of the company's articles of association provided that:

> 'In the event of a resolution being proposed at any general meeting of the company for the removal from office of any director, any shares held by that director shall on a poll in respect of such resolution carry the right to three votes per share ...'

The House of Lords upheld the validity of such an article, despite the obvious conflict of interests.

It is also quite common for members of management to be given preferred voting rights as attached to so-called 'management shares'. In *Investment Trust Corpn Ltd* v. *Singapore Traction Co. Ltd* [1935] Ch 615 one 'management share' was enabled to outvote the remaining 399,999 shares. In *Rights and Issues Investment Trust Ltd* v. *Stylo Shoes Ltd* [1965] Ch

250, Stylo Shoes Ltd was allowed to alter its articles of association in order to double the votes which might be cast in respect of management shares held by directors of the company.

(E) Preference shares

Preference shares can be defined as shares which confer on their holders some 'right of preference', whether as to participation in profits (normally expressed as a percentage of the nominal value of the share, e.g. 7 per cent) or return of capital or both, over other shares. The holder is usually entitled to a dividend of a fixed amount before any dividend is paid on the ordinary shares. Under articles in the usual form the shareholder is entitled to a dividend and can sue for it only if a dividend has been declared in general meeting (see Chapter 2). However, the articles may provide a contractual right to a dividend by laying down the manner in which the profits are to be applied (see, for example, *Evling* v. *Israel & Oppenheimer Ltd* [1918] 1 Ch 101). Where preferential dividends are payable 'out of profits' this means net distributable profits. The company must write off previous year's losses against the current year's profits (section 263, 1985 Act). Also, if the board have the power under the articles to create reserves and they exercise the power properly (see [3.4]) the preference shareholder may not complain that this leaves insufficient 'profits' to pay his dividend (*Bond* v. *Barrow Haematite Steel Co.* [1902] 1 Ch 353; *Fisher* v. *Black and White Publishing Co.* [1901] 1 Ch 174; *Re Buenos Ayres Great Southern Rly. Co. Ltd* [1947] Ch 384).

Subject to legal requirements (e.g. section 263, 1985 Act, above) and to the variation of class rights procedure, the best guarantee of the payment of a preferential dividend is for express provision to be made in the articles for the application of profits – the declaration of preference dividends being given priority over alternative applications (e.g. transfer to reserves) (see *Evling* v. *Israel*, above.) Table A would need to be adapted to provide such an allocation.

The right to a preference dividend may be *cumulative* (i.e. so that arrears of dividend not declared in previous years remain payable prior to any dividend being paid to ordinary shareholders in any year) or *non-cumulative* (such non-declared dividends being forever 'lost'). Clearly, there could be 'sub-classes' or different classes of preference shares, some being 'cumulative' and others 'non-cumulative', some 'voting' and others 'non-voting' or with limited voting rights.

Preference shares could be 'participating' if they enjoy the additional right to participate with the ordinary shareholders in the profits remaining after they have received their preferential dividend and (usually) the ordinary shareholders have received a dividend equivalent to the preferential dividend rate.

What has been said above regarding preferential rights concerning profits applies *mutatis mutandis* to rights of return of capital. On a winding-up, preference shareholders may enjoy a preferential right to return of capital (i.e. to the extent of the nominal value of their shares) in priority to other shares. They may enjoy the additional right to participate in surplus assets.

(F)   Ordinary shares

These are commonly referred to as the 'residual' category (or class) of shares, in the sense that where a company's share capital is divided into different classes and the special rights of various classes are set out (usually in the articles), the remaining shares are termed ordinary shares. Of course, where all a company's shares are issued on the same terms they will be ordinary shares. However, it is possible that a company will issue ordinary 'A' and ordinary 'B' (and possibly 'C', etc.) shares which have in common that they are not preference shares but whose holders otherwise enjoy different rights. For example, the ordinary B shares may carry restricted voting rights or be redeemable.

Some statutory provisions apply only to 'equity' shares. For the purposes of the 1985 Act 'equity' share capital is defined in section 744 as 'a company's issued share capital, excluding any part of that capital which, neither as respects dividends nor as respects capital, carries any right to participate beyond a specified amount in a distribution'.

7.2.2   The determination of the rights of different classes

In principle, the rights of different classes are ascertained in exactly the same way as are those of shares where there is only one class, that is it is a matter, in particular, of interpreting the terms of issue (as indicated in the 'prospectus' in response to which the member applied for them, usually; see Chapter 10) and the memorandum and articles of association. The name given to shares is not conclusive of the rights attaching to them. Class rights can be defined as the rights attached to each class of shares when there is more than one class of shares. One view, and probably the better view, is that where there is more than one class, even the 'common rights' (identical rights enjoyed by both or all classes) are 'class rights' and can be varied only by the variation of class rights procedure (Pennington, *Company Law*, p.248; Gower, *Principles of Modern Company Law*, p.562). The alternative view is that class rights are those special rights attached to a class of shares, identical rights being excluded (see *Hodge* v. *James Howell & Co.* [1958] CLY 446, CA). This issue is yet unclear but it is of obvious importance to determining which procedure needs to be followed for the variation of particular rights (see [7.2.3] below).

It is not uncommon for different classes of shares to be issued in circumstances where the terms of issue and the memorandum or articles omit to state with precision the respective rights attached to each class, be it in respect of dividend, return of capital or voting. In such cases the courts have applied the 'presumption of equality', i.e. the presumption is that shareholders enjoy the same rights (*Birch* v. *Cropper* (1889) 14 AC 525).

Largely on the basis of this presumption of equality the courts have evolved certain specific rules and presumptions:

(1) All shares are presumed to confer the same rights and impose the same liabilities (*Birch* v. *Cropper* (1889) 14 AC 525).

(2) Preference shares are presumed to be 'cumulative'; i.e. it is presumed that if no preference dividend is declared in any year the unpaid arrears of dividend are carried forward and are payable before any dividend is paid on other shares (*Webb* v. *Erle* (1875) LR 20 Eq 556; *Foster* v. *Coles and Foster* (1906) 22 TLR 555; *Staples* v. *Eastman Photographic* (1896) 2 Ch 303). This presumption is rebutted if, for example, the memorandum or articles give the right to a fixed dividend 'out of yearly profits' or 'out of the net profits of each year' (*Staples* v. *Eastman Photographic* (1896) 2 Ch 303; *Adair* v. *Old Bushmills Distillery Co.* (1908) WN 24).

(3) Arrears of cumulative preference dividend are presumed *not* payable in a winding-up unless previously declared, because dividends only become payable as a debt when declared and are only payable while the company is a going concern (*Re Crichton's Oil Co.* (1902) 2 Ch 86; *Re W.M. Foster & Son Ltd* (1942) 1 All ER 314; *Re Catalinas Warehouses & Mole Co. Ltd* (1947) 1 All ER 51). This presumption is frequently rebutted in the memorandum or articles. This was held to be the case in *Re E.W. Savory Ltd* [1951] 2 All ER 1036, where the articles provided that 'preference shares shall rank both as regards dividends and as regards capital in priority to all other shares (see also *Re Wharfedale Brewery Co. Ltd* [1952] Ch 913; *Re F. de Jong & Co.* [1946] 1 Ch 211; *Re Walter Symons Ltd* [1934] Ch 308).

(4) Preference shares are presumed to rank equally with ordinary shares as to repayment of capital on a winding-up (*Birch* v. *Cropper* above; *Re London India Rubber Co.* (1868) LR Eq 519; *Re Accrington Corp. Steam Tramways* [1909] 2 Ch 40). This is frequently rebutted in the

memorandum or articles, preference shares being given priority as to return of capital over the ordinary shares after payment of the company's debts and liabilities and of any arrears of dividend which may be payable. However, the courts will interpret a provision as to repayment of capital in the memorandum or articles as 'exhaustive', i.e. as defining repayment rights exhaustively. This means that if the articles give preference shareholders preferential rights to return of capital they will be deemed to possess no further rights (rebutting the presumption of equality). For example, there will be no further right to participate in *surplus* assets (i.e. assets remaining after all creditors have been paid and all capital has been returned to the shareholders) if any (*Re Isle of Thanet Electricity Supply Co. Ltd* [1950] Ch 161, 171; *Scottish Insurance Corp.* v. *Wilsons & Clyde Coal Co. Ltd* [1949] AC 462, at 488). This 'presumption of exhaustiveness' is of general application, so that where the terms of issue make some express provision as to the rights of a class in any respect (not just return of capital) then the presumption is that that provision is an exhaustive statement of the rights of that class in that respect (for example, voting or dividend) (*Will* v. *United Lankat Plantations Co. Ltd* [1914] AC 11).

(5) Preference shares are presumed to rank equally with ordinary shares as to participation in surplus assets on a winding-up (*Birch* v. *Cropper*, above). Again, this presumption is frequently rebutted, as we have just seen.

The two cardinal presumptions which assist the court in ascertaining class rights are therefore the presumption of equality and the presumption of exhaustiveness. The latter overrides the former.

7.2.3   The variation of class rights

'Variation' includes 'abrogation' – both under statute and (as a rule) as a matter of interpretation of the memorandum or articles (section 125(8), 1985 Act). Class rights, albeit set out in the articles, may not be varied simply by the passage of a special resolution in general meeting altering the articles. Special protection is afforded the holder of a particular class of shares, notably the requirement that a variation may only occur with the consent of the majority of the holders of that class of share. This applies whether, as is usual, variation is provided for in the memorandum or articles or not (so that the statutory procedure applies). Sections 125-129 of the Companies Act 1985 regulate this matter.

We shall first describe the procedure for variation in brief, moving on to discuss particular issues of interpretation and especially what is meant by the 'variation of a right' and also what is meant by 'class'.

7.2.3.1 Procedure

This is governed by section 125, 1985 Act. The appropriate procedure depends on how the rights which are sought to be varied were conferred. It provides that:

(1) Where the rights are attached by the *memorandum*, and the memorandum or articles do *not* contain provision for variation, those rights are variable only with the unanimous consent of all the members of the company (section 125(5)).

(2) Where the rights are attached by the *memorandum*, and the articles contain provision for variation, *and* this provision was included on the company's incorporation, *and* the variation is *not* connected with the giving, variation revocation or renewal of an authority for allotment under section 80 or with a reduction of capital under section 135, those rights may be varied only in accordance with that provision in the articles (section 125(4)(a)).

Where the final condition is lacking (i.e. the variation is connected with a section 80 authority or a section 135 reduction) the rights may not be varied *unless* section 125(3) is complied with (see (4) below). The same rules apply when the rights are attached otherwise than by the memorandum (i.e. by the articles or under the terms of a resolution of the board or of the general meeting), and the articles contain provision for variation (whenever included) (section 125(4)(b)).

(3) By section 125(2), where the rights are attached *otherwise than* by the memorandum, and the articles do not provide for variation, those rights are variable, but only if:

    (A) (i) the holders of three quarters in nominal value of the issued shares of that class consent in writing; or

        (ii) an extraordinary resolution passed at a separate general meeting of the holders of that class sanctions the variation; *and*

    (B) any additional requirement (howsoever imposed) in relation to the variation of those rights is also complied with.

This statutory procedure is effectively replacing express modification of rights clauses. Even Table A does not contain an express clause.

(4) Where the rights are attached by the memorandum or otherwise,

and the memorandum or articles provide for their variation, *and* the variation *is* connected with a section 80 authority or a section 135 reduction, those rights are variable only if:

(A) (i) the holders of three-quarters in nominal value of the issued shares of that class consent in writing; or

(ii) an extraordinary resolution passed at a separate general meeting of the holders of that class sanctions the variation, *and*

(B) any additional requirement of the *memorandum* or *articles* in relation to the variation of those rights is also complied with (section 125(3)).

(5) It is expressly provided that any alteration of a provision in the articles for the variation of class rights, or the insertion of any such provision into the articles, is itself to be treated as a variation of those rights (section 125(7)).

(6) It is also expressly provided that for the purposes of section 125 and (except where the context otherwise requires) for the purpose of interpreting any provision for the variation of class rights contained in a company's memorandum or articles, references to the 'variation' of those rights are to be read as including references to their abrogation (section 125(8)).

These provisions are not exhaustive. For example, it is still possible for class rights attached by the memorandum to be varied by complying with a procedure set out in the memorandum itself or in the articles if the memorandum refers to such a procedure contained in the articles. The provisions are highly complicated and writers have pointed out difficulties and anomalies, making the seeking of expert advice imperative when drafting memoranda and articles (see, for example, Pennington, *Company Law*, p.240). It may be noted that the powers in section 125(2) and (5) (see above, (1) and (3)) are without prejudice to the court's own powers under sections 4 to 6 (regarding the alteration of a company's objects), section 54 (litigated objection to a public company becoming a private company by re-registration), section 425 (court control of company compromising with creditors and members – see Chapter 9), section 427 (company reconstruction or amalgamation – see Chapter 9) and sections 459 to 461 (protection of minorities – see Chapter 8)

7.2.3.2   *'Variation of a right'*

It is by no means always clear that 'a right is being varied'. The courts have adopted a notoriously narrow interpretation of the phrase under the predecessor of section 125 and to all intents and purposes the statutory wording has not changed. The legislator has not overruled the 'old' case law.

The courts have drawn a distinction between, on the one hand, the 'disturbance' of the right itself and, on the other hand, the 'disturbance' of the *enjoyment* of the right. In the first case there is an attempted variation, the statutory procedure has to be followed, and aggrieved shareholders may invoke the special statutory minority protection provision (formerly section 72, 1948 Act, now reproduced in section 127, 1985 Act, see below). In the second case, there is no variation of a right, no special procedure need be followed, and the general common law or statutory remedies would need to be invoked by an aggrieved shareholder (see below and Chapter 8).

The special statutory minority protection provision, section 127, applies, as did its predecessor whenever rights are *varied or abrogated* either in accordance with a modification of class rights provision in the memorandum or articles or under section 125(2) (section 127(1), 1985 Act). The holders of not less than 15 per cent of the issued shares of the class in question (being persons who did not consent to, or vote in favour of, the resolution for the variation) may apply to the court to have the resolution cancelled. If an application is made the variation has no effect unless and until it is confirmed by the court (section 127(2), 1985 Act). Application must be made within 21 days after the date on which the consent was given or the resolution was passed (depending on the procedure applicable in the particular case) and may be made on behalf of all the shareholders entitled to make such an application by such one or more of their number as they may appoint in writing for the purpose (section 127(3)). The court, after hearing the applicant and any other persons who apply to the court to be heard and appear to the court to be interested in the application may, if satisfied, having regard to all the circumstances of the case, that the variation would unfairly prejudice the shareholders of the class represented by the applicant, disallow the variation and shall, if not so satisfied, confirm it. The decision of the court is final (section 127(4)).

Some points must be noted. This provision can only be invoked if there is a 'variation of a class right' (including abrogation, section 127(6)). When interests or expectations alone are being prejudiced the general common law or other statutory provisions will need to be invoked. The latter include section 459, 1985 Act which offers relief against 'unfair prejudice' (a phrase used in section 127(4)) in the broad context of prejudice to 'interests' (see Chapter 8). Section 459 may take over where section 127 leaves off, and section 127 may 'leave off' at an early stage, for the courts' view has been that class rights are 'varied':

'only if they are different in substance after the alleged act of alteration from what they were before, and so if they are the same in substance but merely commercially less valuable, there is no (variation).'

The courts have taken this restrictive line even where the relevant provision in the memorandum or articles set out a procedure to be followed where rights were 'altered, varied, *affected, modified, dealt with* or abrogated in any manner'. Such a wide clause featured in Re *John Smith's Tadcaster Brewery Co. Ltd* [1953] Ch 308, [1953] 1 All ER 518, and in *White v. Bristol Aeroplane* [1953] Ch 65, [1953] 1 All ER 40. In either case the variation procedure was not complied with by the company. The question was whether it ought to have been followed. This depended on whether class rights were being 'varied' 'affected' etc. In each of these cases the company had issued preference shares which conferred on their holders the right to a fixed preferential dividend and also the right to vote at general meetings if the preference dividend was in arrear.

Taking *White's case* as an example, the company's capital was being increased by the issue of 660,000 £1 preference shares to rank *pari passu* (equally) with the existing 600,000 £1 preference stock and 2,640,000 ordinary shares of 10s. each to rank *pari passu* with the existing £3,300,000 ordinary stock. The new shares were to be issued to the ordinary stockholders and paid for out of the reserve fund. The court held that the rights of the existing preference shareholders did not stand to be affected however much this was the case with the *enjoyment* of the rights, i.e. because their proportional voting *strength* or *power* was being reduced. Their actual rights (e.g. *number* of votes) remained what they had always been. Consequently, it was not necessary for the company to follow the variation of class rights procedure and obtain their consent to the resolution for the issue of the new shares.

Professor Pennington's comment is that there is a sound 'practical' reason for this approach (Pennington, *Company Law*, p.246). He cites Lord Evershed MR in *Re John Smith's case* [1953] Ch 308 at 316, who said:

'It is necessary, first, to note … that what must be "affected" are the rights of the preference stockholders. The question then is … are the rights which I have summarised "affected" by what is proposed? It is said in answer – and I think rightly said – No, they are not; they remain exactly as they were before; each one of the manifestations of the preference stockholders' privileges may be repeated without any change whatever after, as before, the proposed distribution. It is no doubt true that the enjoyment of, and the capacity to make effective, those rights is in a measure affected; for as I have already indicated, the existing preference stockholders will be in a less advantageous position on such occasions as entitle them to register their votes, whether at general meetings of the company or at separate meetings of their own class. But there is to my mind a distinction, and a sensible distinction, between an affecting of the rights and an affecting of the enjoyment of the rights, or of the stockholders' capacity to turn them to account.'

Both Lord Evershed and Professor Pennington see the narrow interpretation of 'variation of rights' as necessary to prevent shareholders acting as a 'second board of directors with a power of veto over the decisions of the duly constituted board' (Pennington, p.246). The force of the argument is undeniable, and particularly so because the board have a duty to act *bona fide* in the best interests of the company which includes a duty to treat all shareholders fairly (*Mills* v. *Mills* (1938) 60 CLR 150 and [7.2.3.3.] below). However, where the power of decision – in this context, the power to issue further shares – lies with the ordinary shareholders these may not be wholly disinterested parties.

It may be that in order that justice be done the law needs to be made more sophisticated. After all, section 127(4) gives the court discretion to set a variation aside if its effect, 'having regard to all the circumstances' (which could be interpreted to include expectations and interests) is 'unfairly prejudicial'. Where a right *is* varied, that variation can be set aside if interests (i.e. legitimate expectations) are being 'unfairly prejudiced', presumably. Surely this test ought to have its day in court – something it is cheated out of by a narrow definition of 'variation of rights'. Nevertheless, it is possible, presumably, for a shareholder who is told that his rights have not been 'varied' to petition under section 459, 1985 on the ground that his *interests* are being unfairly prejudiced (see Chapter 8). A single shareholder may invoke this provision irrespective of the size of his holding and we can probably expect increasing reliance on section 459 in the context of the variation of class rights.

Also, as Pennington writes (p.248), interests (as opposed to rights) may be protected by suitable provision in the memorandum and articles requiring the consent of affected shareholders (e.g. by the same majority as set out for the variation of class rights) before the company may embark on stated operations. These operations might include major acquisitions or disposals of assets, the issue of shares, and voluntary liquidation. As part of the statutory contract such provisions could be enforced by injunction, until the articles were validly altered.

The above comments relate to one example of an area where the conflict between rights and interests emerges. The danger is that the court will fail to apply a test which might prevent the typical shareholder of one class from being unfairly prejudiced by those of another class who also hold the requisite majority of shares of the first class. This brings us to the next topic.

7.2.3.3   'Unfair prejudice'

There is 'unfair prejudice' within the meaning of section 127(4) if the majority who vote in favour of the variation at a class meeting do so in bad faith, or fail to act primarily in the interest of the shareholders of the class in question as a whole. For example, in a 'capital reduction' case which applies a principle applicable in the present context (*Re Holders Investment Trust Ltd* [1971] 2 All ER 289; [1971] 1 WLR 583) the court set aside a resolution reducing the company's capital. In *Re Holders Investment Trust Ltd* the reduction of capital was to be effected by cancelling the 5 per cent £1 cumulative preference shares and allotting the holders an equivalent amount of 6 per cent unsecured loan stock. The majority of preference shareholders also held 52 per cent of the company's ordinary stock and non-voting ordinary shares. They voted for the reduction in a separate class meeting of preference share-holders and carried the day. However, the court refused to confirm the reduction on the basis that the majority had not properly considered what they ought to have considered, i.e. the interests of the class as a whole, but rather had voted in their own interests as equity shareholders.

Therefore, more specifically, there is 'unfair prejudice' if class consent has been obtained by the votes of shareholders who are also shareholders of another class and who vote for the resolution in the expectation of benefiting in that other capacity (*Re Holders Investment Trust Ltd* above; *British America Nickel Corpn* v. *O'Brien* [1927] AC 369; *Re Wedgewood Coal and Iron Co.* (1877) 6 ChD 627). In short, members voting at a class meeting must act primarily 'in the interests of the class as a whole'. Clearly, this is an application in the class meeting context of the principle applied to the power to alter the articles, namely that majorities enabled to bind minorities must act '*bona fide* for the benefit of the whole' (see Chapter 4 at [4.5.3]).

More broadly, as Pennington writes (*Company Law*, p.250) relying on *Re Holders Investment Trust* (above),

'Proof of bad faith is not the only way (of showing unfair prejudice). If (the minority) can show that their rights are being reduced or eliminated without any necessity in the interest of all the shareholders, or if they alone are called on to make sacrifices without compensation, or if they are discriminated against, or if the scheme for the alteration of rights is otherwise unfair, minority shareholders may succeed in having the alteration cancelled without showing that the majority's motives were tainted.'

On this basis, 'unjustified discrimination' (i.e. discrimination not justified by 'reasonable necessity' in the interests of the company as a whole) amounts to unfair prejudice. The court will presumably approach the matter as a reasonable business man would approach it, and ask whether the prejudice being imposed on the class concerned can on any ground be said to be reasonably required in the interests of the shareholders as a whole, including holders of shares in that class. Viewed in this way, the presence or absence of a *'company* interest' (as a point of reference for 'the interests of the shareholders as a whole') is a most important consideration and cases which ignore this dimension, albeit in other contexts, may need to be reconsidered (e.g. *Mills* v. *Mills* (1938) CLR 150; Xuereb (1988) 51 MLR 156).

Nevertheless, however solicitous towards members of a particular class of shares one might be disposed to be, surely there must be circumstances, if the law is to reflect commercial reality, when the interests of a class as a class (let alone those of the minority of that class) can be overridden in the general company interest. All shareholders become members knowing that their rights are in principle variable without their individual consent. They assume, however, and are entitled to assume that they shall be treated fairly by majorities to whose will they may be subject. On one view, the variation of class rights procedure which insists on a separate class meeting's approval already poses too great an obstacle to flexible management. Yet this must be balanced against the difficulty of attracting investors on terms which make them easily exploitable.

It has been pointed out (Pennington, *Company Law*, p.248) that a company may, and regularly will, take action which adversely affects the *interests* of a class of shareholders without altering their rights. Some of the limits on the company's power to do so have already been mentioned (e.g. the obligation on the majority to act *bona fide*) and more will be explored in Chapter 8. Apart from these restraints, which centre around the protection of rights but also go some way to protecting interests, the company acts by majority (the principle of majority rule) and individual or class consent to company policy is not required.

If it is desired to impose further constraints of this kind on general meeting or the board, the memorandum or articles could require the consent of members individually, or of a class of members, for certain important proposed acts, for example major acquisitions or disposals of assets, or the issue of shares or other securities with rights ranking equally with or in priority to the rights of existing members (technically not a variation of the rights of the latter, as we have seen, e.g. *White's case* above, see [7.2.3.2]), or the winding-up of the company. Such a provision would be enforceable by the members concerned as part of the 'statutory contract' (see Chapter 2) and the right of veto given to a class of members would be a class right and could only be varied in accordance with the proper variation of class rights procedure.

7.2.3.4   'Class'

The possible solicitude of the courts for the minority shareholder has, however, been evidenced by the courts' readiness to identify the existence of a separate 'class' (and therefore require variation of class rights procedures to be followed and kindred remedies to be available). For example (in the context of a scheme of arrangement under sections 425-427, 1985 Act – see [9.2]) Lord Templeman held that ordinary shares owned by the subsidiary of the intended purchaser constituted a different 'class' from ordinary shares (with identical rights and obligations) owned by 'independent' shareholders (*Re Hellenic & General Trust Ltd* [1976] 1 WLR 123). Perhaps this case cannot be 'transplanted' and used in a section 127 context (section 425 speaks of classes of members as opposed to classes of shares), but it does show that the courts are not incapable of looking at the realities and of weighing 'interests'. In any case, some recent cases shed new light on the issue and we now turn to these.

7.2.3.5   'Class rights' and 'special rights'

In Chapter 2 (at [2.10]) it was suggested that a shareholder who had the right under the articles to act as director, or solicitor or in some other non-member capacity might possibly argue that this was a membership right. If this were so, would such a right be 'class' right? In one recent case, the court answered this question in the affirmative in principle but in the negative on the facts. In *Re Blue Arrow plc* (1987) 3 BCC 618, petitioner sought relief by injunction under section 459, 1985 Act. Under the articles the president of the company, as she was, could only be removed by resolution in general meeting. The directors convened a general meeting with a view to altering this provision in the articles by special resolution so as to render the president removable by the board. Petitioner claimed that her 'right to remain president until removed by the general meeting' was a class right alterable only by the class rights variation procedure. Mr Justice Vinelott held that as the right was 'unrelated to any shareholding' (and therefore was not even a 'membership' right – petitioner would retain the right even if she sold all her shares) it could not be described as a class right which he described as 'a right attaching, in some way, to a category of the shares of the company'.

His Lordship cited the decision of *Scott J* in *Cumbrian Newspapers Group Ltd* v. *Cumberland & Westmoreland Herald Newspaper & Printing Co. Ltd* [1987] Ch 1, (1986) 2 BCC 99, 227, in support of his conclusion. Here plaintiff had submitted that when rights are conferred by the articles on individuals 'in their capacity as members', the shares which these individuals hold for the time being (and by virtue of which they are for the time being entitled to the rights) constitute a class of shares for the purposes of section 125. Under certain articles adopted at the time when, and as part of the arrangement under which, shares were issued to plaintiff, plaintiff was given, first, rights of pre-emption over the other ordinary shares in the defendant company as well as, second, rights in respect of unissued shares and, third, the right to appoint a director so long as plaintiff held not less than 10 per cent in nominal value of the issued ordinary shares. It was proposed to cancel these special rights by special resolution. Plaintiff sought a declaration that its rights were 'class rights', and an injunction restraining the convening and holding of the threatened general meeting. *Scott J* held that upon a proper construction of the articles plaintiff did indeed enjoy a 'class right'. He held that there is a category of rights which although not attached to any particular shares, was nonetheless conferred on the beneficiary of them in the capacity of member or shareholder of a company. The plaintiff's special rights fell into this category; they were conferred on it in its capacity as shareholder and would not be enforceable by the plaintiff otherwise than as the owner of ordinary shares. If plaintiff were to divest itself of all its ordinary shares it would lose its right to enforce its rights under the articles; although the rights were not strictly 'attached to any particular class of shares', the phrase 'attached to a class of shares' must be regarded as synonymous with 'rights of any *class of members*' for the purposes of section 125.

It was pointed out in Chapter 2 that rights conferred on a member in consideration of his becoming a member (even if relating to a non-member capacity) could in appropriate circumstances be regarded as 'shareholder rights'. It now seems that they may also be regarded as 'class rights'.

7.3   *Application of assets on a winding-up*

Something must be said, albeit briefly, on this topic if only to make the point that shareholders are not the only interested parties. Indeed, in this context, their interests come last. The matter is governed in the main by the Insolvency Act 1986 and the Insolvency Rules, Part IV, made thereunder (as amended by the Insolvency (Amendment) Rules 1987) (in Scotland, the Insolvency (Scotland) Rules 1986 Parts IV – VI).

Secured creditors will realise their securities, proving in the liquidation only for any unpaid balance as unsecured creditors. The order of claims on the company's assets thereafter is broadly this: (1) costs, charges and expenses of the winding-up; (2) the claims of preferential creditors (as to which see section 386 and Schedule 6, Insolvency Act); (3) the claims secured by a floating charge; (4) the claims of ordinary (unsecured) creditors, apart from declared but unpaid dividends payable to members; (5) interest accrued since the company went into liquidation; (6) if the court so orders, any debt owed to a person who has been declared liable to contribute to the company's assets under section 213 (fraudulent trading) or section 214 (wrongful trading) of the Insolvency Act 1986.

Only after payment of the above claims will any available assets be distributed to members in the form of return of capital and, if assets remain, a distribution of surplus assets. It is at this stage that the determination of the rights of the various classes of shares will become relevant and the reader is referred to the outline of the applicable considerations in [7.2.2] above. It may be added here that where the memorandum or articles are silent as to return of capital, then (a) if there are surplus assets, the surplus should be distributed according to the nominal value of shares held by members, not by reference to the amount paid up per share (*Birch* v. *Cropper* above, [7.2.2]); (b)if there are insufficient assets available to return capital fully to all shareholders, those shareholders who have paid up more on their shares than others will receive the difference outstanding on each share owed by the other shareholders (*Re Wakefield Rolling Stock Co.* [1892] 3 Ch 165).

Chapter 8

The Minority Shareholder, Mismanagement and Company Law Remedies

8.1 Introduction

The position of the minority shareholder is not an enviable one. Quite apart from the fact that the principle of majority rule means that his policy views carry no weight unless a majority vote can be mobilised by him, his rights and interests are in principle at the disposal of the majority. At best, special majorities and procedures (e.g. class meetings – see Chapter 7) are required by law or by the articles before his rights or interests can be affected. However, ultimately, affected they can be – for example, through an alteration of the articles of association, or through a majority resolution not to sue directors or third parties for compensation for loss suffered by the company, or a majority refusal to dismiss directors who have acted in breach of duty.

In practice, one of the aggrieved minority shareholder's best weapons is probably that of appealing to powerful regulatory bodies such as the International Stock Exchange, the Panel on Take-Overs and Mergers, The Securities and Investments Board (see Chapter 10) or even The Office of Fair Trading (where there are considerations of competition which may be of interest to this Office). The adverse publicity for the company attached to recourse to such bodies may, of course, indirectly harm the minority shareholder himself, e.g. the listed value of the company's shares may plummet. The threat of appeal to regulatory bodies may be more of a weapon than is actual recourse to such action. We deal with the more directly relevant of such bodies in Chapters 9 and 10.

Company law itself has come to the aid of the minority shareholder although the remedies afforded the minority shareholder against abuse of power and breach of duty by the company controllers are in practice seen very much as measures of last resort. The two major reasons for this are the uncertainty surrounding the scope of the particular remedies and the usual disincentive of the costs involved in litigation, which combine to deter minority legal action.

In this chapter, the principal common law and statutory remedies available to the minority shareholder will be considered. Of crucial importance at common law is the so-called rule in *Foss* v. *Harbottle* (1843) 2 Hare 461, which has proved a formidable obstacle to relief. We shall examine the circumstances in which a personal action (sometimes brought in 'representative' form on behalf of all shareholders who have the same interest) and/or a derivative action (so-called because it is brought by minority shareholders but in order to obtain relief for the company where the wrongdoers are in control of the company) can be brought. Statute then provides major specific remedies, notably in section 459, 1985 Act (petition for relief from unfair prejudice), in section 122, Insolvency Act 1986 (petition for a winding-up order) and in Part XIV, 1985 Act (Department of Trade and Industry investigations). We shall deal with sections 459 and 122 after outlining the common law position. Department of Trade investigations have been treated in Chapter 5.

(A) The common law position on minority protection

8.2.1 The rule in *Foss* v. *Harbottle*

Since the courts are notoriously reluctant to intervene in what they are apt to regard as matters of business judgment, the main obstacle to minority shareholder action takes the shape of a procedural rule known as the rule in *Foss* v. *Harbottle* (see [8.1] above and [8.2.2] below). The minority shareholder will be allowed to sue provided he can convince the court that his case falls within one of the so-called 'exceptions' to the rule in *Foss* v. *Harbottle*. In fact, some of these exceptions concern cases which really fall totally outside the ambit of the 'rule', but they are still commonly referred to as exceptions for convenience.

8.2.2 The rule explained

The rule in *Foss* v. *Harbottle* is in two parts, and the widest statement of the rule came in *MacDougall* v. *Gardiner* (1875) 1 ChD 13 at 25 where Lord Mellish said:

'In my opinion, if the thing complained of is a thing which in substance the majority of the company are entitled to do, or if something has been done irregularly which the majority of the company are entitled to do regularly, or if something has been done illegally which the majority of the company are entitled to do legally, there can be no use in having litigation about it, the ultimate end of which is only that a meeting has to be called, and then ultimately the majority gets its wishes. Is it not better that the rule should be adhered to that if it is a thing which the majority are the masters of, the majority in substance shall be entitled to have their will followed?'

This statement reflects the courts' concern to limit vexatious litigation which can serve no useful purpose and emphasises the 'majority rule' aspect to the rule. There is another aspect to the rule, however. This is sometimes referred to as the 'corporate limb' and it states that since the company is a separate person at law from its shareholders (*Salomon* v. *Salomon & Co. Ltd* [1897] AC 22) then where a wrong is done to the company it is the company and the company alone which may sue.

8.2.3 The questions raised by the rule

In each case, therefore, two questions need to be asked:

(a) Is what is alleged a wrong done to the company (e.g. a breach of duty by a director, who owes his duties only to the company – *Percival* v. *Wright* [1902] 2 Ch 421) or is it a wrong done to the shareholder? If it is only the former, then although the shareholder stands to suffer indirectly as a result of harm to the company, a personal action does not lie and *prima facie* the company should sue through the appropriate company organ (*Prudential Assurance Co. Ltd* v. *Newman Industries Ltd (No. 2)* [1982] 1 All ER 354 at 367); and
(b) Is the alleged wrong 'curable' by the majority? In the words of the classic statement by Lord Jenkins in *Edwards* v. *Halliwell* [1950] 2 All ER 1064:

'First, the proper plaintiff in an action in respect of a wrong alleged to be done to a company or association of persons is *prima facie* the company or association of persons itself. Secondly, where the alleged wrong is a transaction which might be made binding on the company or association and on all its members by a simple majority of the members, no individual member of the company is allowed to maintain an action in respect of that matter, for the simple reason that, if a mere majority of the members of the company or association is in favour of what has been done, then *cadet quaestio.*'

8.3   *The exceptions to the rule in* **Foss v. Harbottle**

The rule is therefore justified on various grounds. Multiplicity of actions, whereby numerous suits are commenced by numerous shareholders, is avoided by insisting that the company sue to redress a corporate wrong (*Gray* v. *Lewis* (1873) 8 Ch App 1035). The possibility of futile and vexatious litigation is allayed (see in addition to *MacDougall* v. *Gardiner* (1875) 10 Ch App 606, *Mozley* v. *Alston* (1847) 1 Ph 790). However, it has a major drawback where the alleged wrongdoers (the board or the majority shareholder(s)) are in control of the power of corporate litigation, i.e. where they are in a position to decide whether the company should sue. Where the sole defender of the company is the minority shareholder he may, by way of exception, be allowed to sue 'derivatively' under the 'fraud on the minority' exception (see [8.3.2.3] below). Therefore, the rule only applies to wrongs done to the company which the majority are in a position to cure. A minority shareholder can sue if:

(1) The wrong is, or involves, the breach of some personal right (see Chapter 2);
(2) A simple majority is not in a position to regularise or to do regularly what has been done 'irregularly'.

The so-called exceptions fall into either of these two categories.

8.3.1   Category 1

A personal action lies for the breach of a personal right. The difficulty is to establish that a personal right has been infringed and reference is made to what was said on this matter in Chapter 2. The remedy is a personal action for a declaration or an injunction (see [2.15] above) but if more than one shareholder has been injured in the same way and have the same interest in the proceedings it is possible for them to group together in a representative action (governed by Order 15, rule 12(1), Rules of the Supreme Court). The action is brought by a shareholder on behalf of himself and all other shareholders who have the same interest against the wrongdoers and the company if relief is also sought against the company.

8.3.2   Category 2

The remaining three 'exceptions' fall within this category, i.e. they deal with wrongs which are 'non-ratifiable' by simple majority. It is unclear why the line was drawn at a *simple* majority and it may be that the 'special majority' exception properly belongs under category 1 (see [8.3.2.2] below).

8.3.2.1 Illegality and ultra vires

In principle, a shareholder may sue:

(1) by way of personal or derivative action to restrain the commission by the company of an illegal or *ultra vires* act (an *'ultra vires'* act is one which the company has no legal capacity to enter into as a matter of interpretation of the objects clause in its memorandum of association – *Simpson* v. *Westminster Palace Hotel Co.* (1860) HL Cas 712; *Hoole* v. *G.W.R. Co.* (1861) 3 Ch App 262);
(2) by way of derivative action to recover company property disposed of to a third party by an *ultra vires* act (*Salomons* v. *Laing* (1850) 12 Beav 377; *Smith* v. *Croft (No. 3)* [1987] 3 BCC 218);
(3) by way of derivative action to compel the directors to compensate the company for loss suffered by it in consequence of an *ultra vires* act (*Spokes* v. *Grosvenor Hotel Co.* [1897] 2 QB 124; *Smith* v. *Croft (No. 3)* above).

The clarity of this exception has become somewhat blurred by recent cases. First came *Devlin* v. *Slough Estates Ltd* [1983] BCLC 497, which sets limits on the capacity of a single shareholder to enforce some statutory provisions (see above, [2.13.1]). Then came *Taylor* v. *N.U.M.* (unreported, but noted in *The Times*, 29 December 1984) where, in a union case, to which analogous principles apply, it was held that individual members were entitled to sue for orders restraining officers from making *ultra vires* payments but that an action to make the officers personally liable to restore company moneys wrongly paid out might be barred if the majority of members voted not to pursue the claim.

This case showed that the traditional approach to the exceptions to *Foss* v. *Harbottle* based on 'non-ratifiability' as the basic justification for allowing minority suit might be a serious over-simplification. Indeed it has recently been recognised in *Smith* v. *Croft (No. 3)* (above) that there is a difference between ratifying (or validating an act) and deciding not to sue (in respect of an act or omission). In this case the court adverted to the majority view among the independent (non-wrongdoing) minority and held that a minority action could not proceed in the face of a decision by the independent majority taken honestly with the interests of the company in view. This case is most important as evidence of the courts' willingness to test the 'independence' of the 'majority' by reference to whether there were reasonable grounds for their decision in the light of the interests of the company. The immediate point of interest here is that although an *ultra vires* act is not ratifiable and can never be ratified even by the unanimous votes of all shareholders (*Ashbury Railway Carriage & Iron Co.* v. *Riche* (1875) LR 7 HL 653) an independent majority among the minority can still block the derivative action. The test shifts from 'non-ratifiability' to 'control by the wrongdoers'. If these are not in control of the litigation decision, the majority's decision will be respected and majority rule will operate.

8.3.2.2   Special majorities

A shareholder may sue derivatively (or in a personal action if personal rights have been infringed) to have a general meeting resolution declared void and to restrain the company from acting on it if it should have been passed as a special or extraordinary resolution but was not (*Edwards* v. *Halliwell* [1950] 2 All ER 1064; *Wood* v. *Odessa Waterworks Co.* (1889) 42 ChD 636). The justification usually given for allowing minority suit in this case is that to allow a simple majority to 'ratify' would be to allow a simple majority to do by ordinary majority what the articles required to be done by a special majority. This begs the question as to why a minority shareholder, as opposed to the company itself, should be allowed to complain. The answer may lie in the words of Lord Jenkins in *Edwards* v. *Halliwell* (above) where two trade union members successfully restrained an attempt by the delegate meeting to increase the members' contribution without obtaining the two-thirds majority required by the rules. Lord Jenkins said:

> 'This is a case of a kind which is not even within the general ambit of the rule (in *Foss* v. *Harbottle*). It is not a case where what is complained of is a wrong done to the union ... it is a case in which ... the union...has invaded the *individual rights of the complainant members, who are entitled to maintain themselves in full membership* ... so long as they pay contributions in accordance with the tables of contributions ... unless and until the scale of contributions is validly altered by the prescribed majority.'

The difficulty is to reconcile such cases as *Edwards* v. *Halliwell* and *Salmon* v. *Quin & Axtens Ltd* [1909] AC 443 with cases like *Grant* v. *U.K. Switchback Rlys Co.* (1888) 40 ChD 135 and *Irvine* v. *Union Bank of Australia* (1877) 2 App Cas 366 (see also [3.8.4]). Presumably, no personal right was involved in either of the latter two cases, so that the 'wrong' would have been regarded as a mere 'internal irregularity' and ratifiable. The difficulty lies in drawing the line between the two kinds of case. This second exception in category 2 certainly overlaps with the 'personal rights' exception.

8.3.2.3 'Fraud on the minority' and 'wrongdoers in control'

(1) The derivative action

The only possible form of action here is a derivative action because the wrong against which relief is sought is always a wrong *to the company*. The action is brought by a shareholder formally on behalf of himself and all other shareholders except the alleged wrongdoers and is brought against the latter and the company. However, the company is only nominally a defendant. It cannot be joined as plaintiff because the minority have no authority to sue on its behalf, but it must be a party to the action if it is to be bound by, and take the benefit of, the judgment. Judgment is given for the company and not for the plaintiff. The essence of this exception, as viewed traditionally, is that the wrong is of a type which the company may not ratify and that the wrongdoers are in control of the power of corporate litigation. We shall look first at the requirement of 'control' and then at the concept of 'fraud on the minority'.

(2) 'Control'

The shareholder must be able to show that the company will be prevented from suing and must therefore have attempted to mobilise the appropriate company organ in whom the power of decision has been vested. The facts indicating this control must be alleged in the statement of claim in a derivative action and a *prima facie* case of control must be made out *in limine* (i.e. at the outset) if defendants seek to have the suit struck out as disclosing no cause of action (*Birch* v. *Sullivan* [1958] 1 All ER 56). If there is any doubt as to the ability of the wrongdoers to control litigation through control over a majority of the votes in general meeting, the court will direct the holding of a general meeting to decide the issue and the burden will fall on the plaintiff to show that control was exercised (*Prudential Assurance Co. Ltd* v. *Newman Industries Ltd* (No. 2) [1982] Ch 204 at 222, CA). By 'control' is usually meant majority voting control. This can be personal ownership of shares carrying voting rights or 'indirect', through voting shares held by nominees (*Pavlides* v. *Jensen* [1956] Ch 565) or where the directors whom it is sought to sue can influence the vote by casting votes attached to shares held by another company on whose board they sit (*ibid.*).

It has been pointed out that there can be control over the power of corporate litigation without voting control in general meeting, as where the articles vest the power exclusively in the board of directors (see Blake (1987) Vol. 5 Co. Law Digest p.19).

At first instance in *Prudential Assurance Co. Ltd* v. *Newman Industries Ltd* (No.2) [1981] Ch 257, Lord Vinelott mused whether 'control by the wrongdoers' might not become the overriding criterion for allowing a derivative action to proceed. He said:

> 'Whether the claim is for property improperly withheld or for damages for negligence or breach of fiduciary duty and, in the latter case, whether those controlling the company have or have not obtained some benefit, the reason for the ('fraud on the minority') exception is the same, namely that the claim is brought against persons whose interests conflict with the interest of the company.'

He had also argued for a wide definition of 'control' to include '*de facto*' control (control in fact) which he defined (at pp.324–325) as the ability of those persons against whom the action is sought to be brought on behalf of the company by any means of manipulation of their position in the company to ensure that the action is not brought by the company, so that there was no real possibility that the issue would ever be properly put to the shareholders. He further indicated that a derivative action might lie whenever justice required it. The Court of Appeal (speaking *obiter*, because by then the company had decided to take the benefit of the action) firmly rejected a general 'justice' exception as an 'impractical' test. Moreover, their Lordships emphasised the need for plaintiff to make out a *prima facie* case not only of control but also of 'fraud on the minority', leaving the scope of this open. It is to this second condition that we turn after pointing out that the 'control' element has been emphasised in the recent case of *Smith* v. *Croft (No. 3)* (above) where a non-ratifiable *ultra vires* act was in issue but the derivative action was not allowed to proceed because an independent majority were against the action.

(3) 'Fraud on the minority'
In *Prudential*, the Court of Appeal affirmed that:

> 'Whatever may be the properly defined boundaries of the exception to the rule (in *Foss* v. *Harbottle*), the plaintiff ought at least to be required ... to establish a *prima facie* case (i) that the company is entitled to the relief claimed and (ii) that the action falls within the proper boundaries of the exception ...'

That is to say that in a preliminary motion to strike out the action on the basis of *Foss* v. *Harbottle*, a *prima facie* case must be made out as to 'fraud' and 'control'.

'Fraud' in this context includes more than fraud at common law. It also covers fraud in the equitable sense of the term, as in the equitable concept of a fraud on a power, an abuse or misuse of power (*Estmanco (Kilner House) Ltd* v. *GLC* [1982] 1 All ER 437 at 445, Chapter 4, [4.5.3]). Applying the traditional 'non-ratifiability' criterion, some wrongs appear to be 'non-ratifiable' (and therefore are 'frauds') while others are not. The question is where to draw the line. As Mr Justice Vinelott put it at first instance in *Prudential*:

[The] authorities show that the exception [to the rule in *Foss* v. *Harbottle*] applies not only where the allegation is that directors who control a company have improperly appropriated to themselves money, property or advantages which belong to the company or, in breach of their duty to the company, have diverted business to themselves which ought to have been given to the company, but more generally where it is alleged that directors though acting 'in the belief that they were doing nothing wrong' (*per* Lindley MR in *Alexander* v. *Automatic Telephone Co.* [1900] 2 Ch 56) are guilty of a breach of duty to the company, including their duty to exercise proper care, and as a result of that breach obtain some benefit. In the latter case it must be unnecessary to allege and prove that the directors in breaking their duty to the company acted with a view to benefiting themselves at the expense of the company; for such an allegation would be an allegation of misappropriation of the company's property. On the other hand, the exception does not apply if all that is alleged is that directors who control a company are liable to the company for damages for negligence, it not being shown that the transaction was one in which they were interested or that they have in fact obtained any benefit from it. It is not easy to see precisely where the line between these cases is to be drawn ... Whether the claim is for property improperly withheld or for damages for negligence or breach of fiduciary duty and, in the latter case, whether those controlling the company have or have not obtained some benefit the reason for the exception is the same, namely that the claim is brought against persons whose interests conflict with the interest of the company.'

The generally accepted position, as approached on the traditional 'ratifiability' analysis, is as follows:

(A)   Non-ratifiable

(a)   Misappropriation of corporate assets and *mala fide* exercise of power
In *Cook* v. *Deeks* [1916] AC 554 the directors diverted a contract, which the company was actively pursuing, to themselves and then purported as majority shareholders to 'ratify' their conduct by passing a resolution declaring that the company had no interest in the contract. It was held that the majority could not be allowed to ratify their own breach of duty and that a derivative action lay. Lord Buckmaster said that:

> 'it appears quite certain that directors holding a majority of votes would not be permitted to make a present to themselves ... a resolution that the rights of the company should be disregarded in the matter would amount to forfeiting the interest and property of the minority of shareholders in favour of the majority, and that by the votes of those who are interested in securing the property for themselves. Such use of voting power has never been sanctioned ... and was expressly disapproved in the case of *Menier* v. *Hooper's Telegraph Works*.'

The reference to *Menier's case* (1874) 9 Ch App 350 indicates that this type of 'fraud' extends to the abuse of power by the majority in general meeting. In this case, a derivative action lay where the majority compromised an action in which the company was involved in return for the grant by the other party of a cable-laying contract to themselves in another guise. This court approach was followed in *Estmanco* v. *GLC* (above) where Megarry J held, in one of the most significant cases on the subject, that a majority resolution ordering the board to discontinue an action brought by the company against the majority (the GLC) amounted to just such a fraud on a power as constituted a 'fraud on the minority' (see further *Millers (Invercargill) Ltd* v. *Maddams* [1938] NZLR 490 (New Zealand Court of Appeal; *Atwool* v. *Merryweather* (1867) 5 Eq 464n).

It is to be noted that *Cook* v. *Deeks* did not clearly answer the question: what if an *independent* majority ratifies or decides not to proceed with action against the wrongdoers? It may be that an independent majority can ratify any 'fraud on the minority', or at least decide not to sue whatever the 'wrong', the assumption being that since they are 'independent' they so decide in the best interests of the company. This was Mr Justice Vinelott's view in *Prudential* v. *Newman Industries (No. 2)*

[1981] 1 Ch 257 at p. 323. Indeed, in *Bamford* v. *Bamford* [1970] Ch 212 the Court of Appeal assumed '*mala fides*' but still allowed ratification and did not disenfranchise the alleged wrongdoers except to the extent of new votes acquired as a result of the alleged breach of duty in issuing new shares for an 'improper purpose'. Perhaps the court was somewhat lax in its use of language. However, *Smith* v. *Croft (No. 3)* now provides support for Mr Justice Vinelott's approach in *Prudential* (see further below under 'Developments').

(b) 'Self-serving negligence'
In *Daniels* v. *Daniels* [1978] Ch 406, directors sold a corporate asset to one of their number for £4,250. Four years later, he sold it for £120,000. Lord Templeman said:

'In *Pavlides* v. *Jensen* [1956] Ch 565, it was alleged that directors had been guilty of gross negligence in selling a valuable asset of the company at a price greatly below its true market value ... Danckwerts J struck out the statement of claim as disclosing no cause of action because no fraud was pleaded ... the authorities which deal with simple fraud on the one hand and gross negligence on the other do not cover the situation which arises where, without fraud, the directors and majority shareholders are guilty of a breach of duty which ... not only harms the company but benefits the directors ... If minority shareholders can sue if there is fraud, I see no reason why they cannot sue where the action of the majority and the directors, though without fraud, confers some benefit on those directors and majority shareholders themselves ... To put up with foolish directors is one thing, to put up with directors who are so foolish that they make a profit of £115,000 at the expense of the company is something entirely different ... *the principle* which may be gleaned from *Alexander* v. *Automatic Telephone Co.*, *Cook* v. *Deeks* and from *dicta* in *Pavlides* v. *Jensen* is that a minority shareholder who has no other remedy may sue where directors use their powers intentionally or unintentionally, fraudulently or negligently, in a manner which benefits themselves at the expense of the company.'

Some commentators argued that after this judgment few wrongs remained 'ratifiable' (Prentice (1979) Conv. 47) but the preponderance of opinion, despite Lord Templeman's clear language, was to the effect that *Daniels* was simply another example of 'non-ratifiable' misappropriation of corporate assets (Boyle (1980) 1 Co. Law 3; Wedderburn (1978) 41 MLR 589).

(B)   Ratifiable (albeit by the votes of the wrongdoers)

(1) Mere negligence is 'ratifiable' (*Pavlides* v. *Jensen*, above).
(2) A *bona fide* exercise of power for a collateral purpose appears to be 'ratifiable' (*Bamford* v. *Bamford* [1970] Ch 212; *Hogg* v. *Cramphorn Ltd* [1967] Ch 254; see Chapter 3, [3.4]).
(3) The making of an 'incidental' secret profit out of one's position as a director in the absence of *mala fides* is ratifiable (*Regal Hastings Ltd* v. *Gulliver* [1967] 2 AC 134n).

(4)   Developments
(A)   Smith v. *Croft (No.3)*
Since, as a matter of additional principle, a shareholder may vote in his own interests even where these conflict with those of the company (see Chapter 4, [4.5.1]) the traditional view has been that a wrong-doing director may vote as a shareholder to ratify his own misconduct. However, we saw in Chapter 4 that the law may be changing. The traditional principle is under attack on several fronts. *Smith* v. *Croft (No. 3)* is the latest development on this issue.

In *Smith* v. *Croft (No. 3)* [1987] BCC 218 the court deferred to the wishes of the independent majority. The allegation in the statement of claim was that the directors had improperly made illegal and *ultra vires* payments. A minority shareholder sued derivatively to recover from the directors the sums so paid out. Knox J held that there was indeed a difference between ratifying and deciding not to sue and that while an *ultra vires* act cannot be 'ratified' (even unanimously) it is open to the company to decide not to sue for the recovery of assets paid out. The court would throw out the derivative action if an independent majority (i.e. a majority of the non-implicated shareholders) so decided. However, the court insisted on 'independence', to be tested by reference to whether it could reasonably be said that those who had voted had done so with the interests of the company predominantly in view. For this purpose, the alleged wrongdoers were 'disenfranchised'; their votes would be ignored, (see also *Prudential* v. *Newman Industries Ltd (No.2)* [1981] 1 Ch 257 at 323).

To put this development in context and thus explain why we have referred to the fraud on the minority exceptions as being 'traditionally' based in the 'non-ratifiability' criterion, we need to refer once again to Mr Justice Vinelott's comments in *Prudential* v. *Newman (No.2)*. There, he said ([1980] 2 All ER 841 at 862; [1981] 1 Ch 257 at 307) that:

'The fraud lies in (the) use of ... voting power, not in the character of the act or transaction giving rise to the cause of action ... (I)f the persons against whom an action might be brought do not control the company there is no obvious limit to the power of the majority to resolve in general meeting to condone the injury to the company or not to pursue the action whatever may have been the act or transaction giving rise to the cause of action and whether fraudulent or not. There may be good practical reasons why the claim should not be pursued, for instance because of the potential injury to the reputation of the company or because the prospect of recovery would not justify the expense of litigation. The difficulty cannot be resolved by defining the limit of the exception to the rule in *Foss* v. *Harbottle* by reference to any category of acts or transactions which are incapable of being authorised or ratified by the majority in general meeting. For, again, there is no obvious limit to the power of the majority to authorise or ratify any act or transaction whatever its character provided that it is not *ultra vires* or unlawful and that the majority does not have an interest which conflicts with that of the company.'

It will be remembered that in *Smith* v. *Croft (No. 3)* the fact that the act complained of was *ultra vires* and therefore non-ratifiable did not prevent the court – once convinced that the independent majority had reasonable grounds for deciding, in the company's interests, not to sue – from disallowing the derivative action. What is most noteworthy is that the non-ratifiability analysis is clearly inadequate. If non-ratifiability is no longer a criterion for allowing a derivative action this leaves only 'control'. This would lead to the highly acceptable result that a derivative action lies whenever the wrongdoers are in control irrespective of whether there had been 'fraud'. The fraud lies in the wrongdoers preventing action against themselves. Thus, principle would not preclude an action against directors simply because they were only being accused of negligence or making an incidental secret profit, or exercising a power *bona fide* but for an improper purpose (see above, [8.3.2.3(3))]).

On the other hand, where the alleged wrongdoers were not in control, majority rule would continue to prevail with one important qualification, namely it would prevail only on the assumption that the majority were 'independent'. For the purpose of testing this independence, votes should be disregarded if the court was satisfied either (a) that they were actually cast with a view to supporting the defendants rather than securing benefit to the company, or (b) that the situation of the person whose vote was being considered was such that there was a substantial risk of that happening. The court has to assess whether the decision-making process was vitiated by being, or being likely to be, directed to an improper purpose – an 'improper purpose' being any other than the securing the interest of the company. All this emerges from *Smith* v. *Croft (No. 3)* (above), which therefore breaks with the 'non-ratifiability' criterion and provides strong recent support for the principle that the views of the majority only demand respect when the majority can be said to have acted *bona fide* in the best interests of the company. The court will clearly conduct an inquiry into the facts in order to establish that the majority can on reasonable grounds be said to have so acted (see *Smith* v. *Croft (No. 3)*).

It would be quite illogical, where ratification by the company is possible, to allow the alleged wrongdoers to do the *ratifying*, while preventing them from participating in the decision as to whether or not the company should sue them. If the courts are finally giving priority to *company* interests, *Smith* v. *Croft (No.3)* is a basis for disenfranchisement in other contexts, and particularly that of ratification.

(B)   The Draft Fifth EEC Directive

Under Article 14 of the Draft Directive (O.J. 1983 No. C.240/2), Member States will be obliged to make such provision relating to the civil liability of members of the management organ and of the supervisory organ (depending on the structure adopted for the public company by national laws) as to ensure that, at minimum, compensation is made for all damage sustained by the company as a result of breaches of law or of the memorandum or articles or of other wrongful acts committed by the members of those organs in carrying out their duties (article 14(1)).

It will be readily noticed that article 14, coupled with article 16 (below) will allow for a derivative action on the widest possible grounds, far wider than those which English law has traditionally provided. Furthermore, any 'discharge', instruction or authorisation given by the general meeting shall not have the effect of exempting the members of the management organ or the supervisory organ from civil liability (article 14(5)). It is provided that proceedings on behalf of the company to enforce this liability shall be commenced not only if the general meeting so resolves by ordinary majority (article 15), but also if requested by a qualified minority of shareholders (article 16(1)).

In the latter case, the shareholders who requested that proceedings be commenced may be ordered to pay all or part of the costs if the court considers that no reasonable grounds existed for commencing the proceedings (article 16(2)). While the company in general meeting may resolve to renounce its right to sue to enforce 'article 14 liability', this will in no way affect the qualified minority right in article 16. Moreover, nothing in the other provisions in any way restricts the personal liability of members of the company's organs towards shareholders personally or towards third parties pursuant to the general civil law set down in national 'legislation' (article 19).

On the last point, saving the word 'legislation' it must be noted that the Draft Directive makes no effort to harmonise the 'civil law' on personal liability towards shareholders personally, and therefore the law as it relates, for example, to enforcement of the articles will remain as expounded in Chapter 2.

However, major developments will ensue in English Law. In particular, Article 18 insists on an express renunciation by the company of the right to sue members of its organs. A qualified minority may sue despite this, and have the company finance the suit provided they act reasonably. However, an individual shareholder who does not qualify under article 16 will not be able to bring a derivative action. This will mark a retrogression in terms of minority protection under English Law. On the other hand, article 14(5) (above) will lead to a different result in such a case as *Multinational Gas and Petrochemical Co.* v. *Multinational Gas and Petrochemical Services Ltd* [1983] Ch 258 where it was held that a company had no remedy because the directors had been authorised in advance by the members to act, effectively, in breach of duty. Their approval, it was held, made the directors' act the act of the company, which was now unable to complain (but see Lord May's strong dissenting judgment at p.280). Furthermore, article 17(1) provides that the bringing of proceedings to enforce article 14 liability may not be made subject (whether by law, the memorandum or articles or any agreement) either to (a) prior resolution of the general meeting or other organ of the company or (b) prior decision of the court in respect of wrongful acts on the part of the members of the management or supervisory organ. However, Member States may provide that the proceedings commenced under article 16 (i.e. at the request of a qualified minority of shareholders) may not be brought without prior court permission, which the court may refuse if the action is 'clearly unfounded'.

Article 17 will do two things. In paragraph (a) it will leave all possible avenues for suit open. In para. (b), it will prevent the sort of exercise which we witnessed at first instance in *Prudential Assurance* v. *Newman Industries* [1981] Ch 257 where the court required to be convinced that there had been a breach of duty before allowing proceedings to be instituted by the minority for the purpose of establishing that breach of duty! The Court of Appeal criticised this approach and clearly stated that the plaintiff must make out a *prima facie* case before the court will go fully into the merits. Article 16 enables a qualified minority to sue and article 17(b) will prohibit the placing of any such obstacles as a need to show 'control by the wrongdoers' in their way. However, the individual shareholder is worse off in so far as he does not qualify under article 16, for in this case he cannot sue except to remedy personal loss caused to himself by a breach of duty owed to himself. But the duties owed by members of the company's organs are owed not to him but to the company, under English law. If a different premise underlies the Draft Fifth Directive it should have been expressly incorporated into a revised article 19.

(5)   Costs

In *Wallersteiner* v. *Moir (No.2)* [1975] 1 All ER 849, the Court of Appeal held that in a minority shareholder's action the court could order that the company should indemnify the plaintiff against the costs of the action. A plaintiff may apply in the initial stages of the proceedings for an order approving their continuance. In any ordinary case, the order should not be made *ex parte* i.e. the company should be joined as a party and be able to lay the facts before the court. The test to be applied by the court in deciding whether the minority shareholders were entitled to an indemnity is whether an independent board of directors, exercising the standard of care which prudent businessmen would exercise in their own affairs, would consider that the shareholders ought to bring their action. The court would take account of the views of the independent majority. Furthermore, it is incumbent on plaintiffs to show that the '*Wallersteiner* v. *Moir* order' is genuinely needed, i.e. that they do not have sufficient resources to finance the action (see, on these points, *Smith* v. *Croft* (1986) 2 BCC 99,010).

A *Wallersteiner* v. *Moir* order is also available where a company action is the relief being sought under section 459 (below), but not where, although there has been a 'theoretical' breach of duty to the company (as where the directors use their power to allot shares for an improper purpose), the substance of the claim is that the personal contractual rights of the petitioner have been infringed and the relief sought is limited to that injury (*Re A Company No. 005136 of 1986*, [1987] BCLC 82).

8.4 (B) Statutory protection of the minority

8.4.1 Section 459, 1985 Act

Section 459(1) provides that:

'A member of a company may apply to the court by petition for an order under this Part (Part XVII of the Act) on the ground that the company's affairs are being or have been conducted in a manner which is unfairly prejudicial to the interests of some part of the members (including at least himself) or that any actual or proposed act or omission of the company (including an act or omission on its behalf) is or would be so prejudicial.'

The provisions of Part XVII apply also to non-members to whom shares in the company have been transferred or transmitted by operation of law (section 459(2)). The mere fact of an agreement to transfer a share, without execution of the transfer, does not entitle the intended transferee to petition under section 459 (*Re A Company No. 003160 of 1986* (1986) 2 BCC 99, 276 and *Re Quickdome Ltd* (1988) 4 BCC 296). Nor will such a share have been allotted to the intended transferee, so that he is not a 'contributory' within section 124, Insolvency Act 1986, and may not petition for a winding-up under section 122, Insolvency Act 1986 (*Re Quickdome Ltd*, above).

'Transmission by operation of law' means some act in law by which the legal estate (legal ownership) passes, even though there might be some further act (such as registration) to be done. The allegation of the existence of a constructive trust could not amount to a transmission by operation of law (*Re A Company No. 007828 of 1985*, (1986) 2 BCC 98, 951). The Secretary of State for Trade and Industry is also empowered to apply for an order (section 460).

8.4.2 Orders for relief: general

If the court is satisfied that a Section 459 petition is well-founded, it may make such an order as it thinks fit for giving relief in respect of the matters complained of (section 461(1)). There are no limits to the court's discretion in the matter of relief orders, but section 461(2) helpfully lists four possible remedies, without prejudice to the generality of section 461(1). These are:

(a) an order regulating the conduct of the company's affairs in the future [In *Re H.R. Harmer Ltd* [1959]] 1 WLR 62, a case decided under section 210, 1948 Act, the forerunner of section 459, the court ordered that the autocratic founder of a successful private company should no longer interfere in the affairs of the company otherwise than in accordance with the valid decision of the board, that he should be appointed president of the company for life and that this office should not impose any duties, rights or powers.];

(b) an order requiring the company to refrain from doing or continuing an act complained of by the petitioner or to do an act which the petitioner has complained it has omitted to do [This includes ordering the company to make, or not to make, an alteration in its memorandum or articles (section 461(3),(4)).];

(c) an order authorising civil proceedings to be brought in the name and on behalf of the company by such person or persons and on such terms as the court may direct [This provides a sort of 'statutory derivative action'.];

(d) an order providing for the purchase of the shares of any members of the company by other members or by the company itself and, in the case of a purchase by the company itself, the reduction of the company's capital accordingly.

8.4.3   The interests *'qua member'* requirement of section 459

8.4.3.1   *Qua member*

The unfair prejudice complained of must affect a member's interests *'qua member'* i.e. enjoyed in his capacity as member. This is as much a requirement under section 459 as it was under the 'old' section 210, 1948 Act, which it replaced (see for example, *Re A Company No. 004475 of 1982*, [1983] 2 All ER 36; *Re a Company No. 002567 of 1982*, [1983] 1 WLR 927; *Re Carrington Viyella plc* (1983) *Financial Times*, 16 February; *Re London School of Electronics* [1985] 3 WLR 474; *Re a Company No. 00477 of 1986* [1986] 2 BCC 99,171). However, the courts are interpreting and applying it liberally. This contrasts with the approach under the old section 210, 1948 Act where the dismissal from directorial or other office of a member was held never to amount to oppression *qua member* (*Elder* v. *Elder & Watson* (1952) SC 49, Scottish Court of Session; *Re Lundie Bros Ltd* [1985] 1 WLR 1051).

Where a member only became such on the understanding that he would be involved in management and in circumstances justifying an expectation on his part that he would be so involved, his unfair exclusion from management amounts to unfair prejudice affecting his interests as a member (*Re a Company No. 002567*, above *obiter*; *Re London School of Electronics*, above; *Re a Company No. 00477 of 1986*, above).

The 'circumstances' which give rise to a legitimate expectation will vary from case to case but in the case of 'managerial expectations' they must come broadly within those sketched by Lord Wilberforce in *Ebrahimi* v. *Westbourne Galleries Ltd* ([1973] AC 360, see [8.5] below) – i.e. the company must be a 'quasi-partnership company' (or an 'incorporated partnership'). Therefore, when the articles of a public company provided that petitioner should be removable by ordinary resolution in general meeting it was held that there could have been no legitimate expectation on her part that the article would never be varied by special resolution to permit removal by the board. No private informal agreement among the directors could justify the holding of that expectation when the circumstances were that outside investors would become shareholders in ignorance of such an agreement (*Re Blue Arrow plc* [1987] 3 BCC 618). While not applied in petitioner's favour in the case last cited the principle of the case is most important. It was set out in *Cumbrian Newspapers* v. *Cumberland & Westmorland Herald* [1987] Ch 1 (see Chapter 7, [7.2.3.5]). 'Outsider rights' which are really 'membership rights' within the reasoning of these two cases are enforceable through section 459 and should be enforceable also by personal action.

8.4.3.2 Interests

Most of the cases mentioned above adopt a liberal interpretation of the *qua member* requirement through reliance on the presence of the word 'interests' (*Re a Company 002567 of 1982*, above). In the relatively recent case of *Re a Company 00477 of 1986* (above) Hoffmann J elaborated. He said:

> '(The application of the *qua member* requirement) must take into account that the interests of a member are not necessarily limited to his strict legal rights under the constitution of the company. The use of the word 'unfairly' in section 459, like the use of the words 'just and equitable' in section (122(1)(g) Insolvency Act 1986), enables the court to have regard to wider equitable considerations.'

Therefore, legitimate expectations and interests are also protected (see also *Re a Company No. 008699 of 1985* (1986) 2 BCC 99,024). To hold otherwise would be to return to the narrow construction of section 210, 1948 Act under which in effect there was a requirement of 'independent (i.e. from section 210 itself) unlawfulness'. However, the question arises whether the use of the word 'unfairly' creates a 'general jurisdiction of unfairness'. In *Re Posgate and Denby (Agencies) Ltd* (1986) BCC 99,352 non-voting shareholders claimed that for the voting members to decide on a particular asset sale without the non-voting shareholders having a vote in general meeting would be 'unfairly prejudicial'. Hoffmann J held that had there not been an express denial of the right to vote he might have superimposed an obligation of fairness using the section 459 jurisdiction so as to require approval of the proposal by equity non-voting shareholders. If this is so, the majority in general meeting is now effectively under an obligation to 'act fairly'. However, it has been pointed out that it is the conduct which must be unfair to membership interests, and that section 459 was never intended to create interests under some general concept of fairness (Jill Poole, (1987) 8 Co. Law 33). In reply it might be argued that the vesting of a right to vote could be the appropriate remedy against 'unfair conduct' affecting interests and certainly the minority members in *Re Posgate and Denby* had an interest in ensuring that the asset sale did not take place at an undervalue.

8.4.4   'Some part of the members (including at least himself)'

The cases suggest that if all members stand to suffer *qua members*, a remedy will not lie (*Re Carrington Viyella plc*, see [8.4.3.1] above). It has been held that the failure by the board to recommend the payment of reasonable dividends does not ground a petition under section 459. This is because, although the legitimate expectations of the members to receive reasonable dividends are thereby ignored, all the members are prejudiced thereby and, there being no discrimination between members the failure to pay dividends is not unfairly prejudicial to some part of the members, as is required by section 459. The appropriate remedy is to petition for the compulsory winding-up of the company under section 122(1)(g) of the Insolvency Act 1986 (see [8.5] below). (*In Re a Company No. 00370 of 1987*, *The Times*, 5 July, 1988). However, one presumes that where the majority have 'other fish to fry', that is where they stand to gain in some other capacity from the conduct complained of, the court will hold that the requirement is satisfied (see *Scottish Co-operative Wholesale Society Ltd* v. *Meyer* [1959] AC 324, AC, decided under the old section 210, 1948 Act).

8.4.5   'Unfairly prejudicial' conduct, acts or omissions
'Unfairness'

Slade J, in *Re Bovey Hotel Ventures Ltd* (31 July 1981, unreported) said:

'The test of unfairness must ... be an objective, not a subjective, one ...(I)t is not necessary for the petitioner to show that the persons who have *de facto* control of the company have acted as they did in the conscious knowledge that this was unfair to the petitioner or that they were acting in bad faith; the test, I think, is whether a reasonable bystander observing the consequences of their conduct, would regard it as having unfairly prejudiced the petitioner's interests.'

Applying this test, Nourse J held, in *Re R.A. Noble & Sons (Clothing) Ltd* [1983] BCLC 273, that no relief lay where petitioner had brought his exclusion from management upon himself through his own lack of interest in the company's affairs. Also, if there is an irretrievable breakdown in relations, exclusion from management of one member is not *ipso facto* (even in *Ebrahimi*-type circumstances) unfair prejudice. That depends on whether it is reasonable that one director should leave rather than the other or others, and upon the terms which the excluded member was offered for his shares or in compensation for his loss of employment (*Re XYZ Ltd* (1986) 2 BCC 99, 520; *Re a Company No. 003096 of 1987*, (1988) 4 BCC 80).

In *Re a Company No. 008699 of 1985* (1986) 2 BCC 99,024, Hoffmann J held that if the directors of a private company chose to advise shareholders on competing take-over offers, fairness required that such advice should be factually accurate and given with a view to enabling the shareholders to sell at the best price.

We saw in Chapter 2 that a qualified minority of shareholders may requisition the convening of a general meeting by the directors under section 132, 1985 Act. The directors have 21 days within which to convene the meeting. In *McGuinness & Anor* (1988) 4 BCC 161 it was held that it was sufficient for section 132 purposes that the meeting was convened or 'called' within 21 days albeit not held within that time (see also *Re Windward Islands (Enterprises) UK Ltd* (1988) 4 BCC 158) but that *prima facie* a delay of seven months between the deposit of the requisition and the holding of the meeting was prejudicial to the interests of the petitioners as being unreasonably long. The court went on to hold that the prejudice was also unfair, on the facts of the case, and granted relief in the form of an order as to the holding of the meeting on a date fixed by the court.

Further Examples of Proscribed Conduct?
In *Re Bovey Hotel Ventures Ltd* (above), Slade J said:

'... without prejudice to the generality of the wording of the section, which may cover many other situations, a member of a company will be able to bring himself within the section if he can show that the value of his shareholding ... has been seriously diminished or at least seriously jeopardised.'

and

'(W)hile I can think of many hypothetical cases that might fall within section (459) but would not fall within section 210, I can think of no hypothetical cases which, though giving rise to the courts' jurisdiction under section 210, would not give rise to such jurisdiction under section (459).'

Section 210 was differently worded and required 'oppressive' conduct. This was defined as conduct which was 'burdensome, harsh or wrongful' importing that the minority were constrained to submit to something which was unfair to them as a result of some overbearing act or attitude on the part of the oppressor (see *Re Jermyn Street Turkish Baths Ltd* [1971] 1 WLR 1042; *Re Five-Minute Car Wash Service Ltd* [1966] 1 WLR 745; *Re H.R. Harmer Ltd* [1959] 1 WLR 62; *Scottish Co-operative Wholesale Society Ltd* v. *Meyer* [1959] AC 324). An allegation of negligence or incompetence would not suffice (*Re Five Minute Car Wash Service Ltd* [1966] 1 All ER 242). An open question is whether it suffices as an allegation of 'unfairly prejudicial' conduct for section 459 purposes, bearing in mind that section 459 is intended as a more liberal measure, but that prejudice must not be suffered, apparently, by *all* members (see [8.4.4] above). At least, the fact that prejudice is 'indirect' is no obstacle (as it is to a personal action – *Prudential Assurance* v. *Newman Industries*, [8.2.3] above). See *Re London School of Electronics Ltd* [1985] BCLC 273.

In *Re Jermyn Street Turkish Baths Ltd* [1971] 1 WLR 1042, no relief was given under section 210 in a case where the majority shareholder had received allegedly excessive remuneration while making a great managerial contribution to the company's prosperity. However, under section 210, petitioner was required to show a course of oppressive conduct and it may be that such a case would be decided differently under section 459.

8.4.6   'Proposed acts or omissions'

It has been held that a vague apprehension in petitioner's mind that at some stage in the future the controllers of a company may harbour an intention to commit an act which would be unfairly prejudicial does not suffice (*Re Gorwyn Holdings Ltd* [1985] 1 BCC 99,47). However, it is not necessary that there be an immediate threat that the offending resolutions will be passed. It is generally sufficient that an act is proposed which, if carried out or completed, would be unfairly prejudicial. Also it is sufficient that the affairs of the company have in the past been conducted in a manner unfairly prejudicial to petitioner even though at the date of the petition the unfairness has been remedied. The question whether an order is required to protect the interests of petitioner from the consequences of unfair conduct or of an act which has been proposed and which may again be proposed is one to be answered at the hearing of the petition (*Re Kenyon Swansea Ltd* [1987] 3 BCC 260).

8.4.7 Petitioner's conduct

It was held in *Re London School of Electronics Ltd* [1985] BCLC 273, [1985] 3 WLR 474, that petitioner's conduct might be relevant in two ways: (a) it might render prejudice 'fair' (see *R.A. Noble & Sons Ltd*, [8.4.5] above) and (b) even if there were unfair prejudice, it might affect the relief which the court might think fit to order.

8.4.8 Orders for relief

8.4.8.1 *Order for share purchase*

Probably, the most common order will remain the order for the purchase of shares (section 461(2)(d)). It has been held that such an order can be made against a person who is no longer a member of the company (*Re a Company [1986]* BCLC 68). As a rule, the shares are to be valued *pro rata*, with no discount for a minority holding (*Re Bird Precision Bellows Ltd* [1984] 3 All ER 414). The valuation will usually be back-dated to the date of commencement of the unfairly prejudicial conduct (*Re O.C. (Transport) Services Ltd* [1984] BCLC 251). If the articles provide a method for determining the fair value of shares, a member seeking to sell them on a breakdown of relations should not ordinarily be able to complain of 'unfair prejudice' if he had made no attempt to use that machinery [*Re XYZ Ltd*, [8.4.5] above; *Re a Company No. 007623 of 1984* (1986) 2 BCC 99,191).

8.4.8.2 *Other orders*

Other possible orders could include the removal of company officers (*Re H.R. Harmer Ltd*, [8.4.2] above); more doubtfully, the appointment of a receiver (*Re Hannetta Ltd* (1953) 216 LT Jo 639), the alteration of voting and class rights (*Re Posgate & Denby (Agencies) Ltd*, [8.4.3.2] above); the reduction of capital, the alteration of the company constitution; the calling of meetings with possible disenfranchisement of certain shareholders to ensure 'independence' in *Smith* v. *Croft No. 3* terms (see [8.3.2.3](3) above).

8.4.8.3   *Corporate action as relief ordered*

Where the court authorises the bringing of a corporate action (section 461(2)(c)), the 'authorised person' will not be liable for costs except to the extent ordered by the court. It remains to be seen how far, if at all, the courts are influenced, consciously or otherwise, by the rule in *Foss* v. *Harbottle* and its exceptions, in considering whether to grant this particular form of relief.

8.4.9   Relationship with other remedies

The availability of a derivative action does not preclude a section 459 petition (*Re a Company* [1986] BCLC 68). Also, a winding-up petition under section 122, Insolvency Act 1986 may be made as an alternative to a Section 459 petition (*Re a Company No. 007828 of 1985* (1986) 2 BCC 98,951). Since winding-up is the remedy of last resort a prospective 'section 122' petitioner may be restrained if 'acting unreasonably' in seeking a winding-up petition in lieu of a share-purchase order under section 459. This is the effect of section 125(2), Insolvency Act 1986 (*Coulson Sanderson & Ward Ltd* v. *Ward* (1987) 3 BCC, 99,207). Section 125(2), Insolvency Act 1986 provides that where a petition is made under section 122(1)(g) of that Act and the court is of the opinion that (a) while petitioner has made out a case for winding-up yet (b) another remedy is available to petitioner and (c) that he is acting unreasonably in failing to pursue that other remedy, then the court is not obliged to make a winding-up order (see also *Re a Company No. 002567 of 1982*, [1983] 2 All ER 854). Therefore, if section 459 is open to petitioner, a winding-up order will probably not be made. Under the old section 210, the courts' narrow interpretation of the section forced petitioner and the courts themselves to order the winding-up of otherwise viable companies. The more liberal the approach to section 459 the less recourse there will be to compulsory winding-up.

The main advantage of a section 459 petition over a personal action is that damages would appear to be available in the former case but not in the latter (see Chapter 2, [2.15] above).

8.5 Winding-up on the 'just and equitable' ground: section 122(1)(g) Insolvency Act 1986

It has been held, without prejudice to the generality of the section, that it is just and equitable that a company be wound up on a minority shareholder petition if:

(1) the company has abandoned its 'substratum', or main objects, or it becomes impossible to pursue them and the objects are not validly altered (Re German Date Coffee Co (1882) 20 ChD 169);

(2) there is no bona fide intention of carrying on business in a proper manner or the company has been formed for an illegal or improper purpose (Re T.E. Brinsmead & Sons [1897] 1 Ch 406);

(3) there is deadlock in the management which cannot be resolved by internal company machinery (Re Yenidye Tobacco Co. Ltd [1916] 2 Ch 426).

(4) a full and impartial investigation into the company's affairs is required (Re Peruvian Amazon Co. Ltd [1913] 29 TLR 384; Re The Varieties Ltd (1893) 2 Ch 235; Re Armvent Ltd [1975] 3 All ER 41);

(5) the articles provide for winding-up in the events which have occurred (Re American Pioneer Leather Co. Ltd [1918] 1 Ch 556),

(6) there has been lack of probity involving serious oppression of the minority, whether as members or in some other capacity (Loch v. John Blackwood Ltd [1924] AC 783, Re Lundie Bros Ltd [1965] 2 All ER 692);

(7) where the legitimate expectations of members have been defeated in circumstances where this was not reasonably required in the interests of the company, a winding-up order may be made. An example of this is where the board fail to recommend reasonable dividends. In Re a Company No. 00370 of 1987 (The Times 5 July, 1988), Harman J said that if the directors simply piled up profits in the company and did not distribute them (subject to the proper needs of the company to ensure that it was not trading in a risky manner and that there were adequate reserves for commercial purposes) the members could, if these facts were adequately proved, petition for a winding-up because the proper and legitimate expectations of members had been defeated.

(8) Where the company is in substance an 'incorporated partnership' and there are grounds on which a partnership would be dissolved. The classic case is Ebrahimi v. Westbourne Galleries Ltd [1973] AC 360, HL, where a minority shareholder was removed from office under what is now section 303, 1985 Act. In substance, this means that

the courts will subject the exercise (even *bona fide*) of legal rights to equitable considerations, i.e. considerations of a personal character arising between one individual and another which might make it unjust or inequitable to insist on strict legal rights or to exercise them in a particular way ([1973] AC 360 at 379). In *Ebrahimi* it was found that there was an underlying agreement that all members would participate in management.

Not every small private company qualifies as an 'incorporated partnership'. Lord Wilberforce suggested ([1973] AC 360 at 379) that one or more of the following elements should occur:

(1) an association formed or continued on the basis of a personal relationship, involving mutual confidence;
(2) an agreement that all or some of the members shall participate in the management of the business;
(3) restrictions on the transfer of the member's interest in the company.

It may be that most of the older cases, particularly those on deadlock and lack of probity can be subsumed under this category for the sake of clarity and convenience of exposition (Farrar, *op. cit.*, p. 375). However, the central point is that the categories are in no way closed, as was emphasised in the *Ebrahimi* case itself.

8.6   Conclusion to Part One

In a book on shareholder rights it is easy to give the false impression that the law in general, and company law in particular, is concerned solely with the rights and interests of the shareholders. This is not so and it is increasingly becoming less so.

Creditors, and this includes debenture holders, have substantial protection – a protection commonly afforded at the expense of shareholders. They can enforce *ultra vires* contracts provided they entered into them in good faith (section 35, 1985 Act). Rigorous rules exist on the maintenance of capital (i.e. the prohibition against its return to members) and at common law it now seems that a company owes a duty to its creditors (exercisable through its directors) to keep its property inviolate and available for the payment of its debts. The directors owe a duty to the company and its creditors to ensure that its property is not dissipated or exploited for the benefit of the directors themselves to the prejudice of its creditors (*Winkworth* v. *Edward Baron*

Development Co. Ltd & Ors (1987) 3 BCC 4). Creditors take priority *vis à vis* members over the company's assets on a winding-up (see Chapter 7, [7.3]).

Countless other legislative provisions ensure that creditors are accorded due protection. It is most noteworthy that in *Brady and Anor* v. *Brady and Anor* (*The Times*, 4 September 1987) the Court of Appeal stated that the phrase 'the interests of the company' in section 153, 1985 Act, involved the interests both of its shareholders *and* of its creditors. (This judgment was reversed on other grounds by the House of Lords, *The Times*, 20 May 1988.)

The interests of customers as potential creditors have claimed and received protection in *R.* v. *Kemp* (1988) 4 BCC 203 where a person was held criminally liable for 'carrying on the company's business for a fraudulent purpose' under section 458, 1985 Act, where the fraudulent purpose was that of defrauding customers.

Employees' interests are also on the ascendant in company law. Section 309, 1985 Act obliges directors, in the performance of their functions, to have regard to the interests of a company's employees in general as well as the interests of its members. While some argue that this prevents directors from prefering the interests of one group to those of the other, it may be that section 309 does not alter the prevalent view of the law, namely that the members' interests are supreme. On this second view, it is said that directors must *have regard* to employee interests (in the same way that in practice they will take account of regional, community and even national interests) but 'act in what they consider to be the best interests of the company as a whole' (meaning the members).

Even if this view is correct, it does not mean that some members may not be prejudiced (for example, through a board refusal to agree to a transfer by them of their shares, or through their expulsion from membership), nor does it mean that all current members may not see their short-term interests postponed to what the board sees as their long-term interests. In *Dawson International plc* v. *Coats Patons plc & Ors* (1988) 4 BCC 305, Court of Session) Lord Cullen held that directors owed their fiduciary duties to *the company*. In discharging this duty they had to *consider* the interests of the shareholders, but this does not mean that the directors are under a fiduciary duty to shareholders in regard to the disposal of shares on a take-over and accordingly obliged to act in such a way as to further their best interests. What was in the interests of current shareholders *as sellers* of their shares might not coincide with what was in the interests of the company (in other words, in the interests of the typical long-term investor in the company). Therefore, directors might on behalf of the company agree to recommend a bid and not to encourage or cooperate with an approach from another would-be bidder without being in breach of a fiduciary duty to current shareholders. Of course, if directors took it upon themselves to give advice to shareholders in a bid, they had a duty to do so in good faith and not fraudulently, and not mislead whether deliberately or carelessly. If they failed in this duty, affected shareholders might have a remedy (*Heron International Ltd* v. *Lord Grade* [1983] BCLC 244). However, this does not mean that directors are under a so-called secondary fiduciary duty to shareholders, but merely that they are under a potential liability based on ordinary principles of law. Nothing prevents directors becoming liable to shareholders, or anyone else, on ordinary principles of agency law or the law of negligence.

In theory, the board must, it seems, balance the short-term and the long-term interests of present members (Savoy Hotel Investigation, HMSO 1954). In practice, however, boards may pander rather more to short-term interests out of fear of removal. Under pressure from the EEC Company Law harmonisation programme we can expect the status of the employee in the company to improve dramatically, with far-reaching effect on many of the current rules of Company Law (see especially the Draft Fifth EEC Directive on Company Law; see generally Xuereb (1988) 51 MLR 156). Even now, employers themselves argue for employees to take a real interest in their company's affairs. In the recent Rowntree take-over battle (as in the BTR/Pilkington Glass take-over battle of some years ago) the employees have played an active part. The National Freight Consortium has sought to protect itself from a hostile take-over bid by introducing a dual voting system in its equity. To this end, it sought approval from the Stock Exchange for employee shareholdings to carry double the votes attached to other shareholdings on any decision as to whether the company should be taken over. All in all, there is a growing awareness that employees are entitled to some say in major company decisions as well as recognition that increased employee interest is salutary in principle.

Part Two
The 'External' Dimension

Chapter 9

Company Reorganisation: Mergers, Reconstructions, Take-overs

9.1 Introduction

9.1.1 The dissenting member

This chapter deals with the principal types of reorganisation within, or involving, a company. It is not the purpose of this chapter to explore the factors which impel a company to reorganise but rather to highlight the position of the shareholders, be they part of the majority or the minority in the event of each type of 'reorganisation', using this word in its widest sense. The emphasis will be on the protection of the minority (often called the 'dissenting') shareholder and can be seen as an extension of Chapter 8 in this respect.

9.1.2 The relevant rules

The relevant rules may be statutory (mainly the Companies Act, 1985) or non-statutory (e.g. the City Code on Take-overs and Mergers) in provenance. In a book of this kind it is possibly only to outline the general framework of legal or City regulation and to point out areas of overlap with other areas of law and in particular with the variation of member's rights (Chapter 7), minority protection (Chapter 8), and disclosure requirements (Chapter 5).

9.2 Schemes of arrangement under sections 425–427, 1985 Act

9.2.1 General

Sections 425–427 set out a mechanism whereby a company may enter into a 'compromise' or 'arrangement' with its members or any class of them (or with its creditors). This can and often will, involve the variation of members' rights. Important safeguards are therefore stipulated including: (1) the provision of adequate information to shareholders; (2) specific voting procedures and majority requirements; (3) the necessity for court approval of the proposed scheme.

9.2.2   Sphere of application

Section 425 applies to (a) any company liable to be wound up under the 1985 Act and (b) to any compromise or arrangement between a company and its members (or any class of members). The provision applies also to creditors but our concern is with members.

Its scope is extremely wide. The term 'member' has been given a wide interpretation in this context, to include, besides registered members, the holders of share warrants to bearer (*Re Wedgwood Coal & Iron Co.* (1877) 6 ChD 627) and the (as yet unregistered) holders of letters of allotment (*Dey* v. *Rubber and Mercantile Corpn. Ltd* [1923] 2 Ch 58). The courts have been encouraged, by the discretionary power to withhold approval, to adopt a broad definition of compromise or arrangement. In *Re NFU Development Trust Ltd* [1973] 1 All ER 135, at 140, Brightman J appeared to accept counsel's submission that 'any transaction affecting the rights of persons in their capacity as members of a company is an arrangement between the company and its members, even if the transaction takes the form of total forfeiture of membership rights', but subject to the following important caveat:

> 'The word 'compromise' implies some element of accommodation on each side. It is not apt to describe total surrender … Similarly, I think the word 'arrangement' in this section implies some element of give and take. Confiscation is not my idea of an arrangement.'

Not all 'arrangements' are 'compromises', however. A transaction is an 'arrangement' if it involves the exchange of one set of rights and liabilities for another. This occurs, for example, where shares in one company are exchanged for shares in another company (see *Re Guardian Assurance Co* [1917] 1 Ch 431; *Savoy Hotel Ltd* [1981] 3 All ER 646). 'Compromise or arrangement' is wider than 'reconstruction or amalgamation', which can be achieved under sections 110-111, Insolvency Act 1986 (see [9.3] below), but if the proposed scheme is in reality a sale of the shares of the company there must be genuine consent to the scheme by the company either through the board or the general meeting (*Re Savoy Hotel Co.*, above), and it seems that section 425 cannot be used in a take-over situation where other provisions which provide particular protection to the dissenting minority (such as sections 428-430 F, 1985 Act as enacted by section 172 and Schedule

12, Financial Services Act 1986, see [9.4.4] below) call for application (*Re Hellenic & General Trust Ltd* [1975] 3 All ER 382).

Section 425 may not be used to implement a scheme which is totally *ultra vires* (i.e. outside the company's legal capacity) or contrary to the general law (*Re Oceanic Steam Navigation Co. Ltd* [1939] Ch 41). Also, if the scheme involves a reduction in the company's capital, the requirements of sections 136-141, 1985 Act – which provide strong safeguards to members and creditors – must be complied with in addition to the requirements of sections 425-426 (*Re White Pass & Yukon Railway Co. Ltd* [1918] WN 323).

Procedure

If a scheme falling within section 425 is proposed, the court may, on the application of the company or any member of the company (or if the company is being wound up, the liquidator) order a meeting of the members, or class of members, concerned to be convened. An explanatory statement must be sent out with the notices convening such a meeting, explaining the effect of the compromise or arrangement and in particular stating any material interests of the directors (in whatever capacity) and the effect on those interests of the compromise or arrangement insofar as it is different from the effect on the like interests of other persons (section 426(2)). Before it can become binding on all members and the company the scheme must be:

(1) approved by a majority in number representing three-fourths in value of the members or class of members present, either in person or by proxy, at the meeting; and
(2) sanctioned by the court; and
(3) a copy of the court order must be sent to the Registrar of companies for registration (section 425(2),(3)).

The court's role

The court is involved at two stages:

(1) when it orders that a meeting (or meetings) be held to consider the scheme (section 425(1)); and
(2) when (a) it ascertains that the requirements of that order have been complied with and the requisite majority obtained for the scheme, and (b) considers whether an order should be made sanctioning the scheme.

In *Re Anglo-Continental Supply Co. Ltd* [1922] 2 Ch 723, Astbury J said:

> 'In exercising its power of sanction ... the court will see: First, that the provisions of the statute have been complied with. Secondly, that the class are fairly represented by those who attended the meeting and that the statutory majority are acting *bona fide* and not coercing the minority in order to promote interests adverse to those of the class whom they purport to represent, and, thirdly, that the arrangement is such as a man of business would reasonably approve.' (See also *Re Alabama, New Orleans, Texas and Pacific Junction Rly. Co.* [1891] 1 Ch 213 at 238 *per* Lindley LJ.)

In performing task 2(a) (above) the court will in particular ensure that separate meetings of separate 'classes' of members affected have been held. A liberal approach to the definition of 'class' has been adopted, namely a 'class' comprises 'those persons whose rights are not so dissimilar as to make it impossible for them to consult together with a view to their common interest' (*Sovereign Life Assurance Co.* v. *Dodd* [1892] 2 QB 573, CA *per* Bowen LJ at 583). *Re Hellenic & General Trust Ltd* [1975] 3 All ER 382 shows that the emphasis is on community of interest rather than similarity of *rights*. There the scheme involved the surrender of their shares by the ordinary shareholders of *Hellenic & General Trust Ltd*. These would be cancelled and new shares issued to Hambros, making Hellenic & General a wholly owned subsidiary of Hambros. The shareholders in Hellenic & General would receive shares in Hambros. The majority shareholder in Hellenic & General was a company called Merchandise & Investment Trust Ltd (MIT) which was wholly owned by Hambros. It was held that MIT constituted a separate class from the other ordinary shareholders in Hellenic & General and that separate class meetings should have been held.

In exercising its discretion to sanction the scheme at stage 2(b) [above], the court will not, as a rule, test the commercial convenience of the scheme. That is a matter for the members to decide (see, for example *Re English, Scottish & Australian Chartered Bank* [1893] 3 Ch 385 at 409, in a creditors' case). However, a limited inquiry into the merits will be undertaken to test the *legitimacy* of the majority decision and prevent a 'fraud on the minority'. There is a clear obligation on all members voting to vote in the interests of members and (in a class meeting) in the interests of members of that class as a whole (*Re NFU Development Trust Ltd* above, *Re Hellenic & General Trust Ltd* above). The test which the court will apply in the context of an arrangement with members is whether the scheme is one which no member voting in the interests of members (or a class of members) as a whole could reasonably approve (*Re NFU Development Trust Ltd* [1972] 1 WLR 1548 *per* Brightman J). The onus is on the company to show that the scheme is fair (*Re Hellenic & General Trust Ltd* above) and the court has wide discretion to approve the scheme subject to conditions imposed in the interests of fairness (*Re Chartered Bank of Australia* [1983] 3 Ch 540).

Section 425 can be used for the variation of class rights, where the statutory provisions considered in Chapter 7 cannot be complied with. We saw that section 127 provides that a qualified minority may challenge the alteration on the grounds of unfair prejudice. The general view is that the good faith or fairness criterion applied in a section 425 context is that applicable under section 127.

The very 'right' to remain a member, in so far as there is such a *prima facie* right, is subject to section 425 being properly invoked by the company. To such arrangements the 'good faith' and 'reasonableness' tests will be vigorously applied by the courts and as we have said a scheme which amounted to uncompensated expropriation would not qualify as a 'compromise or arrangement' at all (see [9.2.2] above). It would seem that section 425 can be utilised by the company to modify shareholder rights which are contained in the memorandum and declared to be unalterable (see Chapter 2, [2.12]). Additionally, Part I of the Insolvency Act 1986 sets out a 'voluntary arrangement' procedure by which a meeting of creditors of a company are enabled to impose a composition or scheme of arrangement on all creditors, with the agreement of the company's members. Provision is made for the protection of any member or members (or contributory or contributories) against unfair prejudice (section 6 Insolvency Act 1986).

The purpose of sections 1 to 7 of the Insolvency Act is to provide a simplified arrangement with its creditors as an alternative to the sections 425-427, 1985 Act or sections 110-111, Insolvency Act (see [9.3] below) methods. Sections 1 to 7 seek to achieve this essentially by substituting the supervision of a qualified insolvency practitioner for that of the court. There is no requirement that separate meetings be held for separate classes of creditors, as is the case under the sections 425-427 procedure. However, besides objecting on grounds of unfair prejudice, a person who was entitled to vote at the members' meeting may challenge the scheme in court on the ground that there has been some material irregularity at, or in relation to, the meeting (section 6, Insolvency Act 1986). If the court is satisfied that the member or contributory's objection is a valid one it may revoke or suspend the company's approval or order that further meetings be held to consider a revised proposal, or to reconsider the original proposal in a proper manner (section 6(4),(5),(6) Insolvency Act 1986).

After the respective creditors' and members' meetings the chairman of the meetings must report the result of the meetings to the court (section 4(6)). Any challenge under section 6 must be made within 28 days from the day on which the reports are made to the court (section 6(3)); in default, no approval given at a meeting can be invalidated by any irregularity given at or in relation to the meeting (section 6(7)).

9.3   Sections 110-111, Insolvency Act 1986

9.3.1   Scope

As an alternative to a 'reorganisation' under sections 425-427, a company which is proposed to be, or is in the course of being, wound up *voluntarily*, may utilise sections 110-111, Insolvency Act 1986. In the absence of unanimous consent, this procedure must be used where the scheme in effect involves the sale of the company's business or property to another company, and the distribution of the proceeds amongst the members, notwithstanding any provision in the company's memorandum and articles purporting to exclude the operation of these provisions in whole or in part (*Bisgood* v. *Henderson's Transvaal Estates Ltd* [1908] 1 Ch 743). The reason is that these provisions afford members particular protection. A dissenting member may therefore obtain an injunction to prevent a reconstruction of this type being effected by simple agreement outside sections 110-111.

If a company's memorandum does not authorise it to sell the whole of its undertaking, sections 110-111 afford an alternative to an alteration of the objects clause under section 4, 1985 Act (*Southall* v. *British Mutual Life Assurance Society* (1871) LR 6 Ch App 614).

9.3.2   Procedure: comparison with section 425 procedure

Section 110 is available whether the voluntary winding-up is a members' or a creditors' voluntary liquidation. In practice, members are only really affected when the voluntary winding-up, actual or proposed, is a members' voluntary winding up and the company is solvent. In such a case, the members of the company being wound up (the transferor company) by special resolution, authorise the liquidator to sell the whole or part of its business or property to another company (the transferee company) in return (a) for shares, policies or other like interests in that other company being issued for distribution among the members of the transferor company and/or (b) of any other arrangement under which the members of the transferor company acquire the right to participate in the profits of, or receive any other benefit from, the transferee company (section 110, Insolvency Act 1986). The transferee company need not be a registered company.

Within seven days of the passing of the resolution, a member who did not vote in favour of the resolution may serve written notice addressed to the liquidator at the company's registered office requiring the liquidator to choose either (a) to purchase his interest at a price to be fixed by agreement or by arbitration or (b) to abandon the proposed reconstruction altogether. The method by which the liquidator is to obtain the purchase money to 'pay off' dissenters must be determined by special resolution and the payment must be made before the company is dissolved (section 111, Insolvency Act 1986).

By contrast to the section 425 procedure, this procedure has the 'advantage' from the company's point of view that the court's sanction is only required in one instance, namely where a winding-up order is made against the company within one year after the adoption of the 'authorising' special resolution (section 110(6), Insolvency Act 1986). On the other hand, it is a requirement of this procedure that the company go into voluntary liquidation with the attendant negative messages which this conveys to the world at large. Moreover, under the section 425 procedure the court is empowered to make orders (which obviate the need for much documentation) whenever a reconstruction or amalgamation involves the transfer of the whole or any part of the undertaking of one company to another (section 427, 1985 Act). From the members' point of view, the courts' approach is to require in its discretion that a scheme proposed under section 425 but which would also fall within the ambit of sections 110-111, Insolvency Act 1986, provides the dissenting member with the same rights to be bought out at a fair price as are given by sections 110 and 111, Insolvency Act 1986 (*Re Anglo-Continental Supply Co. Ltd* [1922] 2 Ch 723).

A reconstruction under section 110 may run into difficulties where there are preference shareholders or other shareholders with special rights involved. It might not be easy to fit these shareholders into the transferee company's share structure. Here again, however, the scheme could succeed under section 425 if protection equivalent to that under section 111 were provided (*Re Tea Corporation Ltd, Sorsbie* v. *Tea Corpn. Ltd* [1904] 1 Ch 12). If a scheme either (a) involves a sale of assets or its business to a company with a view to liquidation and distribution of proceeds but cannot be carried out under section 110 or (b) falls outside the scope of section 110 entirely, the court is able to sanction the scheme under section 425 if the scheme is fair and reasonable. It may, as a condition of approval and in its discretion, require that shareholders receive protection equivalent to that provided by section 110 (*Re Anglo-Continental Supply Co.* [1922] 2 Ch 723 *per* Astbury J at 734-735).

9.3.3 'Reconstructions', 'mergers' and 'divisions'

A 'reconstruction' essentially involves the destruction of the old company (but not its business or enterprise or concern) and the transfer of its business to a new company whose membership is substantially the same as that of the old company. The difference between a reconstruction and a merger (or 'amalgamation') is that the latter involves the blending of two (or more) concerns one with the other(s), but not merely the continuance of one concern (*per* Buckley J in *Re South African Supply & Cold Storage Co.* [1904] 2 Ch 268 at 287). A merger is effected by the shareholders of one or both of the merging companies exchanging their shares (either voluntarily or as a result of a legal operation) for shares in the other or in a third company ... the shareholding in the combined enterprise will be spread between the shareholders of the two companies (Weinberg, Blank and Greystoke, *Take-overs and Mergers*, 4th ed. 1979, paras. 102-106).

A merger may take place (a) either by the transfer of undertakings A and B to a new company C; or (b) by the continuance of A and B's undertakings by Company B upon terms that the shareholders of A shall become shareholders in B, or (c) where the members of Company A transfer their shares to Company B in return for shares in the latter; or (d) by the reduction of the capital of Company A by the surrender of their shares by its members. In return they receive shares in Company B. The surrendered shares are cancelled and the reserve thereby created is used to pay for new shares in B which are alloted to A.

These operations are achievable under one or other of the procedures in section 425, 1985 Act or section 110, Insolvency Act 1986 and sometimes either [as in case (a)]. The courts will ensure that dissenting members are afforded maximum protection. In case (d) the statutory capital reduction provisions (section 135, 1985 Act) must be complied with.

Divisions (or 'scissions' or demergers) are the logical opposite to mergers. They are not common but are likely to become more so. A division takes place either (a) when a company transfers all its assets and liabilities to two or more companies in exchange for the issue of shares in those companies to the shareholders of the original company or (b) when a part of a company's undertaking is transferred to another company, some or all of the transferee company's shares being allotted to a part of the first company's shareholders – the first company's undertaking and shareholders being 'shared' between the transferor and transferee company.

As a rule, the statutory provisions on reconstructions and amalgamations do not apply to divisions since the operation falls outside the definition of a reconstruction as an operation whereby 'substantially the business and the persons interested are the same' (*Re South African Supply and Cold Storage Co. Ltd* above and see *Brooklands Selangor Holdings Ltd v. IRC* [1970] 2 All ER 76). However, general rules on arrangements (sections 425-427, 1985 Act) and on the reduction of capital by repayment (see *British and American Trustee and Finance Corp. v. Couper* [1894] AC 399) could be used to effect a division. These provisions apply to mergers and divisions of public companies subject to the addition of a new section 427A and Schedule 15A of the 1985 Act (which was amended for this reason by the Companies (Mergers and Divisions) Regulations 1987, SI 1987 No. 1991). (See also the Insurance Companies (Mergers and Divisions) Regulations 1987, SI 1987 No. 2118. These Regulations implemented the Sixth EEC Directive No. 82/891. The effect is that the court may not, in exercise of its powers under section 425, sanction a compromise or arrangement which falls within the cases set out in section 427(A)(2) unless: (a) a three-quarters majority of the shareholders of the *transferee* company agree and (b) directors' and experts' reports setting out specified information, and relevant company accounts, are made available to the shareholders.

9.4   Take-overs

9.4.1   Definition

A take-over takes place when one company acquires control of another. It may be defined as a transaction, or series of transactions whereby a person (individual, group of individuals or company) acquires control over the assets of a company, either by becoming the owner of those assets or indirectly by obtaining control of the management of the company. Where shares are closely held (held by a small number of persons) a take-over will generally be effected by agreement with the holders of the whole of the share capital of the company being acquired. Where the shares are held by the public generally, the take-over may be effected (1) by agreement between the acquirer and the controllers of the acquired company; (2) by purchases of shares on the Stock Exchange; or (3) by means of a take-over 'bid'.

The 'take-over bid' is a technique for effecting either a take-over or a merger: in the case of a take-over, the bid is frequently against the wishes of the management of the offeree company; in the case of a merger, the bid is generally by consent of the management of both companies. It may be defined as an offer to acquire shares of a company, whose shares are not closely held, addressed to the general body of shareholders, with a view to obtaining at least sufficient shares to give the offeror voting control of the company. Where a 'take-over bid' is used for effecting a take-over, it may take the form of an offer to purchase shares for cash, or of a share-for-share exchange, or of a combination of these two forms; where used for effecting a merger, it always takes the form of a share-for-share exchange offer (Weinberg, Blank and Greystoke, *Take-overs and Mergers* (1979) 4th ed., paras 102-106). In a take-over by exchange of shares, i.e. where the shareholders in the 'target' company acquire shares in the offeror company in return for their shares in the target company, the result is the same as that achieved under section 425, 1985 Act or section 110, Insolvency Act 1986. The now-common 'management buy-out' and less common 'workers' buyout' involve the acquisition of the majority of the company's shares by directors or workers.

9.4.2   The main rules – legal and non-legal

In the United Kingdom the vast majority of take-overs take place by acquisition of shares, whether this be (1) a private or market acquisition or (2) an acquisition by offer. In the latter case, the first step is the issue by the offeror company of an 'offer document' to the appropriate members of the target company. Take-over offer documents may fall within the prohibition of section 57, Financial Services Act 1986. This prohibits the issue of 'investment advertisements' except by authorised persons or if the contents have been approved by an authorised person (see Chapter 10).

9.4.3   Rules on substantial acquisitions of shares

The first matter to note is that by section 198 of the 1985 Act any 'person' who knowingly acquires or ceases to have, or who becomes aware that he has acquired, or ceased to have, an interest equal to or greater than the 'notifiable percentage interest' (currently 5 per cent in nominal value of the company's share capital, see section 201) in the relevant share capital (see section 198(2)) of a public company, must notify the company of that fact (see sections 198-210). The duty to notify applies if at the time of acquisition or cessation of any interest, or at the time that he becomes aware of that event (the relevant time), his interests in shares which carry the right to vote in all circumstances at general meetings extend to at least 5 per cent of all the issued shares of the company, or all of the issued shares of the same class, which carry the right to vote in all circumstances (sections 198(1)(2), 199(2)(4) and (5), 210(1), 1985 Act).

The duty also arises if a person who has an interest in shares of a public company becomes aware of a change of circumstances or of any fact which is relevant to the application of the obligation to notify his interests (section 198(3)). Further, by section 199(5), the obligation also arises under section 198(1) where (a) the person had a notifiable interest immediately before the relevant time but does not have such an interest immediately after it, or (b) he had a notifiable interest immediately before that time, and has such an interest immediately after it, but the 'percentage levels' of his interest immediately before and immediately after that time are not the same. This is clarified by section 200(1) which provides that the 'percentage level' means the percentage figure found by expressing the aggregate nominal value of all shares comprised in the share capital concerned in which the person is interested immediately before or (as the case may be) immediately after the relevant time as a percentage of the nominal value of that share capital and rounding that figure down, if it is not a whole number, to the next whole number.

The effect of this is that if a person's interest varies by one percentage point and his total interest was at the notifiable level (5 per cent) before the variation, or remains or becomes so after the variation, notification is required. Interests which a person's spouse, infant child or step-child may have are deemed to be that person's interests, as also are interests of a body corporate where (a) that body or its directors are accustomed to act in accordance with his directions or instructions or (b) that person is entitled to exercise or control the exercise of one-third or more of the voting power at general meetings of that body corporate (section 203, 1985 Act).

'Concert parties' are also covered (section 204-206, 1985 Act). These are agreements between two or more persons which include provision for the acquisition by any or more of them of interests in the relevant shares of a particular public company ('the target company'). The principal provision is that each party to such an agreement is taken (for the purpose of the obligation of disclosure) to be interested in *all* shares in the target company in which any other party to it is interested (section 205, 1985 Act). The definition of a so-called 'concert party' agreement in section 204 is narrower than the definition of 'persons acting in concert' in the City Code. The Companies Act provisions on concert parties are in the process of review with a view to their clarification.

The obligation to notify arises as soon as an interested person knows that his interest has exceeded or fallen below the notifiable percentage (sections 198, 199) and parties to a 'section 204 agreement' must keep each other informed about their respective interests (section 206). The interested person has five days within which to make the required disclosure to the company (although a proposal to shorten this period has been made, DTI Press Release, 11 May 1987, para. 11), detailing the information required by sections 203, 205, 210, 1985 Act as applicable. Failure to do so constitutes a criminal offence and the Secretary of State is empowered to impose the restrictions set out in Part XV 1985 Act on the relevant shares (section 210(5), 1985 Act). Every public company must keep a register of substantial interests in shares (section 211, 1985 Act). A listed company to whom such disclosure is made must in turn transmit the information to the Stock Exchange and make disclosure in its annual report and accounts (Admission of Securities to Listing, Sect.5; Ch.2, para 16). A public company may mount its own inquiry into interests in its shares (section 212, 1985 Act). Also, a qualified minority of members (representing one-tenth or more of the amount paid up on shares carrying a right to vote) may requisition the company to carry out such an inquiry (section 214, 1985 Act).

These legal rules are supplemented by the Rules Governing Substantial Acquisitions of Shares, issued and enforced by the Panel on Take-Overs and Mergers (see [9.4.5.5] below). These apply to acquisitions which result in a holding of shares, or rights over shares, which give control over 15–29.9 per cent of the company's voting rights. Subject to limited exceptions (in Rule 2) Rule 1 states that an acquisition in any seven-day period of 10 per cent or more of the total voting rights of a company may not be made if the result is to bring the shareholding of the acquirer (together with persons acting by agreement or understanding with him) to between 15–29.9 per cent. A holding of 30 per cent or over is subject to the City Code itself. Rule 3 of the SARs requires notification (by noon on the business day following the date of the acquisition – though a proposal to change this to 9 AM on that day at the latest has been made: DTI Press Release, 11 May 1987, para. 11) to the company and the Stock Exchange when a person's shareholding reaches (or exceeds) 15 per cent or more of the voting rights in a company (see also rule 8 of the City Code on Take-Overs and Mergers). The EEC is considering a proposal for a Directive on the disclosure of information relating to the acquisition or disposal of significant shareholdings in listed companies (EEC, Com.(85) 791 final, O.J. 1985 No. C.351/35).

9.4.4 The position of the individual member under the law

We have seen that the directors of a target company may owe certain duties to the shareholders of that company (*Gething* v. *Kilner* [1972] 1 WLR 337; *Heron International Ltd* v. *Lord Grade* [1983] BCLC 244; see [8.6]) and that a minority shareholder may seek relief under section 459, 1985 Act for 'unfair prejudice' suffered in a take-over context (*Re a Company No. 008699 of 1985* (1986) 2 BCC 99, 024, and see [8.4.5] above).

The Companies Act 1985 also contains specific statutory provisions designed to balance the interests of the majority and minority shareholders of the target company (sections 428–430 F). The provisions are highly technical. In substance they provide, subject to stringent requirements of substance and procedure, (and with some variation in particular circumstances) that where the offeror has acquired or contracted to acquire not less than nine-tenths in value of the shares to which the offer relates (i.e. all the shares, or all the shares of any class or classes, in the target company) then (a) the offeror may by notice to the dissenting member(s) seek to buy out compulsorily the dissenting minority and (b) any dissenting member may require the offeror to buy him out. The court is in ultimate control of the terms of the acquisition in either case. The court has the power to fix terms of acquisition in the event of such applications as a dissenting member may make in either case and the offeror may make in hypothesis (b) (the so-called 'reverse acquisition' hypothesis).

In addition, the court has the power to prevent the compulsory acquisition in hypothesis (a), on the application of the recipient of a compulsory acquisition notice. The test under the previous law (the 'old' section 428 which was replaced by the new sections 428–430 F) was whether what was then called the 'scheme or contract' (now the 'take-over offer'; section 428) was 'fair' to the relevant body of members (*Gething* v. *Kilner* [1972] 1 WLR 337; *Re Hoare & Co. Ltd* (1933) 150 LT 374; *Re Grierson Oldham and Adams Ltd* [1968] Ch 17), in the sense that the consideration offered is substantially less than the real value of the shares concerned (*Re Press Caps Ltd* [1949] Ch 434) although it was not enough for applicants to show simply that the scheme was open to criticism and that a higher price could have been obtained for the shares (*Re Sussex Brick Co. Ltd* [1961] Ch 289; see also *Re Hellenic & General Trust Ltd* 1975] 1 WLR 123). Now that the court has the power to revise the terms of the offer made to a dissenting member on an application under hypothesis (a) this will probably lead to very little use of the power to prevent the compulsory purchase.

9.4.5 City self-regulation

9.4.5.1 The City Code on take-overs and mergers

The rules of the City Code are critical to take-over practice where public companies (listed or unlisted) or private companies which have had certain kinds of public involvement during the ten-year period preceding the bid (Introduction, City Code, para. 3) are involved as offerees, potential offerees, or in which control may change or be consolidated. They are 'extra-legal' rules administered by a body representative of the City 'players' called the Panel on Take-overs and Mergers, with the help of such City institutions as the Stock Exchange and the Bank of England. It is proposed here to summarise the principles and main rules of the Code, the violation of which can lead, in serious cases, to the withdrawal of the City's facilities from the culprit. Although having no direct legal effect the City Code is recognised by the courts as denoting 'good business practice and standards' (Lord Denning, MR in *Dunford & Elliott Ltd* v. *Johnson & Frith Brown Ltd* [1977] 1 Lloyds Rep 505 at 510).

The introduction to the Code admonishes that the spirit of the Code, as well as its letter, must be adhered to. Although non-legal, the City Code has now received legal backing. Persons breaking the Code may find that by way of sanction, access to the facilities of the securities markets in the United Kingdom is barred. In particular, the new City self-regulatory organisations (e.g. the Securities and Investments Board and the Self-Regulating Organisations) set up under the Financial Services Act 1986 (see Chapter 10) may require that those subject to their jurisdiction should not act in a take-over for any person who does not appear likely to comply with the standards reflected by the Code. Furthermore, if a person authorised by the SIB or an SRO to carry on an investment business fails to comply with the Code or a ruling of the Take-over Panel, that may lead to withdrawal of the authorisation to carry on investment business (see Introduction to the Code, para.1). The Code's Introduction further provides (in para. 2(c)) that the SIB and SROs will require, through their rules, investment businesses to co-operate with the Panel in enquiries and investigations, and the Panel has been designated under the Companies Act 1985, the Financial Services Act 1986 and the Banking Act 1987 to receive regulatory information, the disclosure of which is restricted by statute.

It may be noted here that this system of self-regulation with legal backing will give way to outright statutory regulation if and when an EEC proposal for a Directive on take-over and other general bids is agreed. The proposal covers many issues now dealt with by the City Code (see (1988) 9 Co. Law 56).

9.4.5.2 Layout of the Code

The Code consists of an Introduction (listing the constitution of the City Panel, the nature and purpose of the Code, the scope of the Code, its enforcement, co-operation with other authorities – see further Chapter 10 – and a comprehensive definition section), 10 General Principles, 38 Rules (with Notes) and three Appendices. The overriding principles are the protection of the shareholders in the offeree (target) company and the equal treatment of those shareholders. To this end, the conduct of the take-over bid by the offeror and the conduct of the board of the offeree company are subjected to constraints by the City Code.

9.4.5.3 The general principles

(The following is reproduced with the kind permission of the Panel on Take-overs and Mergers.)

Introduction

It is impracticable to devise rules in sufficient detail to cover all circumstances which can arise in offers. Accordingly, persons engaged in offers should be aware that the spirit as well as the precise wording of the General Principles and the ensuing Rules must be observed. Moreover, it must be accepted that the General Principles and the spirit of the Code will apply in areas or circumstances not explicitly covered by any Rule.

While the boards of an offeror and of the offeree company and their respective advisers have a duty to act in the best interests of their respective shareholders, these General Principles and the ensuing Rules will, inevitably, impinge on the freedom of action of boards and persons involved in offers; they must, therefore, accept that there are limitations in connection with offers on the manner in which the pursuit of those interests can be carried out.

Each director of an offeror and of the offeree company has a responsibility to ensure, so far as he is reasonably able, that the Code is complied with in the conduct of an offer (see Appendix 3 for Guidance Note). Financial advisers have a particular responsibility to comply with the Code and to ensure, so far as they are reasonably able, that an offeror and the offeree company, and their respective directors, are aware of their responsibilities under the Code and will comply with them. Financial advisers should ensure that the Panel is consulted whenever relevant and should cooperate fully with any enquiries made by the Panel. Financial advisers must also be mindful of conflicts of interest (see Appendix 3 for Guidance Note).

General Principles

(1) All shareholders of the same class of an offeree company must be treated similarly by an offeror.

(2) During the course of an offer, or when an offer is in contemplation, neither an offeror, nor the offeree company, nor any of their respective advisers may furnish information to some shareholders which is not made available to all shareholders. This principle does not apply to the furnishing of information in confidence by the offeree company to a *bona fide* potential offeror or *vice versa*.

(3) An offeror should only announce an offer after the most careful and responsible consideration. Such an announcement should be made only when the offeror has every reason to believe that it can and will continue to be able to implement the offer: responsibility in this connection also rests on the financial adviser to the offeror.

(4) Shareholders must be given sufficient information and advice to enable them to reach a properly informed decision and must have sufficient time to do so. No relevant information should be withheld from them.

(5) Any document or advertisement addressed to shareholders containing information or advice from an offeror or the board of an offeree company or their respective advisers must, as is the case with a prospectus, be prepared with the highest standards of care and accuracy.

(6) All parties to an offer must use every endeavour to prevent the creation of a false market in the securities of an offeror or the offeree company. Parties involved in offers must take care that statements are not made which may mislead shareholders or the market.

(7) At no time after a *bona fide* offer has been communicated to the board of the offeree company, or after the board of the offeree company has reason to believe that a *bona fide* offer might be imminent, may any action be taken by the board of the offeree company in relation to the affairs of the company, without the approval of the shareholders in general meeting, which could effectively result in any *bona fide* offer being frustrated or in the shareholders being denied an opportunity to decide on its merits.

(8) Rights of control must be exercised in good faith and the oppression of a minority is wholly unacceptable.

(9) Directors of an offeror or an offeree company must always, in advising their shareholders, act only in their capacity as directors and not have regard to their personal or family shareholdings or to their personal relationships with the companies. It is the shareholders' interests taken as a whole, together with those of employees and creditors, which should be considered when the directors are giving advice to shareholders.

10. Where control of a company is acquired by a person, or persons acting in

concert, a general offer to all other shareholders is normally required; a similar obligation may arise if control is consolidated. Where an acquisition is contemplated as a result of which a person may incur such an obligation, he must, before making the acquisition, ensure that he can and will continue to be able to implement such an offer.

General Principles 1, 2, 5 and 10 are directly concerned with equality of treatment of shareholders. Principle 2 again, and also Principles 4 and 5 deal with the breadth and accuracy of information which is to be made available to shareholders. Principle 3 ensures that frivolous (non *bona-fide*) offers are not made. Principle 5 again, together with Principles 7 and 9 set constraints, and impose requirements of independence and standards of care, upon the offeree company's board, and also on the offeror company's board in relation to its company's shareholders. Principle 6 seeks to prevent the creation of a false market in shares. Principle 8 prohibits the exercise of rights of control in bad faith, prohibiting 'oppression of the minority' and in effect imposing a duty of good faith on the majority shareholder(s) in an offeree company in a take-over context at least. Principle 9 obliges boards to consider the interests of employees and creditors as well as those of the shareholders taken as a whole when advising shareholders. This is most interesting, for it acknowledges that other interests besides those of the shareholders must also be at least 'considered', if not acted upon. The City Code appears to accept that these other legitimate interests may impose constraints on the boards' freedom of action to act in the best interests of their respective shareholders (General Principles, Introduction, para. 2, City Code). This non-legal rule raises once again the whole question as to how directors should act when competing interests conflict – a question also being raised in other contexts (see Chapter 8, [8.6]). Principle 10 deals with the 'mandatory bid' which must be made when effective (*de facto*) control is acquired or consolidated.

9.4.5.4 The Rules

The Rules (which number 38) and the three Appendices set out in detail the procedures to be followed in the conduct of a take-over bid. It is not possible to set them out here. They deal with the whole procedure including the 'approach' phase where the offer is put to the offeree company's board, announcements of offers and possible offers, the obtaining of independent advice (Section D); dealings and restrictions on the acquisition of shares and rights over shares (Section E); the 'mandatory offer' and its terms (Section F); the voluntary offer and its terms (Section G); the provisions applicable to all offers (Section H); conduct during the offer (Section I); documents from the offeror and the offeree board (Section J); profit forecasts (Section K); asset valuations (Section L); timing and revision (Section M); restrictions following offers (Section N); partial offers (Section O); redemption or purchase by a company of its own securities (Section P); dealings by connected exempt market-makers (Section Q).

9.4.5.5   *The City Panel's rules governing substantial acquisitions of shares*

Like the City Code, these rules (known as the SARs) are published by the City Panel. They are designed to prevent the covert acquisition of a shareholding of between 5 per cent and 29.9 per cent. At 30% the City Code takes over. The SARs restrict the speed with which a person may increase his holding of shares and rights over shares to an aggregate of between 15 per cent and 30 per cent of the voting rights of a company. They also require speedy disclosure of the acquisitions of shares or rights over shares relating to such holdings (see [9.4.3] above). Provision is made for tender offers (rule 4) and for persons acting 'by agreement or understanding' in the acquisition (rule 5). The exceptions to the prohibition made in rule 1 are set out in rule 2.

9.4.5.6   *The Stock Exchange's rules*

Under the Stock Exchange requirements, if a listed company is involved as bidder or 'target', the Stock Exchange requirements as set out in Section 6, Chapter 2 of the Yellow Book (Admission of Securities to Listing) must be complied with on penalty of suspension of listing. For example, the offer document must be forwarded to the Stock Exchange for approval and must, *inter alia*, detail (para. 3):

(1) the precise terms of issue of the securities for which the offer is made;
(2) any payment proposed for compensation for loss of office;
(3) in the case of a partial offer, the reason for not making a full offer;
(4) middle market quotation, going back for six months before the date of the offer, and if the relevant securities are not listed any information as to the number of, and price at which, transactions have taken place during the preceding six months.
(5) the nature and particulars of the business and financial and trading prospects of the offeror company.

The Stock Exchange regulations relevant to take-overs are contained in Section 6, Chapter 2 of the Yellow Book and are based on the City Code on Take-overs. Section 6, Chapter 1 of the Yellow Book deals with acquisitions and realisations and includes rules on very substantial acquisitions or reverse take-overs. It is to be noted that paragraph 3 of Section 6, Chapter 2 requires that certain particulars need to be contained in offer documents 'in addition to any further requirements set out in the City Code' (as to which see City Code, rule 24). This means that the sanctions which the Stock Exchange is empowered by the Yellow Book to impose, including withdrawal or suspension of a company's listing, are available to enforce the provisions of the City Code (see also Introduction to the City Code, para. 2).

9.5 EEC law

Three EEC Company Law Directives deal with mergers and 'scissions' (divisions). These are the Third (Directive No. 78/855/EEC; O.J. 1978, 1295/36) Sixth (Directive No. 82/891/EEC; O.J. 1982, 2.378, pp.47-54) and Tenth (O.J. 1985, C.23 pp.11-15) EEC Directives. The Third Directive deals with 'internal' mergers i.e. mergers taking place between companies within the same EEC Member State. It only covers mergers between public companies, of the share exchange type – that is where shares in one company are exchanged for the assets and liabilities of the other. In the United Kingdom the merger by take-over has been the more common form of merger. The Directive affects reconstructions under sections 425-427 but not take-overs by acquisition of shares. Its main thrust is to require independent experts to be appointed to study the terms of the proposed merger and to advise whether in their opinion the share exchange is fair and reasonable (article 10).

The Sixth Directive deals with the division (scission) of public limited companies and complements the Third Directive. It deals with the operation whereby a public limited company transfers to a number of companies within the same Member State all of its assets and liabilities in exchange for the issue of shares to the shareholders of the divided company. Its main thrust is to ensure that fair value is given by, for example, requiring the directors of all the public companies involved to draw up detailed draft terms of division showing, *inter alia*, the criteria for the allocation of shares in the recipient public companies among the shareholders of the public company being divided. This information would be published at least one month before the draft terms come up for consideration by the general meeting of any public company involved in the division. The subsequent approval of the general meeting of the public company being divided is required, all the shareholders involved having had the benefit of a report by an independent expert.

The Third and Sixth Directives were implemented by the Companies (Mergers and Divisions) Regulations 1987 (SI 1987 No. 1991) which came into force on 1 January 1988.

The Tenth Directive is still being discussed in Europe. It deals with 'international mergers' and is intended to facilitate on a Community-wide basis the type of merger dealt with in the Third Directive (above).

Work continues in the Commission on a Draft Directive to control the conduct of take-over bids throughout the EEC. The Directive proposes a virtual statutory code regulating take-overs. The main aim is shareholder protection with the emphasis on disclosure of information to shareholders (see (1988) 9 Co. Law 56). Also, work is well under way on the development of an EEC policy for the control and vetting of large-scale industrial take-overs and mergers with a view to ensuring free and fair competition in the EEC (Com. (88) 97 final, *Official Journal of the European Communities*, 1988 No. C.130/4 of 19.5.88 – Draft Council Regulation on the Control of Concentrations between Undertakings).

Chapter 10

The Financial Services Act 1986 and Investor Protection

10.1 Introduction

The potential investor has never been better protected, although the old adage – 'a fool and his money are soon parted' – remains true. Whether he is better *served* in future by the securities industry will depend on the operation in practice of the new Financial Services Act 1986.

The Act's purpose is the protection of the investor. First, it sets out what was billed as a new 'self-regulatory regime within a statutory framework', providing for the proper authorisation of investment services and setting down rules of best practice (Part I of the Act).

Second, it seeks to achieve this aim through the rules on the admission of securities to listing on the Stock Exchange and counter-part provisions relating to the prospectus requirements for the issue of unlisted securities (Parts IV and V).

Third, the Act amends the law on insider dealing which is largely embodied in the Company Securities (Insider Dealing) Act 1985. This latter Act makes insider dealing an offence in the circumstances set out therein. It does not impose civil liability and the law is unclear as to whether and in what circumstances a civil remedy is available to a shareholder or investor under English law, although, *pace Percival* v. *Wright* [1902] 2 Ch 41, the seeds for the development of such a remedy can be said to exist (see the Privy Council case of *Allen* v. *Hyatt* (1914) 30 TLR 444 and the New Zealand case of *Coleman* v. *Myers* [1977] NZLR 25). The Law of the United States of America has long offered a remedy (see *SEL* v. *Texas Gulf Sulphur Co.* (1968) 401 F 2d 833 and *Diamond* v. *Oreamuno* (1969) 24 NY 2d 494). Also, there is the theoretical possibility that sections 61 and 62 of the Financial Services Act may be used to afford compensation to such victims of insider dealing as can be identified (see [10.5.5.5] below and B. Rider, D. Chaikin and C. Abrams, *Guide to The Financial Services Act 1986*, p.121). It may be mentioned here that work is advanced in the EEC on a Draft Directive which is intended to co-ordinate the laws on insider dealing of the

Member States and which will prescribe arrangements for cooperation between regulatory authorities in Member States (see Com (87) 111 final and CES (87) 1165).

Fourth, the Financial Services Act introduces a new 'investment advertisement regime' which imposes tight controls over the advertising of investments. In general (and this is the 'Marketing Prohibition'), investment advertisements must be issued by authorised persons or with the approval of an authorised person (section 57). The Securities and Investment Board, the SIB (see [10.5.3] below), is empowered to make rules regulating the form and content of advertisements (section 48(2)(e)) and the manner in which persons may hold themselves out as carrying on investment business (section 48(2)(c)). This is all without prejudice to the specific provisions of the Act dealing with public issues of listed and unlisted securities in Parts IV and V of the Act (see sections 58(1)(d), 58(2) and 58(6) and the exceptions listed in section 58).

Fifth, the Act to all intents and purposes bans 'unsolicited calls' (i.e. 'cold calling') except where permitted by the rules of the Securities and Investment Board or those of a Self-Regulatory Organisation or Recognised Professional Body (see [10.5.3 below]). It achieves this by rendering unenforceable agreements entered into in breach of the prohibition (section 56).

Finally, the Act (in Chapter VIII, Part I) introduces a completely new regime to regulate 'Collective Investment Schemes' (e.g. unit trusts, open-ended investment companies). This regime is additional to the general marketing rules just referred to (e.g. the 'marketing prohibition'). All collective investment schemes have to be 'authorised' (or 'recognised' in the case of overseas schemes) (section 76). Strict controls are imposed on the marketing of such schemes, e.g. the SIB can require that 'scheme particulars', containing specified information, be published (sections 85(1), 87(5), 88(10)). The prevention of restrictive trade practices is covered in Part I, Chapter XIV of the Act. Parts II (and Schedule 10) and III (and Schedule 11) provide respectively for the regulation of the insurance business and friendly societies.

In a book of this scope one has to content oneself with a review of Part I of the Act in general terms, and with outlining the new law on listings and prospectuses in Parts IV and V. The reader is referred to the excellent works on the Financial Services Act for a broader and deeper review of the Act (e.g. B. Rider, D. Chaikin, C. Abrams, *'Guide to the Financial Services Act 1986'*, CCH Editions 1987; Wedgwood, Pell, Leigh and Ryan, *'A Guide to the Financial Services Act 1986'*, Financial Training Publications, 1986). It must be noted that some of what follows regarding Parts IV and V of the Act may be modified as a result of ongoing work in the EEC to produce a Directive regulating the offer to the public of transferable securities within the EEC. This will, for example, have implications relating to the content of prospectuses but in general it is not anticipated that major changes in the Financial Services Act will be required.

10.2   Listings and prospectuses

10.2.1   General

Part IV of the Financial Services Act 1986 replaced the Stock Exchange (Listing) Regulations 1984 and implements the three harmonising EEC Directives (namely, Directive No. 79/279 on the conditions for the admission of securities to official Stock Exchange listing, O.J. 1979 L.66/21 – The 'Admissions Directive'; Directive No. 80/390 on listing particulars, O.J. 1980 L 100/1 – the 'Listing Particulars Directive'; and Directive No. 82/121 on information to be published on a regular basis by listed companies, O.J. 1982 L.48/26 – The 'Interim Reports Directive'). The Council of the Stock Exchange is given statutory official status as 'Competent Authority' with power to make legally binding rules implementing the detailed requirements of the Directives, and the Yellow Book is officially recognised.

Part V of the Financial Services Act 1986 updates and sets out the rules relating to prospectuses issued in relation to unlisted securities. It replaces the relevant provisions of the Companies Act 1985 and the Prevention of Fraud (Investments) Act 1958 and is due to come into force in the latter half of 1988. For this reason the 'old' law is not being covered here.

Both Parts IV and V apply whether securities are issued as consideration for a take-over or for cash. However, Part IV applies to the procedure for admission to listing (whether accompanied by an offer to the public or not) while Part V only applies where an offer of unlisted securities is made.

10.2.2   The aim of Parts IV and V

The aim of Parts IV and V is adequate disclosure to potential investors, i.e. purchasers. The two parts are broadly in line with one another. Continuing obligations of disclosure are imposed on listed companies. Compliance with rules laid down by recognised investment exchanges and 'equivalent' to the statutory rules in Part V may be deemed sufficient compliance (e.g. such rules as may be laid down by the Stock

Exchange in relation to prospectuses where dealings are to be carried out on the Unlisted Securities Market (USM) or on the Third Market).

As far as listed securities are concerned, the Stock Exchange is designated as the competent authority to issue rules governing the admission of securities to listing, the contents of listing particulars and the continuing obligations of listed companies. Its 'Yellow Book' (official title: *Admission of Securities to Listing*) generally imposes stricter obligations than the Directives envisaged. Part IV came fully into force on 16 February 1987 while Part V was to come into force in the latter half of 1988. All the references to sections in what follows are to the relevant provisions in the Financial Services (or 'F.S.') Act, unless otherwise stated.

10.2.3   (A) Part IV of the Act: official listing of securities

10.2.3.1   *Admission to listing*

Section 142(1) of the F.S. Act 1986 provides that no investment to which section 142 applies (see section 142(2) and paras. 1, 2, 4 or 5 of Schedule 1 for these) shall be admitted to the Official List of the Stock Exchange except in accordance with Part IV of the Act. This means that, subject to the overriding authority of the Secretary of State (section 192, F.S. Act), the Stock Exchange may not admit any securities to the Official List unless (1) an application is duly made in accordance with section 143 (i.e. as set out in the Listing Rules) and (2) the Stock Exchange is satisfied that (a) the listing rules' requirements in force at the date of the application and (b) any other requirements imposed by the Stock Exchange in relation to that application have been complied with (section 144(1), F.S. Act).

10.2.3.2   *The Stock Exchange rules*

The Stock Exchange is free to make such rules as appear appropriate but the Act specifies (in section 144(2)) that those rules may, in particular, require as a condition for admission to listing (a) the submission to, and approval by, itself of a document (referred to in the Act as 'listing particulars') in such form and detailing such information as may be specified in the rules and (b) the publication of that document; or, in such cases as may be specified by the rules, the publication of a document other than listing particulars. No application may be made except by, or with the consent of, the issuer of the securities which must be a public company (section 143, F.S. Act).

10.2.3.3 Refusal of application

In any event, the Stock Exchange is empowered to refuse an application (a) if it considers that by reason of any matter relating to the issuer the admission of the securities would be detrimental to the interests of investors; or (b) in the case of securities already officially listed in another EEC Member State, if the issuer has failed to comply with any obligations to which the issuer is subject by virtue of that listing (section 144(3), F.S. Act). The discretion accorded by ground '(a)' is apparently unlimited, while in contrast ground '(b)' has been restricted to breaches of the rules laid down in EEC Member States, but perhaps breaches of the rules of a non-EEC Member State would be relevant to a refusal under ground (a). The Stock Exchange is of course entitled to refuse admission for non-compliance with its rules. Judicial review is available to an aggrieved applicant whose application is refused. In the converse case where admission has been wrongly granted, investors may not challenge the validity of the listing as a means of evading liability on transactions, since admission is conclusive evidence that all the listing requirements applicable to a particular application have been complied with (section 144(6), F.S.Act).

10.2.3.4 Liability of person responsible: general

This does not affect the civil liability of the 'person responsible' to make compensation when an investor suffers loss as a result of a failure to supply information under the general duty of disclosure (section 146), the failure to supply supplementary listing particulars, the failure to supply the information required by the listing rules and the making of false and misleading statements (see [10.2.4], [10.2.6] below).

10.2.3.5 Securities to which the Act applies

The securities to which the Act applies are shares and stock, debentures, instruments entitling the holder to acquire shares or securities, and certificates representing securities (section 142(2), F.S. Act). The Act (section 142(4)) also empowered the Secretary of State to include in this list units in a collective investment scheme (including shares in, or securities of, an open-ended investment company, e.g. an offshore fund).

10.2.3.6 Suspension and discontinuance of listing

The Stock Exchange has the power, in accordance with the listing rules, to suspend or discontinue a listing of securities. This occurs, in essence, where normal and regular dealing in those securities is temporarily or permanently precluded (section 145(3), F.S. Act). The circumstances in which listing may be suspended will be wider than those allowing discontinuation, which are limited to the preclusion of normal regular dealings in the securities in question (section 145(1)).

10.2.4   The 'listing particulars'

10.2.4.1   *Disclosure requirements*

Besides such information as may be required by the listing rules and, as may be the case, such as is specifically required by the Stock Exchange in a particular case (see [10.2.3.1] above) any listing particulars must also contain 'all such information as investors and their professional advisers would reasonably require, and reasonably expect to find there, for the purpose of making an informed assessment of: (a) the assets and liabilities, financial position, profits and losses, and prospects of the issuer of securities; and (b) the rights attached to those securities' (section 146(1), F.S. Act). The factors which will determine what information ought reasonably to be disclosed are set out in section 146(3) and include the nature of the securities and of their issuer; the nature of the potential investor in those securities; the existing availability, or knowledge of, information to or by investors and their likely professional advisers; the fact that certain matters may reasonably be expected to be within the knowledge of professional advisers of any kind which potential investors may reasonably be expected to consult. The general obligation of disclosure under section 146(1) is, in any event, restricted to that information which is within the knowledge of any person responsible for the listing particulars or which it would be reasonable for him to obtain by making inquiries (section 146(2), F.S. Act).

10.2.4.2   *Supplementary listing particulars*

Supplementary listing particulars will have to be submitted to the Stock Exchange, and published, if, between the date of the preparation of the listing particulars and the commencement of dealings in the relevant securities following their admission to the Official List, either (a) there is a significant change affecting any matter required to be contained in those particulars (e.g. the issuing company's prospects) or (b) a significant new matter arises information about which would have been required if it had arisen at the time when the particulars were in preparation (section 147, F.S. Act). The issuer of the securities is excused from this obligation if he was unaware of the change or 'new matter', but a duty is cast on 'any person responsible for those particulars' (see section 152) who is aware of any such change or 'new matter' to give notice of it to the issuer (section 147(3), F.S. Act). We deal with the liability of these persons to investors below.

10.2.4.3 Exemption and registration

In three cases, the Stock Exchange may authorise the omission of information from the listing (and supplementary listing) particulars, namely (a) where disclosure would be contrary to the public interest, (b) where its disclosure would be seriously detrimental to the issuer (but not if its non-disclosure would be likely to mislead a potential investor as to any facts which he must have in order to make an informed assessment), and (c) in the case of debt securities (other than those issued by the government of, or a local authority in, an EEC Member State) which are of a kind normally dealt in only by those expected to understand the risks involved (e.g. Eurobonds) (section 148(3), F.S. Act).

On or before the date on which listing (or supplementary listing) particulars are published in accordance with the listing rules, a copy of the particulars must be delivered to the Registrar of Companies for registration. A statement that a copy has been so delivered must appear in the particulars (section 149, FS Act).

10.2.5 Continuing obligations

The Listing Rules may impose continuing obligations on the issuers of listed securities (section 153, F.S. Act). The Yellow Book indeed does so. They relate to the disclosure of specified matters at half-yearly intervals.

However, the Act does not expressly declare breaches of these continuing obligations to be actionable (as it does with regard to breaches of the SIB's conduct of business rules, see [10.5.5.5] below). It remains an open question whether investors could bring civil actions for compensation for resulting loss. One possible ground might be breach of statutory duty. However, the Act does allow for the imposition of 'self regulatory sanctions' by and at the dispensation of the Stock Exchange and, without prejudice to this general power, expressly empowers the Stock Exchange to take upon itself the authority to publish the fact that an issuer has breached the rules and also itself to publish information which an issuer has failed to publish (section 153(1), F.S. Act).

10.2.6   Investor remedies

The question arises as to what rights of redress are available to an investor in the event of incorrect and misleading information being supplied by an issuer of securities, or a failure on the latter's part to supply required information.

Section 150, F.S. Act provides that, subject to certain defences, the person(s) responsible for the listing (or supplementary listing) particulars relating to any securities is liable to compensate any person who acquires any of those securities and suffers loss in respect of them as a result of either (a) any untrue or misleading statement in the particulars and/or (b) the omission from them of any matter required to be included by sections 146 or 147 (see [10.2.4] above) or by the listing rules (Yellow Book). It may be noted here that no person shall, by reason of being a promoter of a company or otherwise, incur any liability for failing to disclose any information which he would not be required to disclose in listing particulars in respect of a company's securities if he were responsible for those particulars or, if he is responsible for them, which he is entitled to omit by virtue of section 148 (section 150(6)).

The loss to the investor will result from the fact that the securities are worth materially less to the investor than it was represented that they would be worth. The loss will be the difference between the share price at the time of purchase and the share price at the time of issue. The phrase 'acquires securities' includes entering into a contract to acquire securities or an interest in them (section 150(5), F.S. Act). It does not matter that the investor did not actually rely on the listing particulars in deciding to invest, but no compensation is payable if the defendant proves that the investor acquired his securities knowing that a statement was false or misleading or knowing of the omitted matter or of the significant change or new matter – depending on whether the complaint refers to the listing particulars or to the supplementary listing particulars (section 151(5), F.S. Act).

The 'persons responsible for the particulars', and therefore the persons who are potential defendants, are:

(a) the issuer of the securities in question;
(b) where the issuer is a body corporate each person who is a director of that body at the time when the particulars are submitted to the Stock Exchange; but not if the particulars were published without

the knowledge or consent of such person and, on becoming aware of their publication, that person forthwith gave reasonable public notice that they were published without his or her knowledge or consent (see also (c) below);

(c) where the issuer is a body corporate, each person who has authorised himself (etc.) to be named, and is named, in the particulars as a director or as having agreed to become a director of that body either immediately or at a future time;

(d) each person who accepts, and is stated in the particulars as accepting responsibility for, or for any part of, the particulars;

(e) each person not falling within (a) to (d) above who has authorised the contents of, or any part of, the particulars.

(Section 152(1) F.S. Act)

It must be noted that when a person accepts responsibility for, or authorises, only a part of the particulars, that person is liable only in connection with that part, and only if it is included in the particulars at least substantially in the form and context to which that person has agreed (section 152(3), F.S. Act). Also, a person does not become responsible for any particulars simply by giving advice as to their contents in a professional capacity; something more is required to bring such an expert within paragraph (d) (section 152(8), F.S. Act). In a take-over situation, paragraph (d) will cover a target company and its directors who expressly accept responsibility for any part of the particulars as relate to the target company, in which case no other person is responsible for that part under paragraphs (a), (b) or (c) but without prejudice to liability under paragraph (d) (section 152(4) F.S., Act). There is a dispensation from section 152(1) for international securities (Eurobonds) (section 152(5)(6), F.S. Act).

10.2.7 Defences

Certain defences are available, however. The burden lies on the defendant to bring himself within one of them. They are set out in section 151, F.S. Act, namely:

(1) Reasonable belief

If, at the time when the particulars were submitted to the Stock Exchange, the defendant reasonably believed, having made all reasonable enquiries, that the statement was true and not misleading or that the matters whose omission caused the loss was properly omitted. But this is not enough. He must also satisfy the court:

(a) either that he continued in that belief until the time when the securities were acquired; or
(b) that they were acquired before it was reasonably practicable to bring a correction to the attention of persons likely to acquire the securities in question; or
(c) that before the securities were acquired he had taken all such steps as it was reasonable for him to take to secure that a correction was brought to the attention of those persons; or
(d) that he continued in that belief until after the commencement of dealings in the securities following their admission to the Official List and that the securities were acquired after such a lapse of time that he ought in the circumstances to be reasonably excused (section 151(1) F.S. Act).

(2)   Experts' statements

Where the loss is caused by a statement purporting to be made by or on the authority of an expert, and included in the particulars with the expert's consent, no other person (the issuer) will be liable under section 150(1) if he can satisfy the court that at the time when the particulars were submitted to the competent authority (Stock Exchange) he reasonably believed that the 'expert' was competent to make or authorise the statement and had consented to its inclusion in the form and context in which it was included. Again this is not enough. The defendant must also show either:

(a) that he continued in that belief until the time when the securities were acquired; or
(b) that they were acquired before it was reasonably practicable to bring the fact that the expert was not competent or had not consented to the attention of persons likely to acquire the securities in question; or
(c) that before the securities were acquired he *had* taken all reasonable steps to secure that that fact was brought to the attention of those persons; or
(d) that the had continued in that belief until after the commencement of dealings in the securities after their admission to the Official List and that the securities were acquired after such a lapse of time that he ought in the circumstances to be reasonably excused.

(3) Publication, or reasonable steps to publicise, the defect

A person shall not be liable under section 150(1) for loss caused by any statement or omission as is mentioned in that provision if he satisfies the court either:

(a) that before the securities were acquired, a correction, or where the statement was such as is mentioned in (2) above, the fact that the expert was not competent or had not consented, had been published in a manner calculated to bring it to the attention of persons likely to acquire the securities in question; or
(b) that he took all such steps as it was reasonable for him to take to secure such publication and reasonably believed that it had taken place before the securities were acquired (section 151(3), F.S. Act).

(4) Fair reproduction of official statement

A person shall not be liable under section 150(1) for any loss resulting from a statement made by any official person or contained in any public official document which is included in the particulars if he satisfies the court that the statement is accurately and fairly reproduced (section 151(4), F.S. Act).

(5) Plaintiff's knowledge

A person shall not be liable under section 150(1) or under section 150(3) (failure to submit supplementary listing particulars) if he satisfies the court that the person suffering the loss acquired the securities with knowledge that the statement was false or misleading, or with knowledge of the omitted matter or of the change or new matter, as the case may be (section 151(5), F.S. Act).

(6) Reasonable belief in relation to supplementary information

A person shall not be liable under Section 150(3) (failure to submit supplementary listing particulars) if he satisfies the court that he reasonably believed that the change or new matter in question was not such as to call for supplementary listing particulars.

10.2.8 Other grounds of liability

Civil liability under the general law, common law or statute, is expressly retained by the Act. Section 150(4) provides that section 150 (compensation for false or misleading particulars) does not affect any liability which any person may incur apart from this provision. This would mean that actions could lie (1) against the company for rescission of the contract of allotment, or damages in lieu of rescission under the Misrepresentation Act 1967 (section 2(2)], or damages for negligent misrepresentation under Section 2(1) of that Act. In the latter case, it may be that damages are not available without rescission; (2) against individuals (i.e. directors, promoters, experts, persons making offers for sale) for damages for deceit (*Derry* v. *Peek* (1889) 14 App Cas 337), negligent misrepresentation, or possibly, for breach of statutory duty (section 2, Misrepresentation Act, does not apply to Scotland).

The saving for the general law is perhaps, an unnecessary complication, though only time and experience will tell. Surely the new self-regulatory statutory regime was really intended to be comprehensive, as witness section 150(6). This provides that no person shall (by reason of being a company promoter or otherwise) incur any liability for failing to disclose information which he would *not* be required to disclose in listing particulars if he were responsible for those particulars or, if he is responsible for them, which he is entitled to omit by virtue of section 148 (see [10.2.4.3] above).

10.2.9   Criminal liability

Besides incurring civil liability, to make compensation under the general law or under section 150, a person who knowingly or recklessly makes an untrue or misleading statement in listing particulars is liable to criminal prosecution (i) under section 200 for presenting false particulars in an application for listing, or (ii) under section 47 for any publication of those particulars which induced a person to subscribe for the securities in question (see further below, [10.5.5.3], [10.5.5.4]). In addition, criminal liability may arise under section 15 (obtaining property, including money, by deception) or section 19 of the Theft Act 1968 which provides that an officer of a body corporate or unincorporated association (or a person purporting to act a such) who, with intent to deceive (existing) members or creditors about its affairs, publishes or concurs in publishing a written statement or account which to his knowledge is or may be misleading, false or deceptive in a material particular, commits an offence punishable by up to seven years' imprisonment (this provision does not apply to Scotland). (See also sections 1 and 2 of the Theft Act 1978.)

10.2.10   Advertisements, etc. in connection with listing

By section 154(1), F.S. Act, where listing particulars are (or are to be) published in connection with an application for the listing of any securities, no advertisement or other information *of a kind specified by listing rules* shall be issued in the United Kingdom unless the contents of the advertisement or other information have been submitted to the Stock Exchange and the Stock Exchange has either approved those contents or authorised the issue of the advertisement or information without such approval. Any person, other than a person authorised to carry on investment business (see [10.5.2] below), who contravenes this section commits a criminal offence.

An 'authorised person' who contravenes this section will be treated as having contravened the SIB's conduct of business rules or those of his Self-Regulating Organisation (SRO) as the case may be (see section 154(2), and [10.5.3], [10.5.4] below). This means civil liability (see [10.5.5.5] below).

Defendants may establish any of the defences set out in section 154(4) and (5). Under section 154(5), where information has been approved or authorised by the Stock Exchange, neither the issuer nor the person responsible for the particulars will incur any civil liability if that information and the listing particulars, taken together, would not be likely to mislead persons of the kind likely to consider acquiring the securities in question.

10.3   (B) Part V of the Act: offers of unlisted securities

10.3.1   Introduction

Part V of the 1986 Act, expected to come into force in 1988, introduces a new regime to regulate offers of unlisted securities (i.e. securities which are not listed on the Stock Exchange and for which a listing is not being sought – section 158(1)(a), F.S.Act). It does not apply if the offer is conditional on listing and the securities fall within the Part IV definition. It replaces the prospectus provisions in the Companies Act 1985 and is broadly in line with Part IV. It applies in principle to all marketing documents (even if they contain no offer), whether or not there is an offer 'to the public', and whether or not the consideration is for cash, but will not apply where securities are merely introduced on to an exchange.

Part V applies to the following investments: (a) shares and stock; (b) debentures and other instruments creating or acknowledging indebtedness; (c) warrants or other investments entitling the holder to subscribe for such securities; and (d) certificates or other investments representing such securities (section 158(1)(b), section 158(2) and paragraphs 1,2,4,5 Schedule 1, F.S. Act). This includes securities in international companies listed on any overseas exchange, securities to be listed on the Stock Exchange's Unlisted Securities Market (USM) or Third Market (coming within the definition of 'approved exchange' in section 158(6), F.S. Act) securities on an over-the-counter market, Eurobond issues, securities offered under the Business Expansion Scheme, offers of commercial paper or certificates of deposit.

The crux of Part V is the obligation to draw up a 'prospectus', containing information about the securities. The 'prospectus', which is *not* an offer document, is the equivalent for unlisted securities of the listing particulars required for listed securities.

10.3.2   The 'prospectus'

The prospectus must contain such information, and comply with such other requirements, as may be prescribed by rules made by the Secretary of State for Trade and Industry. These rules may regard compliance with the rules applicable in a country or territory outside the UK as equivalent to compliance with the UK rules, and the Secretary of State may direct that compliance with the rules made by an approved exchange is equivalent to compliance under such rules as he may make (section 162, F.S. Act). The Secretary of State is also empowered to make rules (a) regulating the terms on which a person may offer securities by an advertisement to which Part V applies and (b) otherwise regulating such a person's conduct with a view to ensuring that the persons to whom the offer is addressed are treated equally and fairly. Rules under this power may, in particular, make provision with respect to the giving of priority as between persons to whom an offer is made and with respect to the payment of commissions (section 169(1) and (2)). As with the power under section 162 (above), the rules made under section 169 may provide that compliance with certain 'foreign' law requirements is tantamount to compliance with these rules (section 169(3)).

A general duty of disclosure is imposed in similar terms to that imposed with regard to the listing particulars for listed securities (section 163 F.S. Act; see also [10.2.4] above regarding section 146, F.S. Act). Equally, provision is made for a 'supplementary prospectus' in terms similar to those regarding 'supplementary listing particulars' (section 164 F.S. Act; see also [10.2.4] above and section 147, F.S. Act). Also, an 'approved exchange' may, on certain conditions, authorise the omission of information which would otherwise be required (section

165, F.S. Act; see also [10.2.4] above). Similar provisions to those affecting listed securities deal with 'the persons responsible for a prospectus' (sections 166-168, F.S. Act) and contraventions (section 171, F.S. Act). It is to be noted that such liability for misstatements and omissions as does arise is incurred not only towards original subscribers to the issue but also towards any person who subsequently purchases the relevant securities on the strength of the prospectus. It may further be noted here that, as in the case of Part IV ([10.2.8] above) it is expressly provided that the liability to make compensation under section 166 for untrue or misleading statements in, or omissions from, a prospectus or supplementary prospectus does not affect any liability which any person may incur apart from Section 166 itself (section 166(4)]. It should be added that existing shareholders in a company who find that their position has been prejudiced as a result of the issue of a misleading prospectus could conceivably petition for relief under section 459, Companies Act 1985 (see Chapter 8).

10.4 The mechanics of disclosure

10.4.1 (A) Offers of securities on admission to an approved exchange (section 159, F.S. Act)

Only if the securities are to be dealt in on an approved exchange will the prospectus need to be submitted and approved by the exchange concerned as well as delivered to the Registrar of Companies before any agreement can be entered into. Indeed, in general, no person may issue or cause to be issued in the United Kingdom an 'advertisement offering any securities' (as defined in section 158(4), F.S. Act) on the occasion of their admission to dealings on an approved exchange or on terms that they will be issued if so admitted unless either the above obligation is fulfilled or the advertisement is such that no agreement can be entered into in pursuance of it until it has been fulfilled (section 159(1), F.S. Act).

The *exceptions* to this are where: (1) a prospectus relating to those securities has been issued in the previous 12 months and the Exchange certifies that that prospectus taken together with any information published in connection with the admission of the securities provides sufficient information to persons likely to consider acquiring them (section 159(2), F.S. Act); (2) the offer is conditional on the admission of the securities to listing under Part IV (section 161(1), F.S. Act); (3) the securities have been listed in accordance with Part IV in the previous 12 months and the approved exchange in question certifies that persons likely to consider acquiring them will have sufficient information to enable them to decide whether to do so (section 161(1), F.S. Act); (4) where the offer document is a prospectus or short-form offer document relating to offers for subscription in cash which are issued (or caused to be issued) by the issuer of the securities (section 161(2) and section 58(2) F.S., Act); (5) other securities issued by the same persons are already dealt in on an approved exchange and the exchange certifies that sufficient information is already available (section 161(3), F.S. Act – this would presumably cover rights issues, for example).

10.4.2   (B) Other offers of securities (section 160, F.S. Act)

If the securities are not to be dealt in on an approved exchange, section 160 applies. In this context, a distinction is drawn between 'primary' and 'secondary' offers. A 'primary offer' is an advertisement either (a) inviting persons to enter into an agreement for or with a view to subscribing (whether or not for cash) for or underwriting the securities to which it relates or (b) containing information calculated to lead directly or indirectly to their doing so (section 160(2), F.S. Act). A 'secondary' offer is any other advertisement inviting persons to enter into an agreement for, or with a view to, acquiring the securities to which it relates or containing information calculated to lead directly or indirectly to their doing so, but which is issued or caused to be issued by (a) a person who acquired the securities from the issuer with a view to issuing such an advertisement (this 'view' is rebuttably presumed to have been held in the circumstances set out in section 160(4)), (b) a person who, with that same thing in view, acquired them otherwise than from the issuer but without their having been admitted to dealings on an approved exchange or held by a person who acquired them as an investment *and* without any intention that such an advertisement should be issued, or (c) a person who is a controller of the issuer or has been such a controller in the previous 12 months and who is acting with the consent or participation of the issuer in issuing the advertisement (section 160(3), F.S. Act).

In these circumstances, and subject to the following exceptions, no person may issue, or cause to be issued, in the United Kingdom, an advertisement offering any securities which is a primary or secondary offer unless (a) he has delivered for registration to the Registrar of Companies a prospectus relating to the securities and expressed to be in respect of the offer, or (b) the advertisement is such that no agreement can be entered into in pursuance of it until such a prospectus has been so delivered (section 160(1), F.S. Act). The exceptions are (1) in the case of a secondary offer, where a prospectus has been delivered in accordance with section 160(1) in respect of an offer of the same securities made in the previous six months; (2) where the offer is conditional on the admission of the securities to listing under Part IV; (3) where the offer document takes the form of a prospectus or short-form offer document relating to offers for subscription in cash which are issued (or caused to be issued) by the issuer of the securities (sections 161(2) and 58(2), F.S. Act]; (4) where the Secretary of State has by order excluded the prospectus provisions because, (a) the advertisements have a 'private character', (b) they deal with investments only incidentally, (c) are addressed to persons who are sufficiently expert to appreciate the risks or (d) the advertisement belongs to a class which he sees fit to exclude from the operation of the prospectus provisions (section 160(6)(a),(b),(c),(d), F.S. Act); (5) where other securities issued by the same person are already dealt with on an approved exchange which certifies that sufficient information is available.

An important point to note is that secondary offers are not regarded as offers by the issuer but as offers by the person who in fact makes the offer. This explains why the issuer is not a 'person responsible' in the context of a secondary offer. There are certain points of difference of principle between the Part V and Part IV regimes, for example in Part V there is no equivalent to the express exclusion of liability for failure to disclose information in the circumstances detailed in section 150(6) (see [10.2.6] above) As with Part IV, so section 170, F.S. Act, for the purposes of Part V, prohibits a private company or an old public company from issuing in the United Kingdom any advertisement offering its securities (and this includes a promotional as well as an offer document) except as provided by regulation made by the Secretary of State. The Secretary of State is empowered to exempt private companies from this prohibition in the same three expressly defined cases in which he may exclude the application of the prospectus provisions in the case of securities not to be listed on an approved exchange (section 170(2) – see section 160(6)(a),(b),(c) and above). He may make the exemption subject to conditions (section 170(3), F.S. Act).

10.5 *The new authorisation structure and best practice rules*

10.5.1 Background

In July 1981, Professor L.C.B. Gower was charged by the Government with undertaking a review of the securities industry. Meanwhile, some major investment firms were collapsing and investors were losing their money at a time when political and economic considerations were dictating a radical review of the City's operations, leading directly to 'Big Bang'. The official date for 'Big Bang' was 27 October 1986, a year before the 'October Crash'. On that date, the Stock Exchange abolished its system of minimum commissions for stockbrokers in the domestic securities market and introduced a new dealing system. It also abolished its traditional code which segregated the broking and dealing functions on its markets (so-called 'single-capacity' dealing). The admission of 'outsiders' into member firms and the introduction of high technology followed. The overriding need was that of 'internationalisation' in the context of the internationalisation of world securities markets and the maintenance of the competitiveness of the City as a world financial centre.

It is this revamped and aggressive industry which the Gower proposals, now in the shape of the Financial Services Act 1986, seek to regulate. The Act sets out a comprehensive system of self-regulation within a statutory framework involving overall government supervision and control through the Secretary of State who has delegated central functions and powers to the Securities and Investments Board. The following is only a summary of the Financial Services Act's provisions.

10.5.2 Scope of regulation

The crux of the Act is that, as from 29 April 1988, no person may carry on an investment business in the United Kingdom unless he is either an authorised person or is exempt (section 3). To do so otherwise is to commit a criminal offence (section 4) and any investment agreement entered into by any such person is unenforceable by him, except in certain cases (section 5(1)). Obviously, much depends on whether one's activity amounts to 'the carrying on of an investment business'. The Act therefore goes to great pains to define 'investment' (Schedule 1, Part I and Part V, F.S. Act) and for our purposes clearly included are shares and stock in the share capital of a company, including the shares and stock of foreign companies and unincorporated bodies; warrants or other investments entitling the holder to subscribe for such shares and stock; certificates or other instruments conferring rights to acquire, dispose of, underwrite or convert any such shares and stock. Units in collective investment schemes are also included (i.e. units in unit trusts, and shares in or securities of, an open-ended investment company). Generally included are rights to, and interests in, investments falling within any of the categories of investment expressly listed in Schedule 1 of the Act (see Schedule 1, paras. 1-11, 33 and section 63). 'Investment business' is also defined, as a crucial criterion for the scope of the Act's application (Schedule 1, Part II, F.S. Act, to be read in conjunction with Schedule 1, Part III, entitled 'Excluded Activities' and Part V, entitled 'Interpretation'). The Secretary of State has the power to restrict or extend the definitions in the light of experience and new developments (section 2). These definition provisions can be expected to cause difficulty in practice as some seek to evade the regulatory regime.

10.5.3 The Regulatory Structure

What we have under the Act is a vesting of all regulatory powers in the Secretary of State for Trade and Industry, who in turn is empowered to delegate a large number of his powers to a 'designated agency' (section 114, Schedules 7, 8 and 9). This now is the Securities and Investments Board, which remains subject to the supervision of the Secretary of State (section 115). What has emerged in the Act is not so much 'self-regulation within a statutory framework' as, in Professor Gower's own words, 'statutory regulation monitored by, and under the surveillance of, a self-standing Commission' ((1988) 51 MLR 1 at 11).

The powers made transferable to the SIB are as follows:

(1) The power to grant recognition to a Self-Regulating Organisation (SRO), to withdraw it, to seek a court order against an SRO, and to direct an SRO to change its rules or itself change the rules of an SRO (sections 10-14). (There are five SROs; see [10.5.5.7] below.)

(2) To recognise, or withdraw recognition from, a professional body (RPB) (sections 17-21). (There are nine RPBs.)

(3) To grant, suspend or withdraw authorisation in respect to an investment business (sections 25-30).

(4) To grant recognition to an investment exchange (IE) and clearing house (CH) (sections 37-39). (There are seven RIEs and two RCHs.)

(5) To withdraw recognition from a person authorised in another EEC Member State (section 33).

(6) To call for information from authorised persons and recognised bodies (section 104).

(7) To investigate the affairs of any person so far as relevant to any investment business which such person is or has been, or appears

to be or to have been, carrying on (section 105).

(8) To make 'conduct of business rules' regulating the conduct of investment business by authorised persons (section 48).

(9) To make 'financial resources rules' requiring authorised persons to have and maintain minimum financial resources (section 49).

(10) To vary the rules referred to in 8 and 9 above in certain cases (section 50).

(11) To make rules relating to: the cancelling of agreements (section 51), the notification by authorised persons of the occurrence of specified events (section 52), indemnity against the civil liability of authorised persons (section 53), a Compensation Fund for compensating investors where authorised persons are unable to pay compensation (section 54), unsolicited calls (section 56), clients' money (section 55).

(12) To direct that unfit and improper persons be not employed in investment business (or that of a particular kind) (section 59); to publish statements to the effect that an authorised person has been guilty of certain contraventions (section 60); to seek injunctions and restitution orders against likely contravenors of the Act or rules or regulations made thereunder (section 61); to intervene in various ways in the business of an authorised person, in the interests of investors (sections 64-71).

(13) To approve, and make rules relating to, the promotion of unit trust schemes (sections 77-85).

The SIB has recognised five SROs. A list of the SROs, their addresses and scope of authority is given at the end of the chapter and inquiries by investors regarding the authorisation of persons with whom they are dealing can be made directly to the SIB which is obliged to keep appropriate registers. A computerised information system known as the Investor Protection Register allows the public to discover by means of telephone and teletext (PRESTEL) whether investment businesses are authorised, though the register does not provide the names of individuals in investment businesses. The SROs have drawn up their own rules, modelled on those of the SIB. Persons carrying on investment business must become members of the SRO regulating their sphere of activity. On satisfying a 'fit and proper' test they will be admitted to membership and become bound by the rules of that SRO. In this way they become 'authorised persons' (section 7). The detailed provisions of the Act relating to the rules are set out in Schedule 2. The SIB is empowered to alter an SRO's rules, seek 'compliance orders', and in extreme cases withdraw its recognition of an SRO (sections 10 to 13). Similar provisions govern the recognition of professional bodies (with ensuing authorisation of their members, sections 15 to 21 and Schedule 3); and provision is made for the authorisation of insurance companies (section 22 and Schedule 10), friendly societies (section 23 and Schedule 11); collective investment schemes (sections 86 and 24), as well as generally for individuals, bodies corporate, partnerships or unincorporated associations who may apply to the SIB for authorisation directly (sections 25 to 30). Persons authorised in another EEC Member State are covered by sections 31 to 34. 'Exempted Persons' are those listed in Chapter IV of the Act and include recognised investment exchanges and clearing houses (and see Schedule 4). With certain exceptions (section 58(3)) no unauthorised person may issue or cause to be issued an investment advertisement in the United Kingdom unless its contents have been approved by an authorised person (section 57).

At the time of writing, the DTI was still considering views on its draft Order making exempting regulations under section 58(3). This would exempt certain advertisements on similar lines to the system under the old Prevention of Fraud (Investments) Act 1958 and General Permissions. The DTI proposals covered advertisements (a) by a company to its own shareholders and creditors; (b) in connection with employees' share schemes; (c) in connection with certain agreed take-overs of private companies; (d) in connection with the sale of private companies as a whole or substantially as a whole and (e) to professional and business investors.

10.5.4 Obligations flowing from authorisation

In general, authorised persons will have to comply with the rules of the SRO to which they belong or, if directly authorised by the SIB, with those of the SIB itself. SRO rules should provide at least equivalent protection for investors as the SIB's own rules. It is not possible to detail here the provisions applicable to the rules which are required by the Act to be (and which have been) drawn up by the SIB and the SROs. These are available on application to the appropriate body at the addresses at the end of this chapter. They will cover the conduct of business; financial resources; unsolicited calls; cancellation; clients' money and advertising.

In summary, the conduct of business rules will require compliance by authorised persons with the following principles of good market practice:

(a) the avoidance of conflicts of interest. All investment businesses will need to observe principles of fair dealing, owe duties of skill, care and diligence, and of disclosure (i.e. the best advice and 'best efforts' rule). For agency business, this will also involve a 'best execution' principle and a 'subordination of interest' principle;

(b) protection of client's assets;

(c) compensation for investors;

(d) investment and dealing advice should be adequate and reasonable, having regard to the nature of the investment and the circumstances of the client (the 'know your customer' and 'suitability of investment' rules);

(e) disclosure of terms of business to customers (e.g. charges, commissions);

(f) the keeping of proper records;

(g) arrangements to ensure the orderly conduct of business (including rules on advertising, which must be fair, contain suitable risk warnings and disclose the capacity of the advertiser).

10.5.5 Consequences of breach: investor remedies

10.5.5.1 *SIBs' enforcement powers*

We have briefly touched on the SIB's enforcement powers, including the power to prevent breaches of the Act, of its own rules, and of the rules of an SRO or a PB, for example the prohibition against employment of 'unfit' persons (section 59); the making of public statements regarding contraventions (section 60); the seeking in court of injunctions and restitution orders without prejudice to the rights of any other person including an aggrieved investor (section 61); powers of intervention (Chapter VI); powers of investigation; the power to apply for a winding-up order against a company or partnership which is an authorised person on the ground that is unable to pay its debts or that it is just and equitable to wind-up that authorised person (section 72); in certain cases, to apply for an administration order (section 74). The SIB's rules make provision for a complaints procedure to deal with complaints made against any directly authorised business, SRO or PB, IE or CH. This is without prejudice to a complainant's rights of redress in the ordinary courts. SROs are also obliged to provide for dispute settlement procedures in their rules.

10.5.5.2 *Criminal liability*

In addition, certain breaches of the Financial Services Act constitute the commission of a criminal offence. Criminal prosecutions may be brought by either the Secretary of State (SIB) or the Director of Public Prosecutions. The principal offence is that of carrying on an investment business and/or advertising when not authorised (sections 4, 57). Of more immediate concern to the investor is the fact that any investment agreement entered into by an unauthorised person is unenforceable against the investor. This also applies to an agreement entered into by an authorised or exempted person in consequence of anything said or done by an unauthorised person. The investor will be able to recover any money or other property paid or transferred by him under the agreement. In addition, he is entitled to compensation for any loss incurred through having parted with his money or other property (section 5(1)). However, the court may allow an agreement to be enforced in such circumstances as amount to a finding of good faith on the part of the party seeking to enforce it (section 5(3)). If the investor chooses not to perform an unenforceable agreement he must, of course, hand over anything received under it (section 5(4)). Restitution orders, on the application of the SIB, may follow, requiring the contravenor to pay such sum as appears just into trust for distribution among investors who have suffered loss as a result of the contravention (section 6).

10.5.5.3

Criminal offences are also committed by a person who (1) makes a statement, promise or forecast which he knows to be misleading, false or deceptive or who dishonestly conceals any material fact(s) or who (2) recklessly makes (dishonestly or otherwise) a statement, promise or forecast which is misleading, false or deceptive, for the purpose of inducing, or being reckless as to whether it may induce, others to enter (or not enter) any investment agreement, offer (or not offer) to do so, or to exercise (or not exercise) any rights conferred by an investment (section 47(1)). It does not matter that the person induced was not the person to whom the statement was made or from whom the facts were concealed.

10.5.5.4

Another offence under the Act is committed by a person who does any act or engages in any course of conduct which creates a false or misleading impression as to the market in, or the price or value of, any investments if he does so for the purpose of creating that impression and of thereby inducing another person to acquire, dispose of, subscribe for or underwrite those investments or to refrain from doing so or to exercise, or refrain from exercising any rights conferred by those investments (section 47(2)).

10.5.5.5   *Civil liability*

More to the point as far as the individual victim is concerned is the vital new provision in section 62. Whatever other action, criminal or disciplinary, may be taken by any other person or body under the Act the individual investor is now able to sue for damages in a wide range of cases. Section 62(1) provides, in effect, that any contraventions of:

(a) the rules and regulations of the SIB, and SRO or a PB (other than the financial resources rules);
(b) the requirements specified in an order exempting certain advertisements from the section 57 prohibition against advertising by unauthorised persons (see [10.5.3] above);
(c) the duty imposed on authorised persons and appointed representatives to take reasonable care not to employ or continue to employ a person in contravention of a disqualification direction made under section 59 (see [10.5.5.1] above);
(d) any conditions attached to permission granted under Section 50 to alter the conduct of business rules in any particular case, are actionable at the suit of a person who suffers loss as a result. This is without prejudice to such other remedies as may be available (injunctions, restitution orders; sections 62(1), 61(9)).

10.5.5.6   *Compensation funds*

As stated earlier, investment businesses may be required to take out appropriate liability insurance cover by the SIB under its rules. More importantly, investors will be able to seek compensation from a compensation fund to be set up by the SIB, and individual SROs may make their own arrangements. Detailed information about these schemes can be obtained from the SIB or SROs.

10.5.6   Where to seek information or complain

Securities and Investments Board

Address: 3, Royal Exchange Buildings
London EC3V 3NL.
Tel: General Enquiries: 01-283 2474
Authorisation Enquiries: 01-929 3652

SROs

(1)   *Association of Futures Brokers and Dealers*
This association covers firms broking and dealing in financial and commodity futures and options and providing investment management and advice incidental to that range of business.
Address: B Section, Fifth Floor,
              Plantation House,
              528, Mincing Lane,
              London EC3M 3DX.
Tel: 01-626 9763

(2)   *The Securities Association*
This was formed by the merger of ISRO (the International Securities Regulatory Organisation) and the Stock Exchange. It is the SRO to which shareholders will look. It covers firms dealing and arranging deals in domestic and international securities and advising corporate finance customers. This includes not only firms which were previously members of the Stock Exchange, but also the international banks and securities houses trading in the Eurobond and international capital markets.
Address: The Stock Exchange,
              Old Broad Street,
              London EC2N 1HP.
Tel: 01-256 9000

(3)   *Financial Intermediaries, Managers and Brokers Regulatory Association*
This body covers independent intermediaries advising on, and arranging, deals in investments, particularly in life assurance and unit trusts, or providing investment advice and management services to retail customers.
Address: Hertsmere House,
              Marsh Wall,
              London E14 9RW.
Tel: 01-538 8860
              01-895 1229

(4)   *Investment Management Regulatory Organisation*
This covers investment managers and advisers, particularly institutional fund managers, unit trust managers and pension fund managers.

Address: Centre Point,
         103, New Oxford Street,
         London WC1A 1PT.
Tel: 01-379 0601

(5)   Life Assurance and Unit Trust Regulatory Organisation
This covers the marketing of life assurance and unit trusts.
Address: Centre Point,
         103, New Oxford Street,
         London WC1A 1QH.
Tel: 01-379 0444

Recognised Professional Bodies

The Law Society of England and Wales (*Tel*: 01-242 1222)
The Law Society of Scotland (Edinburgh) (*Tel*: 031-2267411)
Law Society of Northern Ireland (Belfast) (*Tel*: 0232 231614)
The Institute of Chartered Accountants in England and Wales
    (*Tel*: 01-628 7060)
The Institute of Chartered Accountants in Ireland (Dublin)
    (*Tel*: 0001 680400)
Insurance Brokers Registration Council (*Tel*: 01-588 4387)
Chartered Association of Certified Accountants (*Tel*: 01-242 6855)
Institute of Actuaries (*Tel*: 01-242 0106).

Appendix: Table A

The following is the text of Table A set out in the Schedule to the Companies (Tables A to F) Regulations 1985 (SI 1985 No. 805) as amended.

REGULATIONS FOR MANAGEMENT OF A COMPANY LIMITED BY SHARES

Interpretation

1. In these regulations—

'the Act' means the Companies Act 1985 including any statutory modification or re-enactment thereof for the time being in force.

'the articles' means the articles of the company.

'clear days' in relation to the period of a notice means that period excluding the day when the notice is given or deemed to be given and the day for which it is given or on which it is to take effect.

'executed' includes any mode of execution.

'office' means the registered office of the company.

'the holder' in relation to shares means the member whose name is entered in the register of members as the holder of the shares.

'the seal' means the common seal of the company.

'secretary' means the secretary of the company or any other person appointed to perform the duties of the secretary of the company, including a joint, assistant or deputy secretary.

'the United Kingdom' means Great Britain and Northern Ireland.

Unless the context otherwise requires, words or expressions contained in these regulations bear the same meaning as in the Act but excluding any statutory modification thereof not in force when these regulations become binding on the company.

Share capital

2. Subject to the provisions of the Act and without prejudice to any rights attached to any existing shares, any share may be issued with such rights or restrictions as the company may by ordinary resolution determine.

3. Subject to the provisions of the Act, shares may be issued which are to be redeemed or are to be liable to be redeemed at the option of the company or the holder on such terms and in such manner as may be provided by the articles.

4. The company may exercise the powers of paying commissions conferred by the Act. Subject to the [provisions[1]] of the Act, any such commission may be satisfied by the payment of cash or by the allotment of fully or partly paid shares or partly in one way and partly in the other.

Note
1   Word substituted for 'provision' by SI 1985 No. 1052, reg. 2(a) with effect from 1 August 1985.

5. Except as required by law, no person shall be recognised by the company as holding any share upon any trust and (except as otherwise provided by the articles or by law) the company shall not be bound by or recognise any interest in any share except an absolute right to the entirety thereof in the holder.

Share certificates

6. Every member, upon becoming the holder of any shares, shall be entitled without payment to one certificate for all the shares of each class held by him (and, upon transferring a part of his holding of shares of any class, to a certificate for the balance of such holding) or several certificates each for one or more of his shares upon payment for every certificate after the first of such reasonable sum as the directors may determine. Every certificate shall be sealed with the seal and shall specify the number, class and distinguishing numbers (if any) of the shares to which it relates and the amount or respective amounts paid up thereon. The company shall not be bound to issue more than one certificate for shares held jointly by several persons and delivery of a certificate to one joint holder shall be a sufficient delivery to all of them.

7. If a share certificate is defaced, worn-out, lost or destroyed, it may be renewed on such terms (if any) as to evidence and indemnity and payment of the expenses reasonably incurred by the company in investigating evidence as the directors may determine but otherwise free of charge, and (in the case of defacement or wearing-out) on delivery up of the old certificate.

Lien

8. The company shall have a first and paramount lien on every share (not being a fully paid share) for all moneys (whether presently payable or not) payable at a fixed time or called in respect of that share. The directors may at any time declare any share to be wholly or in part exempt from the provisions of this regulation. The company's lien on a share shall extend to any amount payable in respect of it.

9. The company may sell in such manner as the directors determine any shares on which the company has a lien if a sum in respect of which the lien exists is presently payable and is not paid within fourteen clear days after notice has been given to the holder of the share or to the person entitled to it in consequence of the death or bankruptcy of the holder, demanding payment and stating that if the notice is not complied with the shares may be sold.

10.   To give effect to a sale the directors may authorise some person to execute an instrument of transfer of the shares sold to, or in accordance with the directions of, the purchaser. The title of the transferee to the shares shall not be affected by any irregularity in or invalidity of the proceedings in reference to the sale.

11.   The net proceeds of the sale, after payment of the costs, shall be applied in payment of so much of the sum for which the lien exists as is presently payable, and any residue shall (upon surrender to the company for cancellation of the certificate for the shares sold and subject to a like lien for any moneys not presently payable as existed upon the shares before the sale) be paid to the person entitled to the shares at the date of the sale.

Calls on shares and forfeiture

12.   Subject to the terms of allotment, the directors may make calls upon the members in respect of any moneys unpaid on their shares (whether in respect of nominal value or premium) and each member shall (subject to receiving at least fourteen clear days' notice specifying when and where payment is to be made) pay to the company as required by the notice the amount called on his shares. A call may be required to be paid by instalments. A call may, before receipt by the company of any sum due thereunder, be revoked in whole or part and payment of a call may be postponed in whole or part. A person upon whom a call is made shall remain liable for calls made upon him notwithstanding the subsequent transfer of the shares in respect whereof the call was made.

13.   A call shall be deemed to have been made at the time when the resolution of the directors authorising the call was passed.

14.   The joint holders of a share shall be jointly and severally liable to pay all calls in respect thereof.

15.   If a call remains unpaid after it has become due and payable the person from whom it is due and payable shall pay interest on the amount unpaid from the day it became due and payable until it is paid at the rate fixed by the terms of allotment of the share or in the notice of the call or, if no rate is fixed, at the appropriate rate (as defined by the Act) but the directors may waive payment of the interest wholly or in part.

16.   An amount payable in respect of a share on allotment or at any fixed date, whether in respect of nominal value or premium or as an instalment of a call, shall be deemed to be a call and if it is not paid the provisions of the articles shall apply as if that amount had become due and payable by virtue of a call.

17.   Subject to the terms of allotment, the directors may make arrange-

ments on the issue of shares for a difference between the holders in the amounts and times of payment of calls on their shares.

18. If a call remains unpaid after it has become due and payable the directors may give to the person from whom it is due not less than fourteen clear days' notice requiring payment of the amount unpaid together with any interest which may have accrued. The notice shall name the place where payment is to be made and shall state that if the notice is not complied with the shares in respect of which the call was made will be liable to be forfeited.

19. If the notice is not complied with any share in respect of which it was given may, before the payment required by the notice has been made, be forfeited by a resolution of the directors and the forfeiture shall include all dividends or other moneys payable in respect of the forfeited shares and not paid before the forfeiture.

20. Subject to the provisions of the Act, a forfeited share may be sold, re-allotted or otherwise disposed of on such terms and in such manner as the directors determine either to the person who was before the forfeiture the holder or to any other person and at any time before sale, re-allotment or other disposition, the forfeiture may be cancelled on such terms as the directors think fit. Where for the purposes of its disposal a forfeited share is to be transferred to any person the directors may authorise some person to execute an instrument of transfer of the share to that person.

21. A person any of whose shares have been forfeited shall cease to be a member in respect of them and shall surrender to the company for cancellation the certificate for the shares forfeited but shall remain liable to the company for all moneys which at the date of forfeiture were presently payable by him to the company in respect of those shares with interest at the rate at which interest was payable on those moneys before the forfeiture or, if no interest was so payable, at the appropriate rate (as defined in the Act) from the date of forfeiture until payment but the directors may waive payment wholly or in part or enforce payment without any allowance for the value of the shares at the time of forfeiture or for any consideration received on their disposal.

22. A statutory declaration by a director or the secretary that a share has been forfeited on a specified date shall be conclusive evidence of the facts stated in it as against all persons claiming to be entitled to the share and the declaration shall (subject to the execution of an instrument of transfer if necessary) constitute a good title to the share and the person to whom the share is disposed of shall not be bound to see to the application of the consideration, if any, nor shall his title to the share be affected by any irregularity in or invalidity of the proceedings in reference to the forfeiture or disposal of the share.

Transfer of shares

23. The instrument of transfer of a share may be in any usual form or in any other form which the directors may approve and shall be executed by or on behalf of the transferor and, unless the share is fully paid, by or on behalf of the transferee.

24.   The directors may refuse to register the transfer of a share which is not fully paid to a person of whom they do not approve and they may refuse to register the transfer of a share on which the company has a lien. They may also refuse to register a transfer unless—

(a)   It is lodged at the office or at such other place as the directors may appoint and is accompanied by the certificate for the shares to which it relates and such other evidence as the directors may reasonably require to show the right of the transferor to make the transfer;

(b)   it is in respect of only one class of shares; and

(c)   it is in favour of not more than four transferees.

25.   If the directors refuse to register a transfer of a share, they shall within two months after the date on which the transfer was lodged with the company send to the transferee notice of the refusal.

26.   The registration of transfers of shares or of transfers of any class of shares may be suspended at such times and for such periods (not exceeding thirty days in any year) as the directors may determine.

27.   No fee shall be charged for the registration of any instrument of transfer or other document relating to or affecting the title to any share.

28.   The company shall be entitled to retain any instrument of transfer which is registered, but any instrument of transfer which the directors refuse to register shall be returned to the person lodging it when notice of the refusal is given.

Transmission of shares

29.   If a member dies the survivor or survivors where he was a joint holder, and his personal representatives where he was a sole holder or the only survivor of joint holders, shall be the only persons recognised by the company as having any title to his interest; but nothing herein contained shall release the estate of a deceased member from any liability in respect of any share which had been jointly held by him.

30.   A person becoming entitled to a share in consequence of the death or bankruptcy of a member may, upon such evidence being produced as the directors may properly require, elect either to become the holder of the share or to have some person nominated by him registered as the transferee. If he elects to become the holder he shall give notice to the company to that effect. If he elects to have another person registered he shall execute an instrument of transfer of the share to that person. All the articles relating to the transfer of shares shall apply to the notice or instrument of transfer as if it were an instrument of transfer executed by the member and the death or bankruptcy of the member had not occurred.

31.   A person becoming entitled to a share in consequence of the death or bankruptcy of a member shall have the rights to which he would be entitled if he were the holder of the share, except that he shall not, before being registered as the holder of the share, be entitled in respect of it to attend or vote at any meeting of the company or at any separate meeting of the holders of any class of shares in the company.

Alteration of share capital

32.   The company may by ordinary resolution—

(a)   increase its share capital by new shares of such amount as the resolution prescribes;

(b)   consolidate and divide all or any of its share capital into shares of larger amount than its existing shares;

(c)   subject to the provisions of the Act, sub-divide its shares, or any of them, into shares of smaller amount and the resolution may determine that, as between the shares resulting from the sub-division, any of them may have any preference or advantage as compared with the others; and

(d)   cancel shares which, at the date of the passing of the resolution, have not been taken or agreed to be taken by any person and diminish the amount of its share capital by the amount of the shares so cancelled.

33.   Whenever as a result of a consolidation of shares any members would become entitled to fractions of a share, the directors may, on behalf of those members, sell the shares representing the fractions for the best price reasonably obtainable to any person (including, subject to the provisions of the Act, the company) and distribute the net proceeds of sale in due proportion among those members, and the directors may authorise some person to execute an instrument of transfer of the shares to, or in accordance with the directions of, the purchaser. The transferee shall not be bound to see to the application of the purchase money nor shall his title to the shares be affected by any irregularity in or invalidity of the proceedings in reference to the sale.

34.   Subject to the provisions of the Act, the company may by special resolution reduce its share capital redemption reserve and any share premium account in any way.

Purchase of own shares

35.   Subject to the provisions of the Act, the company may purchase its own shares (including any redeemable shares) and, if it is a private company, make a payment in respect of the redemption or purchase of its own shares otherwise than out of distributable profits of the company or the proceeds of a fresh issue of shares.

General meetings

36.   All general meetings other than annual general meetings shall be called extraordinary general meetings.

37.   The directors may call general meetings and, on the requisition of members pursuant to the provisions of the Act, shall forthwith proceed to convene an extraordinary general meeting for a date not later than eight weeks after receipt of the requisition. If there are not within the United

Kingdom sufficient directors to call a general meeting, any director or any member of the company may call a general meeting.

Notice of general meetings

38. An annual general meeting and an extraordinary general meeting called for the passing of a special resolution or a resolution appointing a person as a director shall be called by at least twenty-one clear days' notice. All other extraordinary general meetings shall be called by at least fourteen clear days' notice but a general meeting may be called by shorter notice if it is so agreed—

(a) in the case of an annual general meeting, by all the members entitled to attend and vote thereat; and

(b) in the case of any other meeting by a majority in number of the members having a right to attend and vote being a majority together holding not less than ninety-five per cent in nominal value of the shares giving that right.

The notice shall specify the time and place of the meeting and the general nature of the business to be transacted and, in the case of an annual general meeting, shall specify the meeting as such.

Subject to the provisions of the articles and to any restrictions imposed on any shares, the notice shall be given to all the members, to all persons entitled to a share in consequence of the death or bankruptcy of a member and to the directors and auditors.

39. The accidental omission to give notice of a meeting to, or the non-receipt of notice of a meeting by, any person entitled to receive notice shall not invalidate the proceedings at that meeting.

Proceedings at general meetings

40. No business shall be transacted at any meeting unless a quorum is present. Two persons entitled to vote upon the business to be transacted, each being a member or a proxy for a member or a duly authorised representative of a corporation, shall be a quorum.

41. If such a quorum is not present within half an hour from the time appointed for the meeting, or if during a meeting such a quorum ceases to be present, the meeting shall stand adjourned to the same day in the next week at the same time and place or [to[1]] such time and place as the directors may determine.

Note

1   Word inserted by SI 1985 No. 1052, reg. 2(b), with effect from 1 August 1985.

42. The chairman, if any, of the board of directors or in his absence some other director nominated by the directors shall preside as chairman of the meeting, but if neither the chairman nor such other director (if any) be present within fifteen minutes after the time appointed for holding the meeting and willing to act, the directors present shall elect one of their number to be chairman and, if there is only one director present and willing to act, he shall be chairman.

43.   If no director is willing to act as chairman, or if no director is present within fifteen minutes after the time appointed for holding the meeting, the members present and entitled to vote shall choose one of their number to be chairman.

44.   A director shall, notwithstanding that he is not a member, be entitled to attend and speak at any general meeting and at any separate meeting of the holders of any class of shares in the company.

45.   The chairman may, with the consent of a meeting at which a quorum is present (and shall if so directed by the meeting), adjourn the meeting from time to time and from place to place, but no business shall be transacted at an adjourned meeting other than business which might properly have been transacted at the meeting had the adjournment not taken place. When a meeting is adjourned for fourteen days or more, at least seven clear days' notice shall be given specifying the time and place of the adjourned meeting and the general nature of the business to be transacted. Otherwise it shall not be necessary to give any such notice.

46.   A resolution put to the vote of a meeting shall be decided on a show of hands unless before, or on the declaration of the result of, the show of hands a poll is duly demanded. Subject to the provisions of the Act, a poll may be demanded—

(a)   by the chairman; or
(b)   by at least two members having the right to vote at the meeting; or
(c)   by a member or members representing not less than one-tenth of the total voting rights of all the members having the right to vote at the meeting; or
(d)   by a member or members holding shares conferring a right to vote at the meeting being shares on which an aggregate sum has been paid up equal to not less than one-tenth of the total sum paid up on all the shares conferring that right;

and a demand by a person as proxy for a member shall be the same as a demand by the member.

47.   Unless a poll is duly demanded a declaration by the chairman that a resolution has been carried or carried unanimously, or by a particular majority, or lost, or not carried by a particular majority and an entry to that effect in the minutes of the meeting shall be conclusive evidence of the fact without proof of the number or proportion of the votes recorded in favour of or against the resolution.

48.   The demand for a poll may, before the poll is taken, be withdrawn but only with the consent of the chairman and a demand so withdrawn shall not be taken to have invalidated the result of a show of hands declared before the demand was made.

49. A poll shall be taken as the chairman directs and he may appoint scrutineers (who need not be members) and a fix a time and place for declaring the result of the poll. The result of the poll shall be deemed to be the resolution of the meeting at which the poll was demanded.

50. In the case of an equality of votes, whether on a show of hands or on a poll, the chairman shall be entitled to a casting vote in addition to any other vote he may have.

51. A poll demanded on the election of a chairman or on a question of adjournment shall be taken forthwith. A poll demanded on any other question shall be taken either forthwith or at such time and place as the chairman directs not being more than thirty days after the poll is demanded. The demand for a poll shall not prevent the continuance of a meeting for the transaction of any business other than the question on which the poll was demanded. If a poll is demanded before the declaration of the result of a show of hands and the demand is duly withdrawn, the meeting shall continue as if the demand had not been made.

52. No notice need be given of a poll not taken forthwith if the time and place at which it is to be taken are announced at the meeting at which it is demanded. In any other case at least seven clear days' notice shall be given specifying the time and place at which the poll is to be taken.

53. A resolution in writing executed by or on behalf of each member who would have been entitled to vote upon it if it had been proposed at a general meeting at which he was present shall be as effectual as if it had been passed at a general meeting duly convened and held and may consist of several instruments in the like form each executed by or on behalf of one or more members.

Votes of members

54. Subject to any rights or restrictions attached to any shares, on a show of hands every member who (being an individual) is present in person or (being a corporation) is present by a duly authorised representative, not being himself a member entitled to vote, shall have one vote and on a poll every member shall have one vote for every share of which he is the holder.

55. In the case of joint holders the vote of the senior who tenders a vote, whether in person or by proxy, shall be accepted to the exclusion of the votes of the other joint holders; and seniority shall be determined by the order in which the names of the holders stand in the register of members.

56. A member in respect of whom an order has been made by any court having jurisdiction (whether in the United Kingdom or elsewhere) in matters concerning mental disorder may vote, whether on a show of hands or on a poll, by his receiver, curator bonis or other person authorised in that behalf appointed by that court, and any such receiver, curator bonis or other person may, on a poll, vote by proxy. Evidence to the satisfaction of the directors of the authority of the person claiming to exercise the right to vote shall be deposited at the office, or at such other place as is specified in accordance with the articles for the deposit of instruments of proxy, not less than 48 hours before the time appointed for holding the meeting or adjourned meeting at which the right to vote is to be exercised and in default the right to vote shall not be exercisable.

57.   No member shall vote at any general meeting or at any separate meeting of the holders of any class of shares in the company, either in person or by proxy, in respect of any share held by him unless all moneys presently payable by him in respect of that share have been paid.

58.   No objection shall be raised to the qualification of any voter except at the meeting or adjourned meeting at which the vote objected to is tendered, and every vote not disallowed at the meeting shall be valid. Any objection made in due time shall be referred to the chairman whose decision shall be final and conclusive.

59.   On a poll votes may be given either personally or by proxy. A member may appoint more than one proxy to attend on the same occasion.

60.   An instrument appointing a proxy shall be in writing, executed by or on behalf of the appointor and shall be in the following form (or in a form as near thereto as circumstances allow or in any other form which is usual or which the directors may approve)—

PLC/Limited

"   I/We,   , of

, being
a member/members of the above-named company, hereby appoint
of
, or failing him,
of   , as my/our proxy to vote in my/our name[s] and on my/our behalf at the annual/extraordinary general meeting of the company to be held on   19   , and at any adjournment thereof.
Signed on   19   ."

61.   Where it is desired to afford members an opportunity of instructing the proxy how he shall act the instrument appointing a proxy shall be in the following form (or in a form as near thereto as circumstances allow or in any other form which is usual or which the directors may approve)—

"   PLC/Limited
I/We,   , of

, being a
member/members of the above-named company, hereby appoint
of
, or failing him
of   , as my/our proxy to vote in my/our name[s] and on my/our behalf at the annual/extraordinary general meeting of the company, to be held on   19 , and at any adjournment thereof.

This form is to be used in respect of the resolutions mentioned below as follows:

Resolution No. 1 *for *against
Resolution No. 2 *for *against.

*Strike out whichever is not desired.

Unless otherwise instructed, the proxy may vote as he thinks fit or abstain from voting.

Signed this   day of   19 ."

62.   The instrument appointing a proxy and any authority under which it is executed or a copy of such authority certified notarially or in some other way approved by the directors may—

(a)   be deposited at the office or at such other place within the United Kingdom as is specified in the notice convening the meeting or in any instrument of proxy sent out by the company in relation to the meeting not less than 48 hours before the time for holding the meeting or adjourned meeting at which the person named in the instrument proposes to vote; or

(b)   in the case of a poll taken more than 48 hours after it is demanded, be deposited as aforesaid after the poll has been demanded and not less than 24 hours before the time appointed for the taking of the poll; or

(c)   where the poll is not taken forthwith but is taken not more than 48 hours after it was demanded, be delivered at the meeting at which the poll was demanded to the chairman or to the secretary or to any director;

and an instrument of proxy which is not deposited or delivered in a manner so permitted shall be invalid.

63.   A vote given or poll demanded by proxy or by the duly authorised representative of a corporation shall be valid notwithstanding the previous determination of the authority of the person voting or demanding a poll unless notice of the determination was received by the company at the office or at such other place at which the instrument of proxy was duly deposited before the commencement of the meeting or adjourned meeting at which the vote is given or the poll demanded or (in the case of a poll taken otherwise than on the same day as the meeting or adjourned meeting) the time appointed for taking the poll.

Number of directors

64.   Unless otherwise determined by ordinary resolution, the number of directors (other than alternate directors) shall not be subject to any maximum but shall be not less than two.

Alternate directors

65.   Any director (other than an alternate director) may appoint any other director, or any other person approved by resolution of the directors and willing to act, to be an alternate director and may remove from office an alternate director so appointed by him.

66.   An alternate director shall be entitled to receive notice of all meetings of directors and of all meetings of committees of directors of which his appointor is a member, to attend and vote at any such meeting at which the director appointing him is not personally present, and generally to perform all the functions of his appointor as a director in his absence but shall not be entitled to receive any remuneration from the company for his services as an alternate director. But it shall not be necessary to give notice of such a meeting to an alternate director who is absent from the United Kingdom.

67.   An alternate director shall cease to be an alternate director if his appointor ceases to be a director; but, if a director retires by rotation or otherwise but is reappointed or deemed to have been reappointed at the meeting at which he retires, any appointment of an alternate director made by him which was in force immediately prior to his retirement shall continue after his reappointment.

68.   Any appointment or removal of an alternate director shall be by notice to the company signed by the director making or revoking the appointment or in any other manner approved by the directors.

69.   Save as otherwise provided in the articles, an alternate director shall be deemed for all purposes to be a director and shall alone be responsible for his own acts and defaults and he shall not be deemed to be the agent of the director appointing him.

Powers of directors

70.   Subject to the provisions of the Act, the memorandum and the articles and to any directions given by special resolution, the business of the company shall be managed by the directors who may exercise all the powers of the company. No alteration of the memorandum or articles and no such direction shall invalidate any prior act of the directors which would have been valid if that alteration had not been made or that direction had not been given. The powers given by this regulation shall not be limited by any special power given to the directors by the articles and a meeting of directors at which a quorum is present may exercise all powers exercisable by the directors.

71.   The directors may, by power of attorney or otherwise, appoint any person to be the agent of the company for such purposes and on such conditions as they determine, including authority for the agent to delegate all or any of his powers.

Delegation of directors' powers

72.   The directors may delegate any of their powers to any committee consisting of one or more directors. They may also delegate to any managing director or any director holding any other executive office such of their powers as they consider desirable to be exercised by him. Any such delegation may be made subject to any conditions the directors may impose, and either collaterally with or to the exclusion of their own powers and may be revoked or altered. Subject to any such conditions, the proceedings of a committee with two or more members shall be governed by the articles regulating the proceedings of directors so far as they are capable of applying.

Appointment and retirement of directors

73. At the first annual general meeting all the directors shall retire from office, and at every subsequent annual general meeting one-third of the directors who are subject to retirement by rotation or, if their number is not three or a multiple of three, the number nearest to one-third shall retire from office; but, if there is only one director who is subject to retirement by rotation, he shall retire.

74. Subject to the provisions of the Act, the directors to retire by rotation shall be those who have been longest in office since their last appointment or reappointment, but as between persons who became or were last reappointed directors on the same day those to retire shall (unless they otherwise agree among themselves) be determined by lot.

75. If the company, at the meeting at which a director retires by rotation, does not fill the vacancy the retiring director shall, if willing to act, be deemed to have been reappointed unless at the meeting it is resolved not to fill the vacancy or unless a resolution for the reappointment of the director is put to the meeting and lost.

76. No person other than a director retiring by rotation shall be appointed or reappointed a director at any general meeting unless—

(a) he is recommended by the directors; or
(b) not less than fourteen nor more than thirty-five clear days before the date appointed for the meeting, notice executed by a member qualified to vote at the meeting has been given to the company of the intention to propose that person for appointment or reappointment stating the particulars which would, if he were so appointed or reappointed, be required to be included in the company's register of directors together with notice executed by that person of his willingness to be appointed or reappointed.

77. Not less than seven nor more than twenty-eight clear days before the date appointed for holding a general meeting notice shall be given to all who are entitled to receive notice of the meeting of any person (other than a director retiring by rotation at the meeting) who is recommended by the directors for appointment or reappointment as a director at the meeting or in respect of whom notice has been duly given to the company of the intention to propose him at the meeting for appointment or reappointment as a director. The notice shall give the particulars of that person which would, if he were so appointed or reappointed, be required to be included in the company's register of directors.

78. Subject as aforesaid, the company may by ordinary resolution appoint a person who is willing to act to be a director either to fill a vacancy or as an additional director and may also determine the rotation in which any additional directors are to retire.

79.   The directors may appoint a person who is willing to act to be a director, either to fill a vacancy or as an additional director, provided that the appointment does not cause the number of directors to exceed any number fixed by or in accordance with the articles as the maximum number of directors. A director so appointed shall hold office only until the next following annual general meeting and shall not be taken into account in determining the directors who are to retire by rotation at the meeting. If not reappointed at such annual general meeting, he shall vacate office at the conclusion thereof.

80.   Subject as aforesaid, a director who retires at an annual general meeting may, if willing to act, be reappointed. If he is not reappointed, he shall retain office until the meeting appoints someone in his place, or if it does not do so, until the end of the meeting.

Disqualification and removal of directors

81.   The office of a director shall be vacated if—

(a)   he ceases to be a director by virtue of any provision of the Act or he becomes prohibited by law from the being a director; or

(b)   he becomes bankrupt or makes any arrangement or composition with his creditors generally; or

(c)   he is, or may be, suffering from mental disorder and either—

(i)   he is admitted to hospital in pursuance of an application for admission for treatment under the Mental Health Act 1983 or, in Scotland, an application for admission under the Mental Health (Scotland) Act 1960, or

(ii)   an order is made by a court having jurisdiction (whether in the United Kingdom or elsewhere) in matters concerning mental disorder for his detention or for the appointment of a receiver, curator bonis or other person to exercise powers with respect to his property or affairs; or

(d)   he resigns his office by notice to the company; or

(e)   he shall for more than six consecutive months have been absent without permission of the directors from meetings of directors held during that period and the directors resolve that his office be vacated.

Remuneration of directors

82.   The directors shall be entitled to such remuneration as the company may by ordinary resolution determine and, unless the resolution provides otherwise, the remuneration shall be deemed to accrue from day to day.

Directors' expenses

83.   The directors may be paid all travelling, hotel, and other expenses properly incurred by them in connection with their attendance at meetings of directors or committees of directors or general meetings or separate meetings of the holders of any class of shares or of debentures of the company or otherwise in connection with the discharge of their duties.

Directors' appointments and interests

84.   Subject to the provisions of the Act, the directors may appoint one or more of their number to the office of managing director or to any other executive office under the company and may enter into an agreement or arrangement with any director for his employment by the company or for the provision by him of any services outside the scope of the ordinary duties of a director. Any such appointment, agreement or arrangement may be made upon such terms as the directors determine and they may remunerate any such director for his services as they think fit. Any appointment of a director to an executive office shall terminate if he ceases to be a director but without prejudice to any claim to damages for breach of the contract of service between the director and the company. A managing director and a director holding any other executive office shall not be subject to retirement by rotation.

85.   Subject to the provisions of the Act, and provided that he has disclosed to the directors the nature and extent of any material interest of his, a director notwithstanding his office—

(a)   may be a party to, or otherwise interested in, any transaction or arrangement with the company or in which the company is otherwise interested;

(b)   may be a director or other officer of, or employed by, or a party to any transaction or arrangement with, or otherwise interested in, any body corporate promoted by the company or in which the company is otherwise interested; and

(c)   shall not, by reason of his office, be accountable to the company for any benefit which he derives from any such office or employment or from any such transaction or arrangement or from any interest in any such body corporate and no such transaction or arrangement shall be liable to be avoided on the ground of any such interest or benefit.

86.   For the purposes of regulation 85—

(a)   a general notice given to the directors that a director is to be regarded as having an interest of the nature and extent specified in the notice in any transaction or arrangement in which a specified person or class of persons is interested shall be deemed to be a disclosure that the director has an interest in any such transaction of the nature and extent so specified; and

(b)   an interest of which a director has no knowledge and of which it is unreasonable to expect him to have knowledge shall not be treated as an interest of his.

Directors' gratuities and pensions

87.   The directors may provide benefits, whether by the payment of gratuities or pensions or by insurance or otherwise, for any director who has held but no longer holds any executive office or employment with the company or with any body corporate which is or has been a subsidiary of the company or a predecessor in business of the company or of any such subsidiary, and for any member of his family (including a spouse and a former spouse) or any person who is or was dependent on him, and may (as well before as after he ceases to hold such office or employment) contribute to any fund and pay premiums for the purchase or provision of any such benefit.

Proceedings of directors

88.   Subject to the provisions of the articles, the directors may regulate their proceedings as they think fit. A director may, and the secretary at the request of a director shall, call a meeting of the directors. It shall not be necessary to give notice of a meeting to a director who is absent from the United Kingdom. Questions arising at a meeting shall be decided by a majority of votes. In the case of an equality of votes, the chairman shall have a second or casting vote. A director who is also an alternate director shall be entitled in the absence of his appointor to a separate vote on behalf of his appointor in addition to his own vote.

89.   The quorum for the transaction of the business of the directors may be fixed by the directors and unless so fixed at any other number shall be two. A person who holds office only as an alternate director shall, if his appointor is not present, be counted in the quorum.

90.   The continuing directors or a sole continuing director may act notwithstanding any vacancies in their number, but, if the number of directors is less than the number fixed as the quorum, the continuing directors or director may act only for the purpose of filling vacancies or of calling a general meeting.

91.   The directors may appoint one of their number to be the chairman of the board of directors and may at any time remove him from that office. Unless he is unwilling to do so, the director so appointed shall preside at every meeting of directors at which he is present. But if there is no director holding that office, or if the director holding it is unwilling to preside or is not present within five minutes after the time appointed for the meeting, the directors present may appoint one of their number to be chairman of the meeting.

92.   All acts done by a meeting of directors, or of a committee of directors, or by a person acting as a director shall, notwithstanding that it be afterwards discovered that there was a defect in the appointment of any director or that any of them were disqualified from holding office, or had vacated office, or were not entitled to vote, be as valid as if every such person had been duly appointed and was qualified and had continued to be a director and had been entitled to vote.

93.   A resolution in writing signed by all the directors entitled to receive notice of a meeting of directors or of a committee of directors shall be as valid and effectual as if it had been passed at a meeting of directors or (as the case may be) a committee of directors duly convened and held and may consist of several documents in the like form each signed by one or more directors; but a resolution signed by an alternate director need not also be signed by his appointor and, if it is signed by a director who has appointed an alternate director, it need not be signed by the alternate director in that capacity.

94. Save as otherwise provided by the articles, a director shall not vote at a meeting of directors or of a committee of directors on any resolution concerning a matter in which he has, directly or indirectly, an interest or duty which is material and which conflicts or may conflict with the interests of the company unless his interest or duty arises only because the case falls within one or more of the following paragraphs—

(a)   the resolution relates to the giving to him of a guarantee, security, or indemnity in respect of money lent to, or an obligation incurred by him for the benefit of, the company or any of its subsidiaries;

(b)   the resolution relates to the giving to a third party of a guarantee, security, or indemnity in respect of an obligation of the company or any of its subsidiaries for which the director has assumed responsibility in whole or part and whether alone or jointly with others under a guarantee or indemnity or by the giving of security;

(c)   his interest arises by virtue of his subscribing or agreeing to subscribe for any shares, debentures or other securities of the company or any of its subsidiaries, or by virtue of his being, or intending to become, a participant in the underwriting or sub-underwriting of an offer of any such shares, debentures, or other securities by the company or any of its subsidiaries for subscription, purchase or exchange;

(d)   the resolution relates in any way to a retirement benefits scheme which has been approved, or is conditional upon approval, by the Board of Inland Revenue for taxation purposes.

For the purposes of this regulation, an interest of a person who is, for any purpose of the Act (excluding any statutory modification thereof not in force when this regulation becomes binding on the company), connected with a director shall be treated as an interest of the director and, in relation to an alternate director, an interest of his appointor shall be treated as an interest of the alternate director without prejudice to any interest which the alternate director has otherwise.

95. A director shall not be counted in the quorum present at a meeting in relation to a resolution on which he is not entitled to vote.

96. The company may by ordinary resolution suspend or relax to any extent, either generally or in respect of any particular matter, any provision of the articles prohibiting a director from voting at a meeting of directors or of a committee of directors.

97. Where proposals are under consideration concerning the appointment of two or more directors to offices or employments with the company or any body corporate in which the company is interested the proposals may be divided and considered in relation to each director separately and (provided he is not for another reason precluded from voting) each of the directors concerned shall be entitled to vote and be counted in the quorum in respect of each resolution except that concerning his own appointment.

98.   If a question arises at a meeting of directors or of a committee of directors as to the right of a director to vote, the question may, before the conclusion of the meeting, be referred to the chairman of the meeting and his ruling in relation to any director other than himself shall be final and conclusive.

Secretary

99.   Subject to the provisions of the Act, the secretary shall be appointed by the directors for such term, at such remuneration and upon such conditions as they may think fit; and any secretary so appointed may be removed by them.

Minutes

100.   The directors shall cause minutes to be made in books kept for the purpose—

(a)   of all appointments of officers made by the directors; and

(b)   of all proceedings at meetings of the company, of the holders of any class of shares in the company, and of the directors, and of committees of directors, including the names of the directors present at each such meeting.

The seal

101.   The seal shall only be used by the authority of the directors or of a committee of directors authorised by the directors. The directors may determine who shall sign any instrument to which the seal is affixed and unless otherwise so determined it shall be signed by a director and by the secretary or by a second director.

Dividends

102.   Subject to the provisions of the Act, the company may by ordinary resolution declare dividends in accordance with the respective rights of the members, but no dividend shall exceed the amount recommended by the directors.

103.   Subject to the provisions of the Act, the directors may pay interim dividends if it appears to them that they are justified by the profits of the company available for distribution. If the share capital is divided into different classes, the directors may pay interim dividends on shares which confer deferred or non-preferred rights with regard to dividend as well as on shares which confer preferential rights with regard to dividend, but no interim dividend shall be paid on shares carrying deferred or non-preferred rights if, at the time of payment, any preferential dividend is in arrear. The directors may also pay at intervals settled by them any dividend payable at a fixed rate if it appears to them that the profits available for distribution justify the payment. Provided the directors act in good faith they shall not incur any liability to the holders of shares conferring preferred rights for any loss they may suffer by the lawful payment of an interim dividend on any shares having deferred or non-preferred rights.

104. Except as otherwise provided by the rights attached to shares, all dividends shall be declared and paid according to the amounts paid up on the shares on which the dividend is paid. All dividends shall be apportioned and paid proportionately to the amounts paid up on the shares during any portion or portions of the period in respect of which the dividend is paid; but, if any share is issued on terms providing that it shall rank for dividend as from a particular date, that share shall rank for dividend accordingly.

105. A general meeting declaring a dividend may, upon the recommendation of the directors, direct that it shall be satisfied wholly or partly by the distribution of assets and, where any difficulty arises in regard to the distribution, the directors may settle the same and in particular may issue fractional certificates and fix the value for distribution of any assets and may determine that cash shall be paid to any member upon the footing of the value so fixed in order to adjust the rights of members and may vest any assets in trustees.

106. Any dividend or other moneys payable in respect of a share may be paid by cheque sent by post to the registered address of the person entitled or, if two or more persons are the holders of the share or are jointly entitled to it by reason of the death or bankruptcy of the holder, to the registered address of that one of those persons who is first named in the register of members or to such person and to such address as the person or persons entitled may in writing direct. Every cheque shall be made payable to the order of the person or persons entitled or to such other person as the person or persons entitled may in writing direct and payment of the cheque shall be a good discharge to the company. Any joint holder or other person jointly entitled to a share as aforesaid may give receipts for any dividend or other moneys payable in respect of the share.

107. No dividend or other moneys payable in respect of a share shall bear interest against the company unless otherwise provided by the rights attached to the share.

108. Any dividend which has remained unclaimed for twelve years from the date when it became due for payment shall, if the directors so resolve, be forfeited and cease to remain owing by the company.

Accounts

109. No member shall (as such) have any right of inspecting any accounting records or other book or document of the company except as conferred by statute or authorised by the directors or by ordinary resolution of the company.

Capitalisation of profits

110. The directors may with the authority of an ordinary resolution of the company—

(a)　subject as hereinafter provided, resolve to capitalise any undivided profits of the company not required for paying any preferential dividend (whether or not they are available for distribution) or any sum standing to the credit of the company's share premium account or capital redemption reserve;

(b)　appropriate the sum resolved to be capitalised to the members who would have been entitled to it if it were distributed by way of dividend and in the same proportions and apply such sum on their behalf either in or towards paying up the amounts, if any, for the time being unpaid on any shares held by them respectively, or in paying up in full unissued shares or debentures of the company of a nominal amount equal to that sum, and allot the shares or debentures credited as fully paid to those members, or as they may direct, in those proportions, or partly in one way and partly in the other: but the share premium account, the capital redemption reserve, and any profits which are not available for distribution may, for the purposes of this regulation, only be applied in paying up unissued shares to be allotted to members credited as fully paid;

(c)　make such provision by the issue of fractional certificates or by payment in cash or otherwise as they determine in the case of shares or debentures becoming distributable under this regulation in fractions; and

(d)　authorise any person to enter on behalf of all the members concerned into an agreement with the company providing for the allotment to them respectively, credited as fully paid, of any shares or debentures to which they are entitled upon such capitalisation, any agreement made under such authority being binding on all such members.

Notices

111. Any notice to be given to or by any person pursuant to the articles shall be in writing except that a notice calling a meeting of the directors need not be in writing.

112. The company may give any notice to a member either personally or by sending it by post in a prepaid envelope addressed to the member at his registered address or by leaving it at that address. In the case of joint holders of a share, all notices shall be given to the joint holder whose name stands first in the register of members in respect of the joint holding and notice so given shall be sufficient notice to all the joint holders. A member whose registered address is not within the United Kingdom and who gives to the company an address within the United Kingdom at which notices may be given to him shall be entitled to have notices given to him at that address, but otherwise no such member shall be entitled to receive any notice from the company.

113. A member present, either in person or by proxy, at any meeting of the company or of the holders of any class of shares in the company shall be deemed to have received notice of the meeting and, where requisite, of the purposes for which it was called.

114. Every person who becomes entitled to a share shall be bound by any notice in respect of that share which, before his name is entered in the register of members, has been duly given to a person from whom he derives his title.

115. Proof that an envelope containing a notice was properly addressed, prepaid and posted shall be conclusive evidence that the notice was given. A notice shall [...¹] be deemed to be given at the expiration of 48 hours after the envelope containing it was posted.

Note

1   The words 'unless the contrary is proved' were deleted by SI 1985 No. 1052, reg. 2(c), with effect from 1 August 1985.

116. A notice may be given by the company to the persons entitled to a share in consequence of the death or bankruptcy of a member by sending or delivering it, in any manner authorised by the articles for the giving of notice to a member, addressed to them by name, or by the title of representatives of the deceased, or trustee of the bankrupt or by any like description at the address, if any, within the United Kingdom supplied for that purpose by the persons claiming to be so entitled. Until such an address has been supplied, a notice may be given in any manner in which it might have been given if the death or bankruptcy had not occurred.

117. If the company is wound up, the liquidator may, with the sanction of an extraordinary resolution of the company and any other sanction required by the Act, divide among the members in specie the whole or any part of the assets of the company and may, for that purpose, value any assets and determine how the division shall be carried out as between the members or different classes of members. The liquidator may, with the like sanction, vest the whole or any part of the assets in trustees upon such trusts for the benefit of the members as he with the like sanction determines, but no member shall be compelled to accept any assets upon which there is a liability.

Indemnity

118. Subject to the provisions of the Act but without prejudice to any indemnity to which a director may otherwise be entitled, every director or other officer or auditor of the company shall be indemnified out of the assets of the company against any liability incurred by him in defending any proceedings, whether civil or criminal, in which judgment is given in his favour or in which he is acquitted or in connection with any application in which relief is granted to him by the court from liability for negligence, default, breach of duty or breach of trust in relation to the affairs of the company.

Index